To Meli'
Not as genuine, be as a smile as bright as the Sun!

WORKING THE HARD SIDE OF THE STREET

SELECTED STORIES • POEMS • SCREAMS

Best wishes,
Kirk
Tucson Oct. 2000

WORKING THE HARD SIDE OF THE STREET

SELECTED STORIES • POEMS • SCREAMS

KIRK ALEX

Tucumcari Press
P.O. BOX 40998
TUCSON, AZ 85717-0998
USA

WORKING THE HARD SIDE OF THE STREET
Selected Stories • Poems • Screams

First Printing, October 1999

With love to Neil, Ziggy & Darcy for bringing this lost and confused whipped dog back from the dead. And to Shannon.

Design: Jean M. Fairclough

Library of Congress Catalog Card Number: 95-91824
ISBN: 0-939122-25-1

WORKING THE HARD SIDE OF THE STREET

SELECTED STORIES • POEMS • SCREAMS

KIRK ALEX

TABLE OF CONTENTS

Poems

Stories

Hollywood

I am northbound at
the corner of Gower and Hollywood.
5 a.m. My stop light is red.
Not much around. It's Sat. morning.
One or two cars drive past.
Just as my light changes to green
I glance to my right and notice a homeless man
sitting on the short brick wall fronting the car dealership.
At first it appears like he might be looking at me
but I'm mistaken. His stare is a blank stare as he
stares straight ahead.
"Hey, man!" I yell out to him, "Can you use some money?"
I don't get a response. I glance around to make sure
there isn't anyone to witness this,
to see a nut like me giving away
money to some filthy bum.
I do it again.
"Hey, man; I'm serious—I can let you have a couple of bucks."
Nothing. The light is red. I hop out of my cab, dig into
my pockets and run over. The guy has warts on his
grimy face, is not wearing shoes. His hair is
long, matted, dirty. There is
what looks like caked blood mixed in with dirt
and chewing gum on his feet. He is staring
down at the sidewalk now, entirely in a
world of his own, and not aware of
my presence at all.
I place two one dollar bills on the brick wall beside him.
"Here," I tell him; "get some coffee or
something." He doesn't move, doesn't say anything.

The light is green again, and I hurry back to my cab, shift into gear—and I need to glance back one final time—his head had not moved an inch, eyes never blinked, as he continued that blank stare that stared at nothing.

Life shouldn't be this bleak
for any of us.
I see too much hopelessness
out here, too much pain & sadness.
Why are human beings permitted to go on in this manner?
Where are the answers? What happened to
compassion?
I know my two bucks
isn't going to do him
much good—
But it's all I can do for now.
Ultimately (not unlike so many of us)
I opt for the coward's way out,
as I drive off,
turning left
onto The Boulevard of Broken Dreams.

(1980)

It Takes Blood

put your bones behind it

put your guts into it

scream and howl until your

heart starts to bleed

and then, only then,

if you are lucky, might you

be able to get a drop of truth

down on that sheet of paper

in front of you.

waiting for a fare

January
Thursday
it's after 3 in the morning
it's a cold night in Bev. Hills
not as cold as the rest of the
country
but I'm shivering
in my cab
(the heater not functioning)
I should have brought a blanket to wrap
myself in
it's a quiet night
no one around
I'm the only cab on the stand
at the Beverly-Wilshire
the dispatcher hasn't got anything
nothing to do
but wait
and wait
and those are the toughest moments to get
through
those are the ones
because that's when you
start thinking about things you
shouldn't start thinking about
the dreams
the false starts
the waste
the wasted hours
efforts
the years

the women
the friendships
the many people who let you down
and the ones you let down as well
you think about words spoken in haste
about words that were never said
and the damage in both cases
      was equally severe
you think about the past
grade school
high school
the fact that you aren't
all that much wiser
    after all these years
you think about the false starts
wrong moves
about the people you trusted
    and never should have
  about the ones who were true
 but were never given a chance by
    you
you stare at the hotel
    and all the success stories
in it
  and some of those success stories
have swollen noses
  from doing too much nose candy

you try and stop that kind of no-where thinking
your main goal should be, must be
to make the rent
the rest is secondary
  make the rent
       pay the phone bill
   and you realize, too, what a tiny grain
    of sand you really are
                what it really comes down to

a grain of sand
  waiting for a fare,
   maybe a $16.00 airport trip

but people don't start coming out of the hotel
  before 5:30 —
            that's three long chilly hours
     away
   on a chilly night
   in Beverly Hills.

(January 1981)

I Almost Made A Suggestion

It was a late Saturday night call,
up in The Hills (of Beverly).
The guy was drunk
and smelled
and was in tears
and he was in love with a prostitute
who didn't give a shit about him.
He owned a house in The Hills, The Hollywood
Hills,
and he was making good money
writing TV sitcoms
and he hated writing TV sitcoms,
he hated it.
He hated L.A.
He hated actors.
And producers,
the people he had to work with.
He'd been married twice,
and his three kids didn't want
anything to do with him.
He was thinking about suicide,
about picking up the blade.

When we got to the house
in Nichols Canyon
I waited in the cab while
he went in to get the
money.
It was $8.50 on the meter.
A moment later
he emerged holding a

sack
    full of dimes, quarters, nickels & pennies, *mostly pennies*.
"There should be more than enough to cover the fare,"
        he said, and staggered back to the house.
        I almost made a suggestion.
        I knew a nice high rise on Wilshire
        he could take a dive from.

Beverly Hills

they come from all over the world:
Australia, France, Holland, New Zealand,
Spain, Italy, Brazil, to see
the famous Rodeo Drive, to take pictures of
the Beverly Hills Hotel;
they buy maps that show them where
the movie star homes are in Bel Air, Trousdale,
Holmby Hills, Beverly Hills; they take
bus tours, they take more pictures, cab
tours, they ask about the stars.
you answer the best way you know—
and what can you really say?
without sounding too maudlin about
it?
hey, these people are usually losers.
they're known the world over—
but they're boozers or dopeheads or
neurotic flakes who never grew up; with
unattractive, unnatural-looking features
as a result
of too many face-lifts, too much dust,
too much everything.
and the tourists want to know about
the famous movie stars and what are
they like, where do they hang
out? are they at home now? can we go
visit? can we take pictures of their
homes?
what can you say?
there are times you just start driving
around on one of these tours—start pointing

out homes at random—there: Doris Day lives
there, that's Kirk Douglas's home, Gene Kelly
lives there, Fred Astaire, Jack Lemmon,
Johnny Carson, and so on—Lucille
Ball, James Stewart, and it goes on—
you're pointing out houses at random—
and your passengers are convinced movie stars
live in all these homes around here—
and none of it makes much difference.
sometimes you try to explain the real
movie stars to you are people from out-of-town,
the only interesting fares are the ones from
out-of-town, just visitors, real people,
from Northern Calif., from New York, from the Mid-
West, from Brazil, from other parts of the
world; the so-called regular people
are about the only treat in this business;
but they take their pictures, and it
goes on this way—the meter keeps ticking
and that's all that finally matters.

XXXXX

drenched in sweat
in the middle of the night
memories
gripping me by the throat
won't let go
i'm seeing images in the dark
gasping for air
gasping
choking
on something in my throat
vomiting my guts out
the grip's got my face turning
crimson
i flip on the light
and there is blood
mixed in with the vomit
i'm freaking out
what's the blood doing there?
i stagger into the shower
turn the cold water on
and start coughing
can't stop coughing
can't stop
why did i say all those
things to you?
after a while
it's ok
i settle down
look at a letter you wrote
to me ages ago
it's your handwriting
it's part of you
and it's signed:
love, April
XXXXX

sergio leone & his flies

waited for night to fall last night
drove out
got a double fatburger, a coke
ate it in the car.
drove to the vista theatre
and sat through *ONCE UPON A TIME IN THE WEST*.
i don't know how many times i must have sat through
that comical scene (over the years) with jack elam
trying to shoo a fly that keeps
buzzing around his head—landing on his lip, chin,
forehead—and he can't get rid of it;
and he keeps blowing air, trying—
and that fly just won't go away
and i can't stop laughing
just laughing my silly ass off.

this was a little nicer than sitting alone
in my apt. taking it out on my sore hunk a meat,
sitting in the dark, dreaming about things that
would never happen.
it was a long show
and finally had to drive back to the apt.,
stayed up
doing nothing . . .
read a book by kerouac,
wanted to weep for all of us
but the tears wouldn't come;
yanked on the hammer,
and finally dropped off
at 2 a.m.

send me a love letter
i'd like to hear from you.

her pictures

you fill the tub with hot water
another hot bath
you soak in it
you shower, wash your hair
you shave
comb your hair
put on Streissand

you sit in your chair
it is 9:30 in the evening
you are alone
another lonely night
a long night ahead

a young man
who had put himself
on the cross
did it himself

you did it
YOU
brought on
the agony

you shaved for the mirror
you showered for the walls

and there isn't anyone
to see your tears
maybe the one above
knows about it
but what if there's no one

there?
what then?

you look at pictures of
your girl
(who is no longer
your girl)
it hits you
like a hot ball of wax
right inside your guts
right in there

and you start thinking again
about not wanting
to go on . . .

just when you thought
you were past it all . . .

All Dues

What it comes down to,
I staggered and I fell
and kept staggering, stumbling and falling.

that's what this life
has been.

running scared . . .
forever running scared.

doomed from the very beginning . . .
just doomed . . .
what a laugh, what a farce,
paying dues

from the cradle to the grave.

Agoraphobia

across and back again—
into the bathroom and out,
this way and that.
not enough room to really
step out
but you do the best you can.
back and forth
the pacing continues
and you pause by the
window, look up,
it is still light out.
you are dressed, ready
to go,
but it is still light out.
you won't have the guts
to get out there,
to face it,
until night falls . . .

Fame At 2 A.M.

It was a late night call and these late night calls can be real beauties sometimes. The dispatcher had one up in Coldwater Canyon. I'd been sitting at the Beverly Hills Hotel doing nothing. It was two in the morning. I took the call, whipped the cab down to the end of the driveway, turned right, made it to Beverly Drive and took it to Coldwater. No cars around. Nothing.

The streets were dark and quiet in an eerie kind of way, and I had the opera going on the radio, with the female voice hitting such high notes it seemed to underscore the other-worldly atmosphere. I don't usually go for opera, but this time it felt right for some reason, even soothing. I stayed on Coldwater for a mile, turned left, and went up this winding, narrow road, all the while wondering what kind of basket case it was going to be this time because that's all you got this late on a Saturday night in Beverly Hills—crank-calls, 8-balls, show biz freaks who were burning themselves out on booze and drugs. And if they hadn't made it yet, they were fame-struck newcomers, a sad, pathetic bunch struggling, doing anything and everything to climb up that ladder and become a star. As usual, I was apprehensive. I wondered what the hell it was going to be as I pulled up to this two-story house with the big garage and the three or four Ferraris or M. Benzes, or whatever, parked in the driveway and along the front of the white picket fence.

The front door was open and the noise coming from it gave the impression somebody was having a wild time of it inside. I didn't bother to get out of my cab.

A tall, middle-aged guy holding a drink in his hand appeared briefly, said that *she* would be out in a second, and disappeared inside.

I waited.

The "*second*" dragged on. I didn't turn the meter on. I didn't feel like getting into a hassle with some drunk over it, didn't feel like having to explain about Waiting Time. When the "*second*" stretched into nearly twenty minutes I turned the meter on and stepped out to stretch my legs. Finally, she staggered out. She was a young woman, early 20s, and she had red hair. The same guy was right behind her, grabbed the drink from her hand, walked back in the house and slammed the door shut. The redhead continued toward my cab and she was having a difficult time of it in her high heels and condition. She'd had one drink too many, it seemed, and she was a mess—tears and makeup streaming down her face.

Jesus, here we go again. You work the night shift and this is what happens. I preferred working nights for two reasons: I couldn't take L.A. traffic during the day and I couldn't take the heat.

I kept looking at her. I didn't know her, but I felt for her just the same. What a shame, another struggling actress, another good-looking, healthy woman that was going to be used and abused, ruined, and she was going to allow this to happen to herself just so that she might get a taste of fame. She would pay for that stardom, if and when she ever got that far—not that many did—(and even if she never got anywhere, she was still going to pay).

I opened the back door for her, helped her in. I hoped she was sober enough to give me the address. I climbed in, turned the key, and pulled out slowly. There was a three- or four-hundred-foot drop on our right; the road was narrow, winding. I had to be careful. You never knew when a possum or a raccoon or even a coyote might suddenly appear and scurry across the road in front of you. These hills around here were full of the little rascals.

I could hear the woman crying in the backseat. When I asked for a destination all I got was a mumble or two. Not until I reached the bottom of Coldwater Canyon did I try again.

"Westwood," she said.

"Where in Westwood?" I needed a street address.

I got nothing. I looked in the rearview and couldn't see her.

I pulled over to the curb, turned my head to get a better look.

The woman had slid off the backseat and was lying on the floorboard, weeping. She could have been in pain; I wasn't sure, had no way of knowing. I kept looking at her and couldn't shake the sadness of it. Hollywood? You want to come to Hollywood? This is what Hollywood was about, the Hollywood I saw, the Hollywood most people didn't know about. Tinseltown. What a crock. I wished something could have been done about the assholes who ran the game.

"Hey, are you all right?"

She looked up, did her best to smile, but it wasn't working.

"Are you okay?" Her eyes blinked and that sad smile remained, but I got nothing.

I pulled away from the curb.

"I'm taking you to the hospital," I told her.

"*No*," came from the backseat. "*I'm okay. Really, I'm fine.*"

"You sure?"

She kept stammering, assuring me that she was fine. Confused, I turned left on Lexington, took it down to Sunset and Sunset west.

"Where in Westwood do you want to go?"

"Just go to Westwood . . . ," she hiccupped. "They're bastards," she said. "All bastards. . . . Got me drunk . . . put something in my drink . . . I don't know what it was—but it screwed up my head, know what I mean? Really fucked me up. Did you see the bastard who took my drink away?"

"Yeah; I saw him."

"He used to sell used cars. He doesn't sell used cars anymore. He's a producer now, so he thinks. . . . He was supposed to help me, give me a break. That's what he said. I do comedy. I've done the Comedy Store a couple of times. You might have heard of me." She told me her name. I hadn't heard of her. "I've been on the Tonight Show," she said.

"Really?" I said.

"Yeah," she said. "The Tonight Show. One time. I'm a comedienne. Anyway, this bastard is really hung, you know? He's really hung. And every girl in town, every starlet supposedly wants to fuck him because he used to go with Elizabeth ———. And he thinks he's hot shit, you know? He's it—because he's hung and he can do as he damn well pleases—and you're supposed to do what he wants. They drugged me." She wiped her tears, did her best to wipe away the smeared makeup. "He wanted me to go to bed with him. There were two other women in bed with him. I didn't want to do it—and I told him I didn't want to do it. . . ." She blew her nose, unable to stop crying. "*Shit*," she said, angry with herself. "That's when they drugged me. I wouldn't fuck him. I wasn't raised like that. I come from a good family. . . ." After a moment, she said: "They pinned me down . . . and he . . . I'm bleeding back there. God, it hurt. . . . What a bastard. *Jesus Christ, I don't even know why I went*. I'm wasting my time."

"You ought to know better," I said. "Lowlifes like that just use people like you. They're screwed up beyond repair."

"He's supposed to help me—get my career off the ground. *Lies*. That's what it was—*all lies. He couldn't help anybody, the sick son of a bitch*."

I knew it wouldn't do any good to say anything. I did anyway. "It's not worth it," I told her. "Forget the whole thing. You'll get used and keep on getting used. That's the way it is. That's Hollywood. You ought to get out—go back where you came from. What happened tonight will happen again."

"Oh no—*never again. No more parties*."

"Sure, it'll happen again."

"I don't need these bastards. I'll make it on my own. I got talent. I'll show them."

I shook my head. "Are you sure you don't want me to take you to the hospital?"

"I'm sure."

I nodded. "Where are you staying?"

She gave me a Hilgard address. The apartment building I stopped the cab in front of was across the street from UCLA.

"Wait," she said, as she got out. "I have to make sure he's home."

I waited and watched her make it up the four or five steps to the lobby entrance. She reached for the receiver there, dialed a number. She spoke into the receiver for several minutes and climbed back down. She was on the sidewalk, pacing nervously, glancing upwards from time to time. Scared. I looked up myself and noticed a man in a dark overcoat standing on the 4th floor balcony. He was about forty and you could tell he was seething with anger, but he held it in check.

"*What do you want*?" he said to her in a rather calm tone.

"What do you think?" she answered.

"Why don't you go stay with your friends?"

"I want to come in," she said, tears rolling down her face. "I'm tired. *I want to come in.*"

The man didn't move. I saw him looking at me, then up at the bleak sky above, and back down again. It must have taken everything in his power to control his anger.

"Are you just going to stand there!?" she cried out.

"I don't want you in here, *bitch.*"

"*Will you let me in*?"

A minute passed, he went inside and reappeared a while later in a white Seville in the garage downstairs. You could hear the iron gate sliding open. The man slowly drove out to the curb.

Perhaps due to the deep tan and short dark hair, but the guy looked like a contract killer out of the Godfather films. He still had the black overcoat on, white T-shirt underneath, and he looked like he was ready to kill. It was all in the face, cold, unflinching—and yet he maintained. I didn't particularly like getting caught in the middle of something like this—still, I wanted to be paid for my time. I had rent to make, and I couldn't help but wonder what would happen to this woman now. Would I be able to help somehow? Hell, I didn't know. I waited.

"Where've you been?" he said to her.

"Are you going to let me in?"

"*You filthy whore.*" The tone was low, controlled, but he meant business. The redhead kept blowing her nose and wiping her eyes. The man finally got out, and as he did, she backed away, nearly losing her footing in the process.

The overcoat walked over to me, asked what was on the meter.

I told him.

"Goddamn broads are all the same," he said, "they'll fuck

anything to get a break."

He paid me.

"Don't get mixed up with these crazy bitches around here," he advised, adding: "It's not worth it."

I got in my cab.

"Don't leave," the woman pleaded after me, clearly frightened of the guy. "*Don't leave.*"

The man took several steps toward her, but she kept backing away, not wanting him to get near her. He walked back to his car.

"What are you going to do?" she yelled after him.

"Taking you to your friends' house."

"I'm staying here."

He shook his head. "*I'm taking you to your friends' house.*"

"*I'm not going anywhere,*" she insisted. "*I don't have any friends.*"

The Seville disappeared inside the garage and the electric gate banged shut. The woman hurried south on Hilgard, staggering along.

I don't think she knew where she was going or even what she was going to do. I pulled a Uie in the middle of the street and tailed after her. There wasn't a soul around. Nobody. It was late.

Her heels clicked along on the sidewalk as she continued to run.

"Look," I said; "this is crazy. Where are you going?" She glanced at me, but wouldn't stop. "It's not safe. I wouldn't be running around like this if I were you. *Believe me, I know what I'm talking about.*"

She slowed down at least.

"*It's after three in the morning, for God's sake.*"

She walked toward my cab, not saying anything.

"*I'll take you where you want to go—no charge. Don't worry about it—but just get in. Please?*"

She climbed in the front seat.

"Do you have any friends that you can stay with? Anybody?"

She wept in silence.

"You must know someone you can stay with."

"You're nice," she said.

"Don't you know anybody? I can't just leave you like this. He looks like he means business." I then asked what the guy did for a living.

"He's a doctor," was her answer.

"Hell, he don't look like any doctor I've ever seen. Think he'll hurt you?"

"I don't know . . ."

"He ever hit you?"

She nodded. "I don't have any other place to stay."

"You don't want to go back there."

She sighed.

The so-called doctor was back on the balcony, watching us.

"He'll probably hit me," she said. "I have no choice."

"You guys married?"

She smiled a weak smile, shook her head. "No. . . . We share the apartment."

I asked how long she'd been in town.

"Eight months," she said.

Again, I tried to talk her into forgetting show business, just dropping it. She said she was from North Carolina, had four brothers and one sister back home—and they all knew she had talent and could make it, and that there was no way in the world she could face them unless she made it.

I didn't know what to say after that.

She kissed me lightly on the cheek. We pulled away from the curb. I didn't know where to take her. She didn't want to go anywhere but back to the apartment building on Hilgard.

I drove her back.

Before she climbed out she told me her name again. "Be sure to watch for me on TV. I'm going to make it. I'm going to be a star." Then added: "This whole thing is incredible." She wiped her face one more time, wanting her true personality to shine through for me. She wanted me to know that everything would work out.

"I'm supposed to make people laugh—that's supposed to be my job—and look at me. . . ."

I wanted to wish her luck, I wanted to wish her the best, to say something, instead I watched her go up the steps.

She pressed a button near the intercom. The buzzer sounded, and she pushed in the door. As she stepped into the lobby I saw her turn, and pausing long enough to wave goodbye to me, she did her best to smile a nervous smile—and continued on in.

• • •

Talking To A Roach

It was nearly four o'clock in the morning. Sam Gruber sat on the edge of his bed staring down at the worn socks on his feet. There was no more beer left. The bars wouldn't be opening until six. What was a man to do? He looked at the clock again, but that only seemed to make the hands move even slower.

Son of a bitch. He got up and walked the short distance to the bathroom to take a leak, and while standing there he spotted a medium-sized cockroach on the wall by the medicine cabinet. Sam finished up and walked over by the roach. Because Sam hadn't turned the bathroom light on the roach didn't try to take off and hide somewhere. Even though it was dark in the john, there was enough light coming in through the open door from the other room.

Sam was careful to move slowly. He leaned in, and blew lightly.

The roach, startled now, moved a fast inch or two, then paused.

His back seemed to arch in the middle as he worked his antennae, checking out a tiny dark speck of something directly before him. A roach turd?

"You don't have to go nowhere, boy," Sam said. "No need to worry. I won't hurt you. Just want to talk to you." Then he thought about all the roaches he'd killed in his lifetime in all the fleabags he'd been in. Lots of roaches, thousands; spiders too. This roach he just wanted to talk to. It was funny, the damn thing appeared intelligent, more so than most. He'd always thought cockroaches clever sons-a-bitches, usually able to outsmart you, as though the getaway had been planned in advance. He'd come in, flip the light switch and the bastards would be inside those cracks in the walls in seconds flat every time.

Sam studied this one.

This one seemed intelligent. He was just as ugly as the others, but he was smart. He seemed to have something on the ball. Sam was seriously considering cultivating a friendship. Hell, why not?

If that kid can do it in that movie, make friends with a filthy rat, he sure as hell could have a roach for a pet. Roaches were smart, damn them. Always know when and where there's food. Always know how to get inside them iceboxes too, always got at the food.

"I ain't gonna hurt you, boy," Sam whispered. "Honest, I ain't. Just want to talk." He hadn't talked to anyone in months. Generally he liked it that way. Hadn't been outside much, only to buy the wine and the beer, couple of cans of soup. The way he liked it, even though he knew it was a sure way of getting the deep blue blues, the kind that put you in Camarillo, the kind that made you feel like you could fly, leap from a skyscraper, bounce up on your feet and walk away, the kind of blues that made you think about reaching for the razor blade and running it across your wrists.

The skyscraper bit he hadn't attempted yet, although he'd toyed with the razor blade several times in the past, made a cut here and there, witnessed his own blood drip down into the tub.

Just then the roach moved about three inches and stopped.

"Don't go, boy," Sam pleaded. He didn't want to lose him. "I'm all right. I ain't got nothing against you. The ones I can't stand are the clever sons-a-bitches. I don't like them 'cause they think they got something on me. I don't like that. Don't like for nobody to act like they got something on Sam Gruber. Hell, if I wanted to I could kill a lot more, you know? I'm not hard to get along with."

The roach hurried up the wall. Sam was in a panic.

"Don't go. Don't be afraid. Don't go, boy."

The roach continued, paid no attention to what Sam Gruber had to say. Sam Gruber was convinced the roach would reach the ceiling in a second and be way beyond his reach. Desperate now, Gruber looked around frantically for something to sap the roach with, a washcloth, anything, but he had to stop him. He couldn't stand it if the roach got away from him this way.

Sam yanked one of his socks off, stretched it end to end, aimed, and snapped it at the roach. The roach fell to the floor.

That made Sam feel real good. Got him. Sam hit the light switch, looking for the roach. "*You motherhumper*!" he said, when he spotted him, and squashed him with the sock—and in order to keep the dead roach from drawing a bunch of ants, he dropped him into the toilet. Flushed him away. Then Sam Gruber found himself shaking his head; incredible, he thought. "Talking to a roach. I'm going crazy. That's what it is. I'm going nuts. Christ; I'm talking to cockroaches now."

He turned out the light and walked back to his bed. He kept staring at the clock. It was only 4:00 a.m.

• • •

Words

"You might as well be getting paid for it now!" I shouted at her. I was talking about her wanting to date. "What do you mean?" she said with a quizzical expression on her face, as she locked herself in the car, an attempt to keep the maniac at bay. We'd never fought like this—but we were doing it now: screaming, shouting, I was anyway; a wounded animal ranting, pleading to the gods, ripping away at the memories that soon would be nothing more than shredded confetti, that already were. Erased. Eradicated. Destroyed. Bogey and Ingrid had managed to resurrect the fond and priceless memories they'd had of the love they'd once shared in *CASABLANCA*. We were chopping our history, our precious history together to bits; I was responsible for the ugly deed more so than she obviously.

The two years we'd lived together we'd had maybe two arguments. Storybook romances don't happen often, but we'd had one. We'd see other couples arguing and we'd look into each other's eyes and say: Not us. That's never going to be us. Men and women were stepping out on each other, hurting each other—we'd see it—look into each other's eyes, kiss: Not us. That's never going to be us. Soulmates. That's what we were. And always would be. We had never loved like this. But there we were—me shouting obscenities at her, calling her a whore, a tramp; that she was a quitter, that she could never truly love anybody, that she was not capable of it.

And she had the car windows rolled up, the key in the ignition, telling me to forget it: It's over; *it's over.*

We'd had it once, but now it was over. Words kept pouring out of my mouth. I was being primitive and knew it, a barbarian, a man who never ran out of patience for his lady, who always had nothing but respect for his lady, who knew deep down that this woman was anything but the ugly words he kept hurling at her, while simultaneously a voice inside of him urged him to stop it; that he was being childish and ugly; that all she wanted was to be on her own for a while.

But the maniac couldn't see it and continued with the barrage of words, words he did not want to say, words that kept pouring out. It's called losing control; it's called breakdown approaching. And there are other names for it.

Sweetheart, love me like you used to! Please, April, please! Please, honey, I'm losing my sanity. . . . Dear God . . . .

Honey, I need you! Bunny, please, PLEASE, BUNNYYYYY!!!!!!!

I don't know what I'm saying . . . everything is coming out wrong. I know this is it—you'll never love me again!

You'll never smile for me again!

Please, honey, give me a minute . . . to compose myself, to hold on to my sanity long enough to say something intelligent, long enough to show you that I'm trying to understand. I'm not trying to make you do anything, honey. . . . Help me, help me. We're breaking up. We promised each other that would never be us, honey. We're breaking up! Just like everybody else, we're breaking up! God, I'm in pain.

Honey, honey! Don't look at me that way, don't drive away! Honey, this is me, honey! Your man, honey! Don't leave me like this!

Sweetheart, please don't go. . . . I can't control these words . . . the words; it's not what I want to say, it's not what's in my heart . . . I can't say the right thing, honey. . . .

• • •

(1980)

One Birthday Present I Could Have Done Without

It was no use. I couldn't go on driving the hack that night and I phoned her from the airport.

"I'm sorry; goddammit, I'm sorry. *Can't you see what I'm going through*? I've lost everything, *everything*. You were my family, you and the dog. I'm a wreck. Everything I say is *wrong*. I never mistreated you the whole time we were together, never cheated. I know life wasn't exactly a picnic—we had good times. Doesn't it mean anything to you? Jesus Christ—"

"You're sick," she said; "*sick*—and quit calling."

CLICK!

We'd had a bad fight—I won't go into it—a real beaut, *the* one. I had had to pack up and go. She got the used Toyota (needed it for work), took the German Shepherd down to the animal shelter, and was planning on moving herself and not letting me know where.

Life is a bowl of cherries.

The only woman I had ever loved, the only one I had wanted to marry.

"You're sick," she had said; "*sick*."

I didn't want anything after that—not the dreams, not to go on, *nothing*.

The one I needed didn't need me; instead, she had a need of a different order, somewhere between her legs. She had an itch to tend to, the one between her thighs. Forget the 7-year itch (she didn't have enough backbone to last that long); so forget the 7-year itch—this was the two-year itch, while eager, salivating L.A. sleaze-hounds awaited impatiently on the sidelines to accommodate her. And she made sure that I heard plenty about their interest in her prior to this row of rows.

Only she needed to make sure I was out of the picture first, ready and willing to throw our precious love away for a quick lay or two (in *El-Lay*).

She had wanted to remain friends, was willing to put me on standby, just in case the Romeos did not measure up.

Thanks, I said to that, *but no thanks*. Once you let some L.A. dirtbag put his hands on you and his meat *in you* you are *damaged goods* to me, you see? A whore is a whore—any way you cut the damn mustard. Still—it was one excruciating task to get through, deal with: confusion, frustration, agony, worthlessness. Combine all—multiply by 1000; that's what it felt like to go through.

I saw to it that she hated me, made sure she hated my guts by saying some of the most hurtful things to her I could think of because I knew I was not tough enough to turn her away should she have wanted to come back—but by making her hate me that problem was solved at least. I would not have to worry about her wanting to return to my arms after she'd slept around with the warped L.A. trash that had put these ugly and destructive ideas in her pliable and simple mind in the first place.

The question remained, poking at my brain: What kind of shallow type had I fallen for? How could I have been so naive? You wait your whole life to give your heart, to connect with that special one, to *the* one—and she turns out to be the type you have *feared* and *stayed away from for 27 years*: the superficial ding-a-ling, the short-distance-running, male-bashing female lacking in character or class, the brain-dead bimbo type with the silly perpetual grin.

How could you have been suckered into this con? Why you?

What had you done to deserve it? Better yet—what did you expect in Southern California? The artificial gold hair had come out of a bottle, did it not?—to match her artificial persona.

Guts aching, brain on fire. That afternoon I did my desperate best to reach the bit of kindness and understanding I needed to believe was there—only I could not have been more wrong.

But you know, what made it even tougher than all that: it was my birthday, my 29th. Her timing was exquisite.

It's not going to matter to her. Why should it? You see, that two-year itch comes first to this empty-headed female with the silly smile.

April, April—you were about as cold and heartless as they come. Believe you me, this was one birthday present I could have done without.

• • •

(4/3/80)

Help Me!

With money I had borrowed from Angus Gladwyn I found a small room on Hauser Bl. I was drinking beer and made the occasional call to her, trying to connect with her somehow, trying to reach her. I refused to accept that she did not feel anything. I refused to accept that she had a heart of stone. . . . A man and a woman do not go through what we went through not to feel anything, a man and a woman do not have the kind of love we'd had for one another the two years we were together and not feel anything. . . .

I was falling apart, drinking, moaning and pacing that little room and trying to stifle my moans so's the other tenants wouldn't think I was losing my mind; which in fact is exactly what was happening. . . .

I kept dialing April's number. And April kept insisting that it was over.

"Forget it," she said. "Just accept it. We never had the real thing. It is all over."

"I just need your help, April," I pleaded on the phone. "Just help me get through it. I won't bother you . . . I won't interfere in your life; God, I promise; I swear to you. Just help me . . . please . . . PLEASE, HONEY . . . HELP ME, HELP ME!"

"Don't call me anymore," she said, and hung up.

I collapsed on the carpet, convulsing with the tears and pain, clutching my guts that kept cramping up on me now, crawling like that, clinging to the carpet, pleading to somebody up there in the heavens to hear me, somebody to get word to her how much I needed her. . . .

A while later the phone rang. And when I lifted the receiver the person at the other end hung up. Was that my April? Did she feel anything at this point? Did she fear that I might do something? April, were you worried that I might actually go through with it and take my life?

I had some more beer, and when the phone rang again it was Red. I let him talk me into going out to a bar on Melrose, and while I talked with Red I had managed to control myself a great deal and I was sure he had no idea the shape I was in. After we hung up, I drank more beer, stripped my clothes off, and walked into the bathroom. I stood in front of the medicine cabinet, stared at the pathetic creature in the mirror. *I was pathetic, no good, a helpless zero* needing to wither away and die. I looked in the mirror. *No wonder she wants no part of you*. Look at you; *LOOK AT YOU, MAN*. I opened the medicine cabinet and got a razor blade out. . . .

I finished off the beer and sat on the edge of the tub. . . .

I held the blade against my right wrist and ran it lightly across my skin . . . tears poured from my eyes. . . . This is what people were capable of doing to one another. I don't care what anybody says, what the shrinks say, what the priests say, what literature tells us—there must be kindness in us, a certain degree of compassion—but me sitting there naked on that tub was the bottom line, *the whole truth*. *Pain*, we were good at causing *pain*. Nobody wants to die. It is just too sad a thing to do to go out like this. You're intimate with that special someone, you tell each other: *I love you*; and then this happens: razor blades and blood, thinking of dying and seeing no other way out of it. I kept running that blade across my wrist and drew a bit of blood. My jaw was tight, I remember that, tight and hurting, my skull aching, my whole body in pain and shaking. . . .

Will she ever know about any of this, I wondered? Will she ever know about any of it?

I did the same with the other wrist, running that blade across the skin and breaking it and watching the blood materialize in the cut, just enough to be visible. . . . This was love, dear romantics, all you tragic romantics out there.

This was love. . . .

I set the blade down before doing any more damage. "Do you

have the guts to do it?" I kept asking myself. "You threaten suicide; *do you really have what it takes*?" Nobody wants to die like this, or any other way, nobody with anything going. The only ones wishing not to go on living were those in such great pain and it being the only way to stop the pain. I put the razor blade down and got another can of beer out of the refrigerator. I sat on the edge of the bed drinking the beer and kissing her picture—that photo we had taken in the phone booth at the miniature golf course in Torrence off the 405. I stared at her smiling, pretty face. . . . I stared and wondered what would happen if she should need me for some reason someday, and I was not around?

What if I killed myself and she suddenly had a change of heart and would want me?—at least just to talk to me? What if she needed me, what if she needed me and wanted to see me and I was dead?

I lowered the photo and drank from the can. But to die would be the answer. She would no longer have to worry about me bothering her, no more worrying about me getting in her way, interfering with her new friends, the things she wanted to do, the parties she wanted to go to, the dating she felt she had to get out of her system. . . .

I made it for the tub again. There was no other way.

The phone was ringing in the other room. I walked back, reached for the receiver. It was Red Gunderson, making sure I would be ready in twenty minutes, as he was coming by to pick me up.

I had a choice: either I chucked it right there and then (and would have to accept the embarrassment of being discovered in a tub of crimson by my friend Red), or I got dressed and went out with him to the singles bar.

I showered, got into some clothes, and waited for Red to show up. We drove to the bar in his silver Volks.

I had been spared. For some reason I was not meant to go under that day.

• • •

Just Around the Corner

Ernie Hummingbird was third up on the Beverly-Wilshire. It was 3:14 a.m. The town was dead, as was the radio. No business. Nothing. Anywhere. The airport fogged-in. Beverly Hills was a cemetery.

The dispatcher called Ernie's number. Ernie responded.

"I got one at the Hilton," the dispatcher said; "wanna go?"

Ernie was unsure. It may be a no-load, it may be a shorty, and then where would he be? If he left the B-W he would lose his position and would not be able to get that early airport run out of the hotel (there would be too many cabs on it by the time he got back), and he was pressured to do something as he had only made enough to cover the lease.

"What do you say, Ernie?"

"It's probably that prostitute that goes around the corner—"

"I don't know . . ."

"I'll go, I guess . . ."

Ernie pulled off the stand and drove the quarter of a mile to the Beverly Hills Hilton. As he passed the cab stand at the Hilton he noticed *three cabs* parked there in the driveway and wondered why the fare had called *his* company. He pulled up to the lobby entrance. The hooker he'd driven "*just around the corner*" in the past was sitting on a sofa talking with some guy with a hard-on. Ernie stared at her, waiting for a yea or nay. She waved: Yes, she had called a cab.

She better not be going *just around the corner*, Ernie thought, not this time, not with those other cabs waiting on the stand.

As she chatted with the dork with the bulge in his trousers the night security guard walked up to Ernie's cab and said:

"Did you see the cabs on the stand?"

Ernie nodded. "Yeah. She called our cab company. You can ask her."

The hooker walked toward his cab. The guard and the hooker exchanged hellos, said a couple other things, and she got in the cab and said to Ernie: "You're gonna be pissed when I tell you where I'm going."

Ernie's jaw got tight and he shook his head.

"I'm going to the 76 station just around the corner."

"*Why do you do this*?" Ernie finally said.

"I'm sorry. I just don't feel it's safe to walk . . ."

"*Why do you call us when there's cabs on the stand*?"

"I didn't see the other cabs. I swear. I'm sorry. . . ."

Ernie pulled away, drove her the half block to the gas station on the west side of the hotel. She said to him that her car was parked in back of Robinson's. When he got her there Ernie stopped the cab.

"Two bucks," he said.

She handed him three.

"I'm sorry," she said, smiling nervously as she got out. Ernie was shaking his head. He reached for the mike. "*It was the goddamn prostitute—wanted to go to the gas station.*"

"*The one by Robinson's*?" the dispatcher inquired.

"Yeah; can you believe it? I'll never be able to get on the BW now."

"Should have charged her ten bucks," the dispatcher said.

"*I should have punched her in the mouth*," Ernie Hummingbird said.

"Hang in there," the dispatcher said. "Maybe we can pick you up."

By the time Ernie got back to the Beverly-Wilshire there were 7 cabs on it. Ernie locked his doors, slumped his body down in the seat and tried to sleep. It was just too uncomfortable a position to get any shuteye. The lousy tramp, he thought. Averages a good grand a night and gives me a dollar tip. The lousy tramp.

He took his money out and counted it.

After gas, he figured he had enough for a couple of *Egg* McMuffins.

By 6:10 he was 4th up. There was no way he would get a trip out of that hotel at this rate (and he had to have the cab back at the office for the day man by 7:00). The day dispatcher (who had come on at 6:00) asked young Ernie if he wanted a run from the Strip to Century City. Not really, Ernie thought, but he took it. The trip would net him about five bucks. Some nights you just can't win, he said to himself.

Standing on the sidewalk in front of the Alta Loma address he had been given was an impeccably groomed older guy in a tan trench coat and full mustache poring over the front page of the newspaper in his hands. The man looked up from the paper just then and waved to the approaching cab. Ernie could not help but notice the folded black umbrella the obvious out-of-towner carried with him.

An umbrella in L.A.? This time of year? It never rained in Southern California, no matter how gray and foreboding the early morning haze occasionally appeared.

Probably a Brit., Ernie thought, a British chap.

The man got in the cab.

"Morning," Ernie said.

"Good morning," the Brit. said, loud enough and peppy enough. "I'd like to go to 1900 Avenue of the Stars."

There was too much pep from where Ernie sat. He nodded, made a U-turn.

"Do you know how to get there?" the man asked.

"Yep."

"The reason I ask is because some cab drivers don't know their way around. You're sure you know how to get to Century City?"

"Oh, yeah," Ernie told the man, made a right on Holloway. As they neared a corner, the man told him to turn left. Ernie did just that, took it down to Santa Monica Boulevard and pointed the cab west, all the way to *Avenue of the Assholes*, er, Stars—made a left, and was instructed to make a U-turn at first opportunity. Ernie did that. Parked. The man gave him six bucks, asked for a receipt.

"Have a good day," Ernie said as the man climbed out.

He filled the tank at a Mini-Mart at Palms and Motor, bought a

HERALD-EXAMINER. He bought two Egg McMuffins at McDonald's, and drove to the cab office on Motor. He parked the cab, cleaned out the ashtrays, ate one of the Egg McMuffins, waited for Dust the day man and read the paper. The sports section had a lot on the megabuck deal Reggie Jackson had signed with the Angels: **THE JACKSON PHENOMENON ARRIVES IN ANAHEIM**, one headline read. **AUTHORITIES CRACK ALLEGED "SLAVE" RING** was another headline. FBI, INS say Indonesians were "sold" to Beverly Hills, L.A. residents. **TWO MISSING IN SATURDAY PLANE CRASH**. Page 2 had a photograph of two koala bears hanging from a tree. The caption underneath read: Whether they like it or not, koala cuties Addie, left, and Bambina will soon be L.A. Zoo-bound. **BOYCE** convicted; finally breaks his courtroom silence. **NANCY ASNER FILES FOR DIVORCE**. **"NO LINK" IN EL MONTE OFFICERS' CANCER**. A couple of El Monte cops felt that the radar guns they'd been using to clock speeding motorists had given them skin cancer and filed claims against that city. The city of El Monte, in turn, had hired experts to look into the matter. **"NO LINK"** the experts said. **"BRAINSTORM" FILMING TO BE COMPLETED**—Director optimistic despite Wood's death.

The movie section had an ad Ernie was interested in:

SEXUALLY SHOCKING!
DESIREE COUSTEAU IS RANDY
THE ELECTRIC LADY
"highest rating"

Someone had given it *four cherries*.

PLUS SECOND SUPER HOT HIT
AT EACH FINE ADULT THEATRE
PLEASE PHONE FOR TITLE

He had seen pictures of the woman in many skin magazines and had masturbated to them on a number of occasions. He thought he might see this movie. Maybe. Maybe he would.

When Ernie looked up, Dust, the tall, bushy-haired and wild-eyed twenty-five-year-old bounded up to the cab. Dust had a larger than average nose, a real schnoz. His real name was Moe Lipschutz. He preferred to be called Dust. Dust lived in Venice. It was rumored he did quite a bit of speed, grass, some nose candy.

"I'll drive," Dust said. He was full of crazy energy and rather likable.

"You got it," Ernie said, and handed him the other Egg McMuffin.

"Thanks," Dust said. He started the cab up, bit into the Egg McMuffin and got them off the cab co. lot. He turned right on Venice, taking them east.

"What do you think I made last night?" Ernie said.

"What'd you make?"

"About five bucks."

"That's what I made the other day. Business is bad."

"I'm thinking about getting another job."

"Don't do that."

"I'm seriously thinking about it. Hell, look at us—we work and work—and got nothing to show for it. It's crazy. I can't even buy a used car, can hardly make the rent. I can't go on like this."

"My social life has picked up a hundred percent since I started driving days. If you quit I'll have to go back to nights."

Ernie told him about the prostitute that had wanted to go to the gas station by the Beverly Hilton Hotel.

"I know, man," Dust said; "that's why I can't go back to nights. I can't deal with those cunts, I can't take that shit anymore. I'm through dealing with the scum. You don't see any of that during the day." At that instant a woman driving a new Cadillac cut them off. She had come to within inches of ramming her car into the cab they were in. Dust punched his horn and stayed on it, blaring, floored the gas pedal to catch up to the Caddy. They were hugging the Caddy's rear bumper, flying well over the speed limit. This went on for several minutes. Finally, there was a red light at the intersection up ahead that forced both cars to come to a screeching halt. Dust jumped out of the cab, ran up to the Caddy in front of them and started shouting at the woman and pounding on her window that she had rolled all the way up. "You could have killed us back there, you stupid bitch! YOU COULD HAVE CAUSED AN ACCIDENT! YOU'RE A MENACE, YOU KNOW THAT? A GODDAMN MENACE!" The woman stared straight ahead, ignoring the diatribe. The light changed. Dust hopped back in the cab. They drove another block. Dust had now swung the cab around to the right and managed to pull alongside the Cadillac. They were neck and neck, doing fifty down Venice Boulevard. The woman never turned once to look at him. Dust had his window down and continued to glare at the woman. "You're a cunt! A fucking cunt! A CUNT!"

At first opportunity, the woman turned left, down a side-street. Dust laughed and shook his head. Ernie had found the incident a bit amusing himself.

"I think we're in the wrong business," Dust said; "it's a lousy way to start a day." He'd been driving a couple of years now. Ernie had been at it for five. They'd both been at it too long, Ernie thought.

They made a left on Hauser, took it north. "Business ought to pick up when the Olympics get here," Ernie said.

"Hell, yes!" Dust seconded. "I figure we'll be able to make about three to four grand a week."

"*Per driver*?"

"Yes—per driver."

"Come on." It was pie in the sky. Ernie let him go on.

"I'm serious. About two to three hundred a day. That's why I want to see if I can hang in there. Think of all the women that'll be in town."

"Yeah; there should be some decent women around here by then."

"Hell, yes. You're not gonna quit, are you?"

"I should get a regular job."

When they reached Ernie's decrepit, two-story, avocado-green, stucco building, Ernie got out.

"See you at seven," Dust said.

"See you at seven," Ernie said, and entered the loony-bin full of the old and crazy. He took a piss in the bathroom, got out of the clothes. He picked up one of the girlie magazines from the pile in the closet, opened it to the centerfold. The woman was beautiful—glorious tits, with a luscious-looking pussy he could have eaten all day and all night.

Ernie plopped down in the uncomfortable vinyl club chair and started stroking.

• • •

A Life of Quiet Desperation

You can only beat meat for so long and then have to find some other way to occupy your time, but there isn't much else. It's 3:16 on an overcast Wednesday afternoon. The room looks a little better since you painted it. Two walls you painted green, and the other two a powder blue. An improvement.

What next Eddy G.? (a poster of "Little Caesar" on one of the walls) What next?

Is there a woman, a decent woman in Spain who would be happy to have someone like me? A woman in France? London? Brussels? Denmark? Somewhere in Africa? Or maybe South America? Is there a decent-hearted lady in Canada who might appreciate someone like me?

We lead exciting lives. Sleep work sleep. Marking time, waiting to die, waiting, at 30, and waiting. And I used to be able to make it happen, but not anymore. Not anymore.

No spunk. No gusto.

I'm thinking how much I'd like to have some ribs—ribs, baked potatoes, pumpkin pie, a glass of milk.

I climb on my bicycle, and ride it the mile and a half to the market. I have to ride through Park La Brea, and Park La Brea is a "cemetery." Always feels that way. The high-rises that house the elderly, the dead. I see them walking around now and then—gray-haired, seeing but not seeing. The walking dead. But their excuse is more legit than mine.

I make it to the market. A quart of milk, the pie, three oranges, the ribs, the baked potatoes. While I am unchaining the bike, a fortyish horror walks up to me asking me the date. "The 27th," I tell her as I walk away.

"Are you sure" she says.

"I'm sure," I say, hop on my bicycle to get away from the madwoman, the lonely madwoman. She knows she hasn't got a prayer.

I ride the bicycle back. I'm in a hurry. Warm ribs, tasty potatoes. I set the food down on the table. There is a message on my answering machine. The message is from the owner of the cab I drive. The cab is in the shop.

"I will call you back at 6."

I dial the day driver's number.

"Dust, what's happening?"

"I only worked four hours today," he says. "The cab broke down again. I can't keep missing days like this."

"I know what you mean," I tell him. "The 1st is just around the corner."

We both agree the owner should get rid of this cab and put a newer car on the road.

"What're you doing tonight?" Dust asks.

"I don't know—probably stay in—write about the sleaze."

Dust laughs. "Why don't you take a bus down to Santa Monica; we'll hit a few bars. It's ladies' night."

"It would take two hours—"

"No it won't."

"I may go to a movie."

"I'm thinking of going back with the company. I'm missing too many days like this."

"What you could do is become a pimp—get yourself a string of women to support you."

"You know where they hang out, don't you? That 7-11 on Sunset. Maybe I'll go over there, start talking shit, offer them protection, offer to bail them out when they get busted. In no time I'd be driving around in a pink Cadillac, wearing expensive suits, bracelets; get one of them hats with a feather in it."

I do my best to imagine Dust, aka Moe Lipschutz, a lanky, hyper, naturally comical nerd with that wild, dark hair flying all over the place, in a pink pimp-mobile. What a sight that would make.

"You got it, Dust."

"Well, if you decide to come down, give me a call."

"Right. Talk to you later."

I should do it, take him up on his offer. It would do me a lot of good to get out of the room, be around some people, have a couple of beers. . . . But I know I won't. Crowds scare me. People were pretty frightening when you thought about it. I didn't like being around a lot of people.

Loneliness was easier to bear, but not by much.

I take the goodies out of the bag, and go after the ribs; eat two, eat three baked potatoes, half the pie, drink two glasses of milk.

Good. Good stuff.

I stash the rest away in the fridge. Light the briar. Sit back. And I wonder if I've got enough juice in me to do it one more time. . . .

• • •

Stop Talking About Her Before You Start Crying

12:30 AM. The Airport Hyatt. A guy in his 50s with a weather-beaten, sunburned face gets in my cab. The suit he's got on is not cheap; white shirt, a tie.

"Where can we find a girl?" he asks in what sounds like a Southern drawl.

"Nowhere around here," I say. "The Strip is about the only place."

He hesitates.

"It's only a fifteen-minute ride," I explain.

He says: "What the hell, why not?"

Twenty-five minutes later we're in West Hollywood. We cruise Sunset Strip. As we near Schwab's a group of hookers spot the potential john in my cab and suddenly come to life as we slow down. I turn the corner at Laurel, and there they are running toward the cab. They smell money; that's all the suit sitting in my cab is to them: $$$.

The first hooker ruins her chances by quoting $200/250. "Depending on what you want and for how long," she explains in an admixture of aggression and desperation. He shakes his head, doesn't like the price and he is not about to pay it. This is a seasoned customer I've got in my backseat and is playing it right. Then another white hooker elbows her way to the man's window and throws herself inside. She's got a lot of makeup on, too much. It's enough to turn your stomach. Maybe some guys like it that way. I don't recognize her right away because she's wearing a type of snug, white hat that resembles a turban, but then she starts talking and I remember picking her up at the Beverly-Wilshire a couple of times a while back. I remember she's the one with the kid and an "old man" she's been with seven years.

"What chu got to spend?" she asks my passenger.

"One hundred," the man answers.

She counters with: "One-fifty."

Another hooker sticks her head in the window, and says: "How about a *menage*?"

The man is not interested and shakes his head.

Danielle, the hooker I know, gets pissed off at the other hookers for moving in on her and rolls her window up.

"Go to hell, bitch!" the other hookers all shout at her right then. Danielle turns to the john. "Can you spend one-fifty, baby?"

"One hundred," the man says.

"But I got to pay for the cab, baby, on the way back."

"I'll pay for the cab."

"It's been a bad night. Can you make it one-fifty?"

"Maybe some other time," the man says. "All right?"

"I just can't do it. It's been a bad night for me."

"Let's forget it," he says, and seems to mean it. Danielle changes her tune. "All right, all right."

I pull away from the curb. She recognizes me, says: "Hi, loverboy."

I say hello, and it does lessen the tension inside the cab.

"I didn't recognize you with the turban," I explain. She counters with: "Why didn't you call me? You got my number."

"I don't keep numbers."

"You do mine."

We laugh at that.

She turns to talk to the fare. He's from Houston, in the construction business. She asks him the usual questions: How long you been in town? How long you staying?, etc., etc. We make it to the hotel. I've got $27.30 on the meter. The man gives me $32.

"You want me to hang around?" I ask Danielle.

"Yeah, baby; wait for me," she says.

I park the cab and wait about a half hour. When she comes out of the hotel and gets in the cab she wants to know if I can give her a discount.

"$20," I say to her. I want to be paid for my Waiting Time.

"$15."

"$20," I repeat. "I think it's fair. Do you know what most charge? About thirty bucks." And it's the truth, because most cab companies have the higher rates.

"Okay, baby."

And we head back to the Strip. We start talking a bit. It turns out her old man was an engineer, used to push dope. I wonder how the guy she's living with is able to cope with what she's doing.

"He don't mind," she says, then chuckles. "Sometimes he do. Sometimes he do, when I get off, know what I mean? He don't like it when I get off with the young guys, know what I mean, baby? I tell him everything."

I'm nodding and saying "Yeah" like I understand, but I don't.

I didn't see how it couldn't bother a guy to have his woman balling a bunch of strange men. And we start talking about relationships, how impossible it seems to keep one going these days.

She readily agrees.

"We had our ups and downs," she says. "We sure did. I ran away twice from that man. *Twice.*"

"What happened?"

"He came and got me. I lived in Florida for four months without telling him. He came and got me."

"He must really love you," I say.

"Of course, baby. Me and that man been through a lot. He shaved my head completely bald once so I wouldn't leave, but he had a good reason because I did him dirty, too. I left that man in a Phoenix motel once, took the car, all the money, and split. I forgave him because I was wrong."

I never expected I'd be talking to a prostitute about relationships, about love, but we're doing it, and I tell her about the woman I had split up with, that I still love, and feel helpless in doing anything about. Guess I'm seeking answers any damn way I can get them.

"Get her back, baby," she says. "If you really love her, get her back."

"How? She doesn't want anything to do with me. I wouldn't know what to do." And I tell her about the Englebert concert I had wanted to take my girl to about a year back, and how she had sent me a letter telling me to leave her alone. That it was over.

Danielle looks at me, and says: "You better stop talking about her before you start crying. Just get her back, baby; don't wait."

We're driving north on La Cienega, and she says: "We get back to the corner I got to tell those bitches to fuck off. I don't like that shit, the way they did me like that. See, all them stupid bitches got pimps. I don't believe in that shit." She had told me once before that she had had a pimp. "I gave that man more money than you ever saw in your life. I don't need that shit."

I turn west on Sunset.

As we near the corner of Sunset and Laurel she asks for a piece of paper and a pen, writes her number down.

"In case you get anybody that wants a date," she explains.

I don't like the idea. I don't want to start doing that. "What if you're not in?" I say.

"Don't worry, baby," she says. "I call in every hour on the hour."

"What if your man answers?"

She says: "So what? If he answers he'll pretend it's a wrong number and talk like a Mexican, you know the way they do—then he'll call right back acting like it's the answering service. You know what I'm saying, baby?"

Not really, but I nod.

She gives me the piece of paper. "Call me if you just want to talk, all right, baby?"

"Okay."

She steps out of my cab, rejoins what's left of the old gang: a couple of shivering, diehard whores on the sidewalk. I can hear the verbal exchanges. Expensive cars are cruising the Strip, johns on the prowl for action. And it's a cold, windy night for L.A. and not much action in sight, not much makes sense in this world.

I take the piece of paper with her number and I stuff it in the ashtray.

I make a U-turn, taking it west, west, to look for another fare.

• • •

Get Married, And Have A Good Life

It was a Benedict Canyon address in Beverly Hills that I drove up to one night. As I pulled up to the mansion a hooker in her early 20s (escorted, roughly at that, by a disgruntled, angry-faced balding man in bathrobe and house slippers who seemed quite intent in getting her off the premises as quickly as possible) hurried toward my cab before I'd even had a chance to come to a full stop.

She was clutching her purse; bloodshot eyes, runny nose, smeared makeup. To say that she was distraught would be putting it mildly.

The man looked like he was relieved to be rid of her and was back inside the house before the hooker had even climbed in my cab.

Sitting in my backseat now she started wailing full force, crying and carrying on as though in great pain.

"TTTTHHHHEEEEEEYYYYYYYYHHHHUUUUURRRRR TTTTTT MMMMEEEEEE!!! TTTHHEY HHHUUUUURRRRR RTTTTTTMMMEEEEEEEE!!!" she screamed hysterically.

I cut the steering wheel, gave it gas. "I'm getting you to a hospital," I told her. She started shaking her head violently.

"*NNNOOOO! DON'T DO THAT! PPPPLLEASSEEE DON'T DO THAT! PPPLEEEASSE?!*"

The screaming had shaken me up quite a bit and I found myself readily nodding my head, going along with her. "All right," I said. "I won't. I promise; I promise. I won't take you to the hospital. Are you going to be okay?"

She was going through her purse now, desperately searching for something. "YYYEESSS, YYESSSI'MFINE!" she snapped.

"You sure?"

"PLEASE TAKE ME AWAY FROM HERE! THEY HURT ME! TTTHHEEYYYHHURT MMEEE!"

It was all I could do to stay calm. I swallowed hard, had no idea what was going on. *Is the woman hurt? If so—why won't she let me take her to the hospital?*

"Where do you want to go?" I asked.

"*PLEASETAKEMEHOME! TAKEMEHOME—PPPLLLEASSE!*"

"Jesus Christ," I sighed underbreath. "Why me? Why is this happening to me? God . . ."

"*HHHEEELLLPPPP MMMEEEEEEE!*"

"Listen to me—I am trying to help you. Where do you want to go?"

"*TAKE ME HOME! TAKE ME HOME!*"

The screaming had me rattled. I couldn't take it. I stopped the cab. "That's it," I said. I had control, but I was firm. "You either stop all this screaming, or you get the hell out of my cab right now. *You got that?*"

She relented to some degree. "Please don't shout," she said. "I just want to get home. Please be nice to me. Just be nice to me. . . ." She found a cigarette in her purse, fumbled with it, continued to search for a light.

A feeling of desperation came over me. I wiped sweat from my forehead. I felt sorry for her. And I felt trapped. The whole goddamn thing was just too sad and had happened so fast. It happened too often. Fares like this chipped at your sanity.

I continued in a calm tone: "I'll be nice—I promise you. Just stay calm—and I will take you anywhere you want to go. *Anywhere.*"

She was screaming again. "*PLEASE TAKE ME HOME!*"

I got out of my cab, turned my head upwards—there was nothing but dark sky up there. Bleakness. What was I doing? Looking for answers?

I would have to solve this one on my own. Stay calm, I kept saying to myself, stay calm. It wasn't easy. I had to maintain just long enough to get her out of my cab and out of my life.

I climbed back in.

"You didn't tell me where you wanted to go."

"*TAKE ME AWAY FROM HERE!*"

"I told you about the goddamn screaming. Gimme a break—please?"

Much calmer now, she said: "The Marina—"

"That's better," I sighed. We rolled.

"Know how to get there?"

I nodded my head.

"Do you know the way?" she asked again.

"*Yes. I know the way.*"

"You really are a grouch—"

"What? Are you serious?"

"Yes, I'm serious. You're so young and such a grouch."

"I promise you—I'll be nice and get you there."

"What's your name?"

I did my best to tune her out. "Mickey Mouse," I said.

"Mickey Mouse," I heard her echo from the backseat flatly. "You think that's cute. Okay; okay. Cute. You won't tell me your name." There was a pause. "Do you have a light, please?"

I did, but I did not want her smoking. "Sorry, no light," I said.

"You promised you were going to be nice."

"Sorry. I'm not going to let you smoke. You're in bad shape. You're freaking out or something. I'm not going to trust you with a lit cigarette."

"I'm not freaking out. I was a half hour ago—inside that house. I'm okay now. . . ."

I glanced back.

"Really," she said.

I got her the lighter.

"Thank you." She was lighting up. "I only had a quarter of a gram of coke and half a qualuude. . . . That's why I'm so paranoid."

I was in my own world, my pain. "Right," I said.

"They took my money," she said. More tears followed. "I don't know what I'm going to do. My money's missing."

She noticed me glancing up at the rearview mirror. "Don't worry," she said. "I got your fare." She showed me a hundred dollar bill and a couple of twenties. "*I had a roll. My roll's missing.*" She was on the verge of hysteria again. I thought if I showed some interest in her problems it would keep her from freaking out again.

"What do you think happened to it? You think that guy took it?"

"No. I don't know." Then: "I don't fuck these guys. I'm just a dinner companion. I know you don't believe me. He wanted to fuck. I just didn't feel like it. *He wouldn't let up, kept after me, kept after me . . . even after I told him I was on my period*. Finally, I got to call a cab when he wasn't looking. He got mad and called me a bitch. *I'm scared*. It was a referral, you see. . . . I had bad vibes from the very first. . . . I'm always right about these things. I had bad vibes. It was a referral. I don't take referrals."

"What happened?"

She started to tell me, then changed her mind. She said: "*I'm scared . . . I'm scared . . . I'm in trouble . . . I'm in deep trouble . . .*"

"Why? What's going to happen? Is someone going to hurt you? What is it?"

She shook her head. "It doesn't matter. It just doesn't matter . . ." Then she added: "You should count your blessings. . . . I know that you hate your job. You hate being a cab driver."

"I don't hate my job." Maybe I did. I didn't feel it was anybody's business.

"Oh, yes you do."

"No, I don't."

"I can tell. You hate your job."

I found myself sighing again. "Okay; I hate my job."

"There's no need to be sarcastic. I'll be out of your life pretty soon—and you'll never see me again. I'm sorry if I got you upset. It's just that I lost my money . . . and I'm so scared. . . ."

A moment went by. "I'm sorry I shouted at you. You shook me up."

"You don't have to apologize. I'll even give you a good tip."

"Look, you don't have to—"

We were in the Marina, pulling into the Marriott parking lot.

"There," she said. "Stop at the door."

"Nineteen eighty," I said. She gave me a twenty and a five. "You really don't have to give me this much."

She insisted. "Take it, take it."

I kept the money. There was something I wanted to say to her in spite of what had happened, in spite of who she was and who I was, in spite of it all, but the words were not coming, and I hoped the expression on my face, perhaps a trace of a smile of sorts did it. I wanted to say—life is tough, no matter how you cut it.

I didn't care for hookers, but she was a human being. I wished I could have done something to get her out of her jam, wished I could have helped myself. Did any of it make any sense?

Why couldn't I formulate the words? Why stuck? Why now?

"Thanks," I said.

She got out of the cab. "Get married, and have a good life," she said as she walked away.

A line I never would have expected after all that had transpired, and not from her, not from a prostitute. Get married, and have a good life.

I suspected she was being facetious and didn't know what to think.

"You're trying to be funny, right?" I said to her.

She shook her head, said sincerely: "No, no—I'm serious." She staggered a bit, continued on toward the entrance.

"*Look, take care of yourself,*" I told her, but was not so sure that she had even heard me, but then I thought: How can you give advice when you're sinking yourself? I sat there, stared blankly, as she disappeared inside the lobby; I sat there like that, wishing I could have eased our pain, delivered us from our burdens; I sat there this way for a while, thinking about it, and then I did the only thing I *could do*—I sighed, and drove off.

• • •

Le Hot Tub Club

"Get Stella at UCLA Medical Center," the dispatcher said.

"Check-check," I said. In five minutes I was there looking for someone named Stella. It was raining that day. A brunette, 28, 29, in a red slicker walked out. She got in the cab and I couldn't help noticing how green her eyes were. The hair was hard black and she had the greenest eyes.

Plenty was worrying her.

"Are you Stella?" I asked.

She said she was, and needed to get to 3rd and Orlando. I pulled away. To break the ice, I said: "So how are you today?"

The woman in the backseat choked on her tears. "I have a brain tumor," she said. ". . . they have to shave my head . . ."

I didn't know what to say. Stunned, that's what I was. I'd had handicapped people in my cab before, people with cancer, people dying from alcohol, drugs and other diseases. You never knew how to take something like this. Here I was disease-free and wanting to die . . . just waiting for it to happen . . . and I suddenly felt so damn bad for this woman I did not know sitting in the back.

". . . I have three months to decide whether to let them do it." Her tears were flowing. I could hear her weeping back there. . . . "Do you have any idea what it's like for a woman to have all her hair cut off . . . ?"

I wanted to say something, to have the right soothing words to say to her, and I did not know what they would be. I stammered, kept my eyes focused on the slick pavement in front of us, all those speeding cars on Wilshire.

Finally, I said: ". . . Are they positive it's a tumor?"

I looked up in the rearview mirror to see her nodding. "They're positive all right. It's a tumor. They're not exactly sure how big it is yet . . . but it's a growth back there. . . ." She indicated the back of her skull. "Back there," she said. "It's up to me now . . . do I let them do it?—or do I just take a chance and let it go and see what happens?"

We were both quiet for a while.

". . . God, Stella, I don't know what to say . . ."

". . . I'm sorry for ruining your day . . . ," she said.

"Oh no, you didn't ruin my day. Please don't say that."

Two strangers sitting in a cab, we didn't know anything about each other, but that did not matter—there was an instant bond, a connection. The human being in my cab was under pressure, so afraid of dying and I felt for her. I did feel like I knew her and wanted to help some way. This sort of thing is rare, a human connection on a human level, but it happens.

Every now and then something like this will happen, a man or woman will get in your cab and you feel totally at ease and comfortable and are grateful for the experience, grateful that there are people out there you can relate to.

We talked some more. She said she had an urge for ice cream, and pointed out that there was a Baskin-Robbins not far from where she lived.

"Great," I said. "I'm treating you to an ice cream cone."

"You really don't have to do that," she said.

"I'm doing it. I'm treating you, Stella."

We drove down Third Street to the ice cream parlor. We got two cones and drove to her house on Orlando. She thanked me, asked me to write down my cab number, and she walked to her door.

I wished her luck.

About three months later, I took another call at UCLA Medical Center. I had no idea it would be Stella again because the dispatcher did not have a name this time. "UCLA Medical Center," he said. That was it.

I drove over to Westwood. Stella was waiting at the door. I recognized her before she recognized me. When I reminded her about last time, the way we talked, going to Baskin-Robbins, her face lit up and she was genuinely happy to see me.

"How's it going, kiddo?" I asked.

"How are you, Chance?"

"Still hanging in. How about yourself?"

"I haven't decided what to do about the tumor yet. I just don't give a damn anymore. I try not to worry about it."

I pulled away from the entrance and while driving through Beverly Hills on Santa Monica Boulevard Stella climbed over the front seat and made herself comfortable in the front with me.

"You're a sight for sore eyes, as they say," she said. "What have you been doing with yourself?"

"Still driving, still trying to sell some of my writing. Not much has changed with me."

"Do you ever hear from your girlfriend?"

"Oh no," I said. "All that is over with. She doesn't need me. She's got guys who can afford to wine and dine her. I'm just a cabbie, Stella. Her family looks down on that. That's the way it is. Life."

"Hell, I wouldn't let it get to me," Stella said. "There's so many women out there who would be grateful to have somebody like you."

"You really think so?" I asked.

"I know so."

She was shaking her head and looking at me and chuckling. "She didn't know what she had," Stella said. "Believe me." Then she said: "And you haven't been with anyone since you broke up with her?"

I nodded.

She was shaking her head some more. "What a waste," she said. "What a waste."

"I appreciate what you're saying . . . it's been so hard to forget what we had, to pretend that it just never happened. I know some people can do that. The past doesn't matter to them much. They just move on. I loved her, Stella. It wasn't just the sex, because, believe me, the sex wasn't always that great anyway. I don't care who you're with, the sex is going to get dull from time to time if you overdo—that didn't matter—because this other thing is what counts, how you feel about one another—that bond, the bond. I couldn't quit being in love with her . . . I've tried . . . I'm still trying to get on with my life. It just destroyed me. Knocked me out and kept me down . . . so help me. . . ."

She was looking at me and no longer smiling, trying to understand. I wondered if she really could. For that matter, I wondered if anybody really could understand. It seemed every time I started talking about this kind of deep love for my former girlfriend, people seemed to nod and try to see, but they really couldn't and I always felt like some kind of freak. My tales of woe, of caring, always made it seem like I was obsessed with her, that it was all a very unhealthy obsession, and not true love at all.

I've said it before—people can think what they want to think.

That's all right. It doesn't bother me anymore. What I felt was love, that's all it was, just pure love for April's soul, her very being, and wanting to do right by her, wanting to correct the mistakes.

It was about eight o'clock and getting dark as we neared Stella's house. "I was in love like that once," she said.

"Oh, yeah?" I said, relieved at last. I could have been wrong about this one. Maybe this other human being had also been there, experienced the same agony.

"Sure," she said. "It lasted six months."

"What happened?" I asked her.

She shrugged. "I don't know really. I got tired of him and started seeing someone else."

I *was* different. I was a freak who would love the one woman I had given my heart to until the day I died.

"I've got an idea," Stella said. "Let's get some beer and go to Le Hot Tub Club."

"I don't know about that . . . ," I said.

"Come on, Chance. It'll be fun."

She went in her house, got beer out of her refrigerator, and we drove on over to the Le Hot Tub Club in West L.A. Stella used to work at the one on Third Street, so we could not get in for free at this particular one. She was tipsy by then. We got back in the cab and drove to Third and Crescent Heights. The guy recognized her and let us in without charging us.

We went in. Our own private little room with the jacuzzi, floor-to-ceiling mirrors on all four sides, soothing music, and the beer. We stripped. Stella was about 5'4", and did not have a bad figure. We got in the water and held. It all happened gradually, slowly. We kissed lightly, and held some more, made small talk and my erection was obvious, only my heart was not in it.

I had no business being here with this woman. The fact was I was there because I had felt sorry for her, felt sorry and obligated because she had that brain tumor—only now I was not so sure what it was she had. We got out of the water and lay on the mat beside the jacuzzi, and tried to make something happen.

I was still hard but my mind was somewhere else. I kept seeing April, nothing but April, what it would have been like with her in my arms just then, the passion we'd had during our lovemaking, the way I liked to hold her, and do all those things to her, just her.

There could never be any substitute, no matter how hard I tried.

My own nervousness caused us both to get awkward, but that did not bother Stella. She wanted to follow through; she needed me to make love to her. I got on top, got it in, tried to please her, to do my duty as a man, or whatever you want to call it. It would not have been right to do otherwise. No matter how hard I tried not to hurt her feelings, I could not get with it, my heart did not want any part of this. This was sex with somebody you did not feel right about, sex with somebody you did not love, and did not know.

I could not help it, and started talking about the one I had split up with again.

"You really are hooked on that girl," Stella said, annoyed by all this.

"I'm sorry, Stella," I said. "You're very attractive and I like you . . . I just . . . I need to be in love . . . God, I'm screwed up. I'm sorry."

"You don't have to explain," she said. She didn't understand.

Not many could.

"I can't stop thinking about her."

"You're monogamous, huh?" she said.

"See, we never cheated on each other, we didn't lie to each other. Nothing like that. We were so kind during most of the time we were together . . . and then there was nothing. I'll never understand it. I told her I wanted to try sleeping with somebody else but I didn't. I couldn't. Even when I got the chance, I couldn't go through with it. What was going through my mind? Just feeling down about not getting anywhere in life . . . money problems . . . that car we had was breaking down all the time."

Stella was listening, but my words were not connecting, because she said: "It's all right, Chance." And lowered her head down toward my groin and awkwardly proceeded to take care of business in this manner. "You deserve it," she said.

That didn't work either. I didn't want that. I wanted nothing, just to get out of there and forget the whole thing had happened. I needed to cleanse myself off and forget I ever did this. I kept explaining, and got her to give it up. As we started dressing I could tell she was hurt and her eyes easily revealed it. There were tears there. She had taken it the wrong way.

"It's me, isn't it?" she said.

"Oh God, Stella, it isn't you . . . there is nothing wrong with you. You're good-looking and you're sexy. There is absolutely nothing wrong with you. It's me. Can't you see that it's just me." In a moment, I said: "Men are supposed to be machines, robots. We're able to screw anything that comes along. We're not supposed to have feelings."

"I never believed that."

"Not you, Stella, but I think a lot of women out there feel this way. That a man can make it with anything in a skirt. Don't you see? Love is so important. Otherwise, we might as well be wallowing in the gutter. It's the most important thing in the world."

Stella wiped her tears with a tissue and found it hard to look me in the eye as we walked back to the cab.

I had my arm around her and hugged her. "Listen to me, kiddo. It's me that's got this hangup. Not you. Do you realize how many guys out there would be so damn grateful if they could make love to you? Do you realize how many out there wish they had somebody like you?"

She looked up, and it made her seem to feel better. But I did not know how to leave well enough alone when we got back to her apartment, sat at her kitchen table and talked some more, Stella confessing her life story to me, the time she had acted like a bitch with men, acted like a real bitch, the men she had used.

But there was an underlying vulnerability there, and I was still trying to make it up to her for what happened in the jacuzzi that I had her clothes off again in her living room and was on top of her there on the foam mattress and sliding it in, trying hard to make her happy, doing my best, the erection held up and then April's image superimposed itself over the whole scene and I knew there was no winning and I had to stop and start with the litany of apologies, and I had Stella in tears all over again.

I held her tight as she cried.

"Why does this always happen to me like this?" she wept; "I'm attracted to a guy . . . and he's not interested in me."

"I am interested in you, Stella. I really am. . . . I can't explain anything anymore. I'm all twisted up inside. I'm a mess, Stella. Please forgive me."

I kissed her on the forehead and walked outside to the cab.

What a bastard you are, I thought; Chance Register, bastard extraordinaire. A girl with a brain tumor and all I had managed to do was make her feel worse.

Do you see now what I mean by wrong moves all the time?

Do you see how I keep piling up the responsibility? You try to do the right thing and it keeps backfiring on you. I had wanted affection as much as Stella, I had wanted to hold a woman in my arms to feel and experience that which has not been mine to experience in such a long time and I had wanted to be good and kind with her, and I had fucked it all up.

This is the story of Chance Register.

I drove to my apartment and took a long shower. I masturbated in the shower leaning against the wall like that and thought of April, and in the end I could not help weeping.

• • •

How Come You Don't Want No Toot?

Fell asleep in the backseat of my cab at the Beverly-Wilshire Hotel, when this black hooker in black spandex pants starts pounding on the passenger side window, literally pounding on the fucking glass. I raise my head just enough, and decide I do not want anything at this particular moment to do with a hooker.

Don't want her bullshit to fuck with my tired head. I lower my head, want nothing but to go back to sleep.

"Come on, man; I need a cab!"

"I'm waiting for a fare. . . ."

It usually works, only not this time.

"Take me to Hollywood, man. I need a cab."

I stagger out of the back, and lower my weary body into the driver's seat. She's shouting for me to unlock the door on her side. I do it, hit the electric switch that unlocks it. She's inside, and keeps on with the frantic shouting; and I've got to tell her to cool it. She does, and says: "Why you so *grumpy*?"

"Hey, man; I'm grumpy because I don't need this fucking shouting at three o'clock in the morning."

She offers me toot. I turn it down.

She says: "How come you don't want no toot?"

"*I don't need that shit.*"

"Okay, I was just asking."

"Thanks, but no thanks."

"Hey, baby, you think I spend my hard-earned money on this shit?—no way. I take it only when it's free. Only time I do it."

Fucking hookers. . . . I know they're human beings—but it is also a fact this is the gutter—and when all you see is the gutter—most of the time—it gets to you, makes you sick . . . makes you wonder about humanity, the human animal. Took her to an apartment building at Hollywood and Gardner, said she had to pay off a debt. It was $7 something on the meter. She gave me a ten, said to wait; said: "Don't you run off now—'cause it won't be worth it nohow."

"Where're you going?" I asked.

"3rd and Vermont. You wait for me, hear?"

She goes in. While I am waiting, a car with Kansas plates pulls up—two drunk hookers in miniskirts wobble out, go in the same building. The car drives off. It is a quiet time of night. There is a black-and-white parked three blocks west of where I am sitting, lights flashing.

A black pimp, wearing a lavender suit and matching tie, steps out of the building, checks his mailbox—this late at night? And I can't help but wonder if this is the debt my hooker was talking about. The pimp gets in the Caddy parked in back of me and drives off.

I'm watching the meter—and have decided I don't want any part of the hooker. As soon as the meter goes over the $10 mark, I'm gone. At $10.20 I do exactly that. I need sleep. Make it back to the Beverly Hills Hotel, park, crawl in the backseat and doze off.

• • •

(Aug. 15, '83)

I'll Be Your Sex Slave

I was sitting in my room on Hauser. The lights out. Drinking beer. As always, I kept wishing and hoping that she would call. If only I could hear the sound of my baby's voice, my Bunny's voice, her voice.

The phone rang.

It was Maxine, a woman I'd driven to the airport in my cab two weeks earlier. Someone had finally decided to call me.

A woman, finally, a woman had decided I was worth calling.

After we'd exchanged hellos, she said: "Bet you thought I'd never call."

She was right. This was L.A., after all. We decided to get together later on in the week, do something. I told her I would call before going over.

Two nights later I was in my cab cruising Beverly Hills. I thought about Maxine. She was not my type, but she was somebody. She was female, a woman I could spend some time with.

Beggars could not be choosers (someone once said). I needed company.

Keep trying, keep trying, I often told myself. Because if you do not try, you will never be able to get on with it.

You're wasting away. Live your life. Live it. You have to.

I called Maxine from a pay phone. She said she was not doing anything. "You're welcome to come over."

I told her I would.

Maxine lived on Rexford Drive, a couple of blocks north of

Wilshire Boulevard in Beverly Hills. She lived in a house in back, second floor. I had parked my cab in the alley, per her instructions (as parking regulations are strictly adhered to in this part of town); walked in through a wooden gate. I climbed a wooden staircase, and knocked.

Maxine was rather plain, early 30s. She had an ugly black mole on her chin. Now, I knew that she was not responsible for that black mole; it was not her fault that she had it, and yet, as hard as I tried to ignore it—I couldn't. There it was, the size of a large nipple, the mole. Right there on her chin. The most unattractive mole I'd ever encountered.

It could not be ignored. I made every effort to pretend it was not there—but every time I would look at her face, the mole stared back. Maxine's hair was a dull dishwater blond with small curls. The hair appeared lifeless; she did not seem to know what to do with it. I was the last guy to be judging anybody. This is what I saw. I knew I was not God's gift to women either. Like I said: observations. I noticed things, I always noticed things. Too perceptive, too something. . . .

One other thing was certain—what Maxine lacked in looks, she surely made up for by being well-endowed. The woman had a bosom, just about as large as my former girlfriend's.

She asked me in.

We got on the topic of animals. Did I like them? I favored dogs and birds; could appreciate the beauty of horses (from a safe distance). Cats didn't do anything for me. They used to; not lately. I felt more at ease around animals than people, generally speaking.

"How do you feel about rabbits?" she asked.

I shrugged.

Before I knew what was going on I heard a loud, silly chuckle (that sounded closer to a cackle) and she was opening a door to a bedroom in back.

"You're kidding?"

"Meet Desiree," she said, indicating a white rabbit that nibbled on celery and carrots in a large wire cage on the floor by the radiator.

Desiree? The heck kind of name was this for a rabbit?

Desiree was too busy working her jaws to pay any attention to us. There was a faint, albeit distinct odor to Maxine's abode.

"Right," I nodded. "Cute-looking rabbit." Come to think of it,

Maxine resembled the rabbit to a good degree: small eyes, small nose; an unattractive, rabbit-like mouth. I did not know what I was doing here.

"She's really neat," Maxine said.

"Yeah; she's all right."

She asked about my name; was it really my name?

I shrugged. "No," I told her. "Had it changed. I guess at the time I didn't want any part of the old man—"

"What was your name before you changed it?"

"It's really not important. I mean, it's been Chance Register for ten years now. I was just trying to forget some things. I guess it doesn't work that way. There's no way to block out your past. It's always there. Always. Unless you can figure out a way to get brainwashed. Anyway, it's not even worth discussing—"

"I'm sorry. I was just curious."

"It's all right. I understand. So you draw, huh?"

"Yeah. Would you like to see some things I've done?"

"Yeah, I really would."

She retrieved a portfolio, opened it; showed me some sketches: birthday cards that she had done, X-Mas cards, and others. She was quite good.

"I'll tell you something right now, Maxine—"

She looked at me. "What?" she said.

"They're terrific—"

"You really think so?"

I was sincere. "Man, you are talented. This stuff will sell like hotcakes."

She was beaming. "Thank you."

"Do you know who to show it to?"

"I may be signing a contract pretty soon—"

"Really?"

"Not for big bucks, I'm sure—but it's a start."

"That is really terrific. I'm really happy for you."

Maxine let Desiree out of her cage. The rabbit took off like a bullet, hopping nervously all over the place: from floor to bed, top of the headboard and back down again, knocking things over. It amused me to see it. The room was about to be left in shambles, unless

Maxine got her hands on her pet and put an end to it. She leapt at Desiree where she paused in a corner of the room to catch her breath, scooped her up, and gently placed her back inside the cage.

I wondered if it was safe for the rabbit to be near the radiator.

"Isn't it too hot for her?"

"No, she likes it. It keeps her warm."

What did I know about rabbits? Maxine sat on the bed. I walked over and sat beside her.

"Were you ever married?" I asked her.

Maxine nodded. "It lasted three years," she said.

"What happened, if you don't mind my asking?"

"No, it's okay. We just—it was all wrong. He was Jewish—and I just—I guess I didn't love him—I was young. I didn't know what I was doing."

"Did he love you?"

"No . . . it was sex mostly. But then that didn't work out either. It eventually all came out. He wasn't my type, and I wasn't his type. He likes a big ass. I guess my ass wasn't big enough. I like a guy to be slim. He's got a potbelly. He just got too sloppy looking. It just didn't work. We've stayed friends and all. That's about it."

I had my arms around her, hugging her. She responded. I had her blouse off. Her tits came spilling out, then I got my hand down under her skirt. She went along with it for a while, then resisted. . . .

"I like it to be an event," she said. "If you know what I mean? Because it should be an event whenever you make love."

"I understand," I said. I sat up. "Listen, I've got to take care of some business. Why don't you get into a sexy nightgown or whatever, and I'll be back?"

"I don't know . . ."

"Why not? It could be a lot of fun."

"We don't really know each other—" she said.

"Sure we do—"

"I suppose—"

I squeezed her waist. "I'll be back with some beer in about an hour."

"Okay," she said. "You sure you want to do this?"

"Yeah. Why not?"

"What should I wear? What would you like to see me in?"

"How about a sexy garter belt?—stockings, heels? All that stuff turns me on—"

Maxine nodded her head. She was getting just as excited. "I've got just the thing."

I kissed her on the cheek. "I'll be right back."

I bought a 6-pack at an AM/PM near Century City. Driving back to her place I was beginning to have doubts. I parked my cab in that alley in back of her place, popped open a can of beer. I pulled on the can, pondering, pondering. . . . I started talking to myself.

"So what are you going to do? What do you think? I'm going to fuck her, that's what. You sure? Yeah, I'm sure. I'm gonna go back there and I'm going to give her a hell of a ride—but first, I'm going to have some beer—then I'm going up there. You're not going up there—you haven't got what it takes. Wanna bet? You're thinking about April, you're thinking about your baby. You want your best. Second best won't do. Maxine might be a nice lady, but look at her—living with a rabbit. Hey, man. Come on. She's a spinster at 28, man. An old maid at 28—and she looks like that rabbit. She's got the nose and that mouth, just like her rabbit. And those eyes—see those eyes? Bloodshot eyes, just like the rabbit. And how about that wart on her chin? How about that ugly wart? Huh, man? It's a mole. Wart/mole, *same difference*. You still gonna fuck her? You gonna do it? Sure. I will. I'm gonna try. I gotta beat this thing somehow. This is the only way. You think. Yeah, I hope. I hope I'm right."

I shook my head, finished off the can, opened another. I needed the guts to go through with it. The brew would give me the guts.

"She's so damn nice. . . . Jeeze. She looks just like the fucking rabbit. Nice tits, I guess."

I rested my forehead against the steering wheel. "I can't do it . . . ," I heard myself say. "I can't go up there. . . . Bunny why did we have to break up? I don't want this . . . I don't want to live like this. . . . You said you'd love me forever, Bunny, . . . I just want my baby. . . ."

I lifted my head. I had an idea, a way out.

"That's what I'll do . . . call Maxine back. Tell her you have to work, they want you to work. Tell her you'll make it some other night. Tell her you're sorry, but that you could get together later on. . . ."

I drove to a pay phone, dropped my dime in. I started dialing Maxine's number—and hung up. I tried again—and could not follow through. I returned to the cab.

"Goddammit; goddammit."

I turned the key in the ignition, pulled away. I was back parking in her alley, got out and climbed her steps to the second floor.

Maxine answered her door all in red—red heels, red garter belt, red bra and panties. The gown she had on was some dreadful-colored thing, see-through. It was all very garish, unappealing. I did my best to conceal my true feelings. I had started it all and I would be a man about it and follow through. I would show some decency and not let this woman down. She was doing her best.

Even her tits, as large as they were, were unappealing to me; not unlike cream cheese in their whiteness were her breasts and lacking any firmness, it seemed. All unappealing, as everything would be after April.

I smiled. I said: "Wow-wee. Lookin' good."

She was pleased to hear that. "You think so? You really think so?"

"For sure. Yeah. I like the outfit."

She could not touch April. I raised my eyebrows, and said, "Yep. Hot stuff all right."

We were over by her bed soon enough. I had my clothes off, and the rest of hers. We were under the sheets. Maxine was breathing heavily.

"*I'll do anything you ask . . . ,*" she said. "*I'll be your sex slave. . . .*"

She worked away at my groin with her lips, trying her best.

She kept asking what I liked. I was at the other end, attempting to conjure up a desire for this woman, for this poor, sad woman. This was how I saw her. A sad being. I guess we were both sad that way. I had no business being here, no business doing this. My heart was not in it. Only Maxine did not pick up on that. My groin was hard, and that was all that mattered to her. She kept working it. I wanted it to end, I needed to get away, rush back to my room and shower, to stay in the shower for a week, a month.

Finally, I got the nerve to sit up. I pulled away from her gently and sat up. She wondered what was the matter.

"What is it, Chance?"

"Nothing . . ."

"Just tell me what you like and I'll do it."

I felt awful. "It's got nothing to do with you, Maxine."

"You sure?"

"Look, I like you. I really do . . . I . . ."

"Are you thinking about her?"

I nodded. "I can't help it. I'm sorry."

"It's all right."

"I know I started all this. I can't get her off my mind. I love her so much. I mean—" At this point I was beaming. "We were really good to one another there for such a long time. We didn't use each other, the way you see people doing all the time."

"Seems you're obsessed with her."

I got dressed. "I should be getting back to work. I'll call you. That's a promise. Maybe we can go out and stuff; you know, a movie—"

"Yeah, sure—"

"I mean it."

"I understand."

She wrapped a sheet around her, walked me to the door.

I hadn't wanted to hurt her feelings. "I do like you," I told her. "I want to see you again. If it's okay?"

"Yeah, I'd like that," Maxine said. "But first you'll have to work out your problems with this other lady—that is, if you intend to have carnal relations with me"

I gave her another nod, solemn as I was. I left. I was in my cab pulling away, heading back to my room. "You couldn't do it, you couldn't do it. . . . Why did you have to go up there? What did it prove? What did it prove? That you could make her? Is that it? No. What then? Nothing. That's what. Nothing. God, I feel dirty, cheap, cheap, like a fucking whore—a fucking whore. You sleazebag, you scum. How could you? How could you? Shut up. Just shut up. She's out there probably doing the same thing."

I kept saying that my April was out there having a good time, so why couldn't I? Why couldn't I? Because I wasn't cut out for it. I couldn't do it.

"*Why not me*? 'Cause you're a fool, kiddo. You've got some stupid rules that you go by and you can't change. That's why, you pathetic mutherfucker! That's why! *Because you love her, because you love her. . . .*"

I was in the shower as soon as I reached my place. I stayed in the shower a long time; I finished off the beer and stayed in the shower, tears streaming from my face along with the water from above that pounded the top of my skull.

Several days passed. I phoned Maxine to explain that I really was not in any shape to be dating anybody. I had made several attempts, but it was just too soon for me. I needed time to heal (I'd no idea then that it would take a total of six years, *six whole years* before the pain would let me be, before I could see some light at the end of that long, dark tunnel).

Maxine said she understood. I hoped that she did.

We hung up.

• • •

Fag

Several nights had passed since I had walked out on Maxine in the middle of our "carnal encounter." I was at the cab stand at the Beverly-Wilshire Hotel in Beverly Hills. The doorman blew his whistle. As I pulled into the driveway I watched a portly Arab attired in suit and tie approach my cab.

"Good evening," said he. A pleasant sounding gent, I thought.

"How are you?" said I.

"Let's go to West Hollywood."

I got us out of the driveway, made a right on Rodeo Dr., and took it north.

"Whereabouts in West Hollywood?" I asked

"Where the action is."

"How do you mean?"

"You know—nightclubs, hot spots."

"They're all over the place. Got a name?"

"Any gay club will do."

I thought about that for a minute. When we reached Santa Monica Bl., I took us east. "There's the Manic Monkey. That's pretty popular."

"Oh yeah?" said he, perking right up. "How do you know?"

"I'm a cab driver—I make it my business to know these things. That's how I make my living."

"Have you ever been inside?"

"No, sir; I've never been inside."

Now, I could have been rude and/or nasty to this chubby guy

sitting in my backseat, but I chose not to be that way. Treat them with respect, courtesy, no matter what their sexual preference happens to be. And I made it a point to be this way at all times—unless they put their hands on me. But that rarely happened. A moment passed before the Arab followed up with: "You have never slept with a man, have you?" The man's questions were beginning to unsettle me.

"*Nope*," said I.

"That's all right," he said, failing to mask his disappointment. "I understand."

I did not know how to respond to that one. You don't have to say anything, Chance. Just keep driving. Take the man where he wants to go, drop him off. Period. Get the next fare.

"Is that a good pickup place?" he asked.

"I wouldn't know, sir. All I know is every time I've gone by there the place was busy, lots of people around—mostly males, some women. My guess is the women who hang out at this place are gay, too."

"What about this gay newspaper? Do you know anything about it?"

"Which one?"

"I don't recall the name. They carry advertisements for male escorts. I have no idea where to get one."

"Oh, those," I said. "You can get those anywhere, any paper rack. They're all over the place."

"Really? I never see them. I have no idea where to get one." He was lying, but it did not matter.

"On any corner. In West Hollywood."

"If I gave you twenty dollars, would you be so kind as to buy a newspaper for me? I truly would appreciate it, sir."

I was in the cab business to make a living. I accepted the twenty.

"No problem," said I; "I can do that for you."

"Fine then. Thank you. I would appreciate it if you would be so kind as to drop me in front of the Manic Monkey while you purchase the newspaper for me. I'm interested in going inside and taking a look."

"Sure thing," I said; drove him to the Manic Monkey, and he got out. I drove off.

Now I had a peculiar problem on my hands—even though I had said to him: *No problem*. What if someone that knew me saw me buying a gay newspaper? What then? It made me nervous as hell. If I were gay it would not have mattered at all, but I wasn't. How was I going to go about buying the newspaper for the Arab?

To hell with it! Do it. What's there to hide? *You know what you are and you are not homosexual—so just do it. Be a man about it and do it*. And if someone should spot you buying a fag rag—so what? Too damn bad. People were so damn quick to put labels on others anyway. Remember Viet Nam?

Remember the way you had intended to lighten your hair with Peroxide to look hip and cool (you were 18, had not been sent to the bush yet, lazying around in that beach town of Cam Rahn). That had been the thing—blond hair and dark sunglasses—and your hair, to your shock and dismay, had gone platinum on you. And the jerks, those ignorant redneck jerks pointing the finger and saying underbreath: "Guy's queer."

And do you recall, months later, in a different part of Nam (in the relative safety of the base camp, away from the boonies for three days of R&R, hot meals and actual showers), do you recall going to see the medic because your testicles ached due to the sixty-five pound ruck you had been lugging around on your back in triple-thick canopy jungle, dodging bullets and sidestepping booby-traps. And the hick medic was convinced you were queer instead, that you had gone into the medic's barracks because you had wanted to be touched down there by another man? And this medic had passed it around to the others in your platoon, spread false rumors about you? Do you remember? And all you had wanted was for a way to end the pain in your groin region, fearing it was hernia. Jockey shorts would have helped you tremendously, but the army did not believe in jockey shorts (and some of those ignorant redneck types were even convinced that if you wore jockey shorts you had to be a "faggot"). All military underwear consisted of green boxer shorts; that was all anybody received in the boonies, as well as when we were allowed our brief three-day stays in the rear.

Do you recall all that? The ignorance? The labels? The accusations? I had tolerated the ribbing, the harassment; never bothered to explain anything to the vacuous white trash I'd been stuck to serve with in the jungles of Nam—not that all were this way. I'd even met some genuine human beings there; only the rest seemed to go out of their way to make your life pretty damn miserable. It always seemed to me the "macho types," the ones obvious about it, were always trying to conceal something. What were *they* hiding?

And this is why I went out of my way to treat human beings with respect. This is exactly why. People were too quick and eager to point the finger.

Buy the paper. Get it over with, I kept saying to myself.

And I wondered what April's reaction would be if she saw me go up to one of those sidewalk racks pulling out a gay paper?

You're making a living. You told the man you would get him a newspaper. He paid you good money for it. Do it.

Just do it.

I was back on Santa Monica Boulevard again, east of Doheny. I noticed a row of paper racks on the sidewalk there on the south side of the street. I parked it at the curb next to the racks, got out. Santa Monica Boulevard was busy, lots of cars driving by (with people in them). I felt intimidated, nervous.

Hell, what did I do? What am I guilty of?

You can't sneak around something like this because that's when you get busted. She'll spot you. April will see you and she'll be convinced you're a homo now, the reason you preferred to masturbate than make love to her (although she would never understand that masturbation was simpler, easier, required a lot less work. If only she could have had some control down there, if only she could have made it possible for me to feel some friction down there, that my groin was rubbing against something down there, instead of empty air. I do not wish to blame here, but this is why lovemaking with her was always so exhausting and finally unfulfilling—unless she got me off orally.).

Would she ever be able to understand this?

I looked the stands over, found the type of cheap, sleazy rag of a paper I thought the Arab might like, dropped my 75¢ in.

I reached for the paper, tossed it in my front seat through the open window, executed swiftly, as though I were stealing something, as though I had just committed some sort of petty crime. As ridiculous as it seems—this is exactly how it had felt for me. I was guilty of a criminal act. Christ. Let me get out of here. I hurried around the front of my cab, slid in, and pulled away. A moment later I was letting out a deep sigh of relief. It was over. What the hell were you so nervous about? You're a man, and it's a free country. The apprehension did not entirely leave me as I was still in West Hollywood, the center of gay life in L.A. I nearly always felt uneasy about having to spend the slightest amount of time in this neighborhood.

I was back at the Manic Monkey. The Arab walked out, climbed in.

"You're right," he said. "It's packed in there, very busy."

"But you didn't like it enough to stay, eh?"

"Some other time. I have to get back to the hotel," he explained half-nervously. "Did you get my newspaper?"

I pulled away from the curb, handed him the paper. I could easily make him out in my rearview mirror, beaming, leafing through the paper. He looked up momentarily. "Was it difficult?" he wanted to know.

". . . No; not at all," I answered.

"Well, I do appreciate it. This is exactly what I had in mind."

Another happy customer.

"You know," he offered; "in my country you can get executed for exhibiting homosexual behavior."

"Oh, yeah?" I said, just to have something to say.

"Oh yes," he said. "It's very strict in the Arab countries, very strict. You don't know how good you have it here in America, the freedom. I do so enjoy my visits here."

I drove him back to the Beverly-Wilshire Hotel. "Is the twenty dollars enough to cover the fare?" he inquired.

"Yes, sir; it is," I answered.

Before he vacated the back he had his coat off and wrapped it hastily around the gay newspaper, doing a competent job of concealing it this way. He thanked me again as he scrambled out of my taxi, and I watched him hotfoot it inside the hotel lobby past the doorman and other people milling about. Well, I was amused. As I said—another happy customer. I drove off.

Later that night there was a message on my answering machine:

"You're a fag," the female voice said. Good old Maxine. And I had been so convinced of her class and decency. I played it again. "You're a fag." Click. There it was. So someone had noticed me buying the fag rag after all. What could I do? I shook my head and laughed. I felt a bit sorry for Maxine and all the other Maxines out there in this town.

• • •

Beverly Hills Was Easy To Hate

I was in the Valley buying Angus Gladwyn a hamburger at Carney's on Ventura Boulevard. I had told him the whole story, everything that had happened with Maxine: the mole on her chin, the rabbit, the red garter belt, all of it, including the little message, the nasty little message Maxine ended up leaving on my answering machine.

We ate our hamburgers. Angus was appreciative of every free meal that came his way, as he had been unemployed for quite some time now. Financial woes. We all had them.

I said to him: "And I'm thinking: God, she's a sweet person; why did I have to hurt her feelings like that? It bothered me. And then the card comes—from her. And the card says: I hate to be left dangling. It didn't make any sense, Angus. I thought I had made it all clear. I'm just not in any shape to be seeing anybody. A one-night-stand—not even a one-night-stand—*half of a one-night stand.*"

Angus was nodding his head, enjoying his burger and fries.

I said: "Here's the topper—the final word from that *sweet lady*; she left a message on my tape—it said, *get this*—'You're a fag.'"

We both had a chuckle.

I shook my head, said: "*You're a fag*? Nice person, huh? Understanding. Sweet through and through. Why there is so much misery in this fucking world."

Angus was laughing by now, and said: "So you going to see this Maxine again?"

"You're pulling my leg, right?"

Angus laughed so hard he damn near choked on a French fry.

I couldn't stop shaking my head, then looked up at the row of silver spoons that had come in, the Silver Spoon Crowd that resided around these parts of the Valley: Studio City, Reseda, Encino, Tarzana—they were just like the Beverly Hills Crowd, Bel Air, Westwood; all the same. Spoiled and stupid-looking. Daddy paid for everything. Everything had been handed to them on a silver platter—and the real thing—like love and decency meant nothing. The whole thought of it always turned my stomach.

I said: "That's Beverly Hills, Angus—the flake capitol of the world."

A month later I was on the cab stand at the Beverly-Wilshire. Last up. Slumped down in my seat. The fares weren't coming. You did your best to detach yourself from it, all of it: the nowhere existence, the lack of progress and the years invested, the haunting past that kept pecking at your brain, by hoping for sleep. . . . Only, as hard as I tried, I could not fall asleep. That pay phone I used to call my girl from every night across the street at the parking lot was there and could not be avoided. I stared at the pay phone. I would not be making any more calls to her from it. Around 8:00 p.m. every night, the nights I worked, I would phone her. It had become a habit, more than a habit—a sort of ritual and a need—even the times I would get an out-of-town trip (and seemed to be annoyed by the fact I'd have to pull off the freeway, if I happened to be on some freeway, to get to a pay phone if it was near eight o'clock simply because my girl had expected me to call her).

But sitting down in my cab like that, able to see the top of the phone, how much I wished I could have called her from it now: *Your Hubby's calling. Hi, Bunny. How are you?*

How's Bridget? (her German Shepherd) *How's things? Everything all right there? I feel so bad because all we have is this one car and you getting stuck at home like this by yourself.*

And April would always respond with: *I don't mind it, honey.* I would say: *Go out with your friends, Bunny. Do things. You don't have to stay in, you know? Go out and do things, April. Some day all this will change for us. You'll see. Things are going to be better.*

Just then I heard a woman giggling outside my cab. It sounded strangely familiar, irksome. I wanted to tune it out of my mind and concentrate on the pay phone across the street and the memories that went with it; this was our pay phone, the pay phone I usually called my girl from every night. I wanted to be left alone with my thoughts. The giggling persisted. There was no shutting it out. It was so incredibly high-pitched and affected it was painful to listen to. And also I knew who it was without having to look up. I lifted my head enough just the same. *Maxine.*

Making out with a guy up against a glass storefront a mere twenty feet from my cab. Why my cab?—and why so close?

Maxine noticed me and cranked up the volume. The guy was in a three-piece suit, white shirt, tie—another slick Beverly Hills phony—and continued to paw at her, lick her neck, earlobes. They worked pretty hard to put on this show. And for what? Maxine, the Rabbit Lady. Her mole was gone.

That ugly, black mole the size of a nipple was no longer there. I guessed she'd had it removed. She had a different hairdo this time, had spent some money on her appearance; her hair was so black now it appeared dark blue in the moonlight. I noticed a tight white blouse that she had on to showcase her figure to the fullest, and a black, tight-fitting skirt that clung to her body. And the "playboy" with her kept pulling her toward him. Hard. Pressed his torso against her enormous bosom.

Bored, I slumped back down in my seat. What they were doing did not bother me. It meant nothing to me. I felt nothing for Maxine, never had.

I did my best to tolerate the artificial laughter for a while; but finally it was her giggle, that nerve-wracking, high-pitched giggle (not unlike chalk being scraped against a blackboard) that made me want to scream out. This was her way of getting back at me for not paying her a return visit, for not being "a man." Now she had a "real man" in her arms: Don Juan of Beverly Hills, who would give her a forgettable ride and forget he ever knew her.

I hated that giggle, and clamped my hands (hard) over my ears. It was no use. I could still hear them. Finally, I shot up in my seat and drove my cab off the stand, eager to leave the two lovebirds behind.

Beverly Hills.
I hated this place.

• • •

Love Did Not Happen This Easily

It was a call on Crescent Heights, north of 3rd Street this afternoon. A gray duplex like all the others in the area. I pulled into the driveway, reached for the mike.

"It's for somebody named Kendall," the dispatcher said. I looked up and a beautiful woman stepped out of the house and climbed into the cab. My heart was in my throat. All she'd had on was a simple pair of tight-fitting gray sweatpants and a white T-shirt. That did not matter. She was a knockout: 5 ft. 8 or 9, a real heart-stopper that took your breath away, she did mine. *Take it easy, Chance; take it easy*. You must know by now only a real sucker dreams of being in love with someone in this town, a real sucker and nothing but a sucker. Love is nonexistent around here; but my God, she looked fine.

"Hi," I said, once I'd recovered.

"Can you take me to the Beverly Hills Cafe?"

So I only had ten minutes to get somewhere with her, if I intended to get somewhere with her; that was the time I had to strike up some kind of conversation, to get to know this woman—and let her know something about me, where I was coming from, my own background, etc.

Do you see what a fool I really am now?

My heart was fluttering, butterflies in my belly, aching to be in love with a decent woman. I had no idea what she was like, but I thought: You can't give up, you just can't.

Keep trying, Register, keep trying. Remember what you used to say to yourself? You're not a quitter! You're not!

You don't quit. Others quit, not you! You lost out to love, but that had not been the real thing; April tried to tell you that. If it had been the real thing it would not have ended the way it did.

I was willing to try again with Kendall. I didn't know her, it was true—but I would make that effort. My guess was she worked as a waitress—as she had indicated she was in a real hurry to get to the place on time. By now I was pretty good at guessing what people did for a living, what part of the country they were from, and at times I could even discern what part of the world they were from. Often, if someone got in the cab and they had energy and were alert—they were not from L.A. Simple as that. If they talked about things that mattered, world affairs, anything of any importance, they were not from Southern California.

The L.A. type talked about modeling, screenwriting, acting, making money and getting a Mercedes, getting that toot.

Kendall had been living here four years, was studying to be an architect, which sounded pretty impressive to me. She was more beautiful than any model I'd ever seen and she had the good sense not to be interested in any of that: *movies or modeling*.

The sucker kept thinking: Maybe we can fall in love and my past won't matter, and maybe we can move out of L.A.

I told her I was writing and not selling anything. When she inquired why I had moved to L.A. from Chicago I told her that I had moved out West believing I would have better prospects out here, and that I had family here. I had moved out after returning from Nam, that was true, but had only seen my parents and younger brother and sister but once.

I did not wish to burden this person that I had just met with further details. I couldn't bring myself to admit either that I had anything to do with movies and that that had been the real pull that had landed me in Tinseltown.

I couldn't admit it, was ashamed to—and as far as the rest of it was concerned: I had told the truth; I no longer had any interest in filmmaking. I had been trying to write fiction, books, stories; nothing remotely to do with Hollywood. Screenplays were not my forte (not that I knew what my *forte* was, or that I even had a *forte*). Hollywood was a ball-buster, simple and true; a jaded, evil whore.

I got Kendall to the coffee shop on time, and hurried back to my apartment to grab a copy of my book, that self-published, self-help book on how to recover from a bad love-affair. I had used a pen name for the cover: Alec Summers; my reason being I wasn't in it for fame and glory—but had sincerely wished to help others who may have been going through the agony of a divorce and/or bad breakup with someone they loved dearly.

I shaved, cleaned up, and drove back to the coffee shop.

I wrote my home phone inside the cover, my name and cab number, and handed it to Kendall.

Later that evening the dispatcher informed me to call Kendall at the coffee shop. "In fact," said he; "she called several times."

I dialed the number, asked to speak to Kendall.

"I'd like to talk to you," she said, no longer sounding indifferent (as before). She was excited about something.

"What do you think of the book?" I asked.

"That's what I'd like to talk to you about," she said. What was she all-aflutter about, I honestly wondered.

I stopped by the coffee shop and, although she was quite busy, I was given special attention by her as I sat there at one end of the counter. She was wide-eyed, curious and excited and wondered why I had given her the book.

I shrugged, grinning sheepishly. "I just thought you might like to read it," I said, not knowing how to break it to her or whether I even should, that I had written it and paid for the actual printing. . . .

I didn't know what her reaction would be if I'd confessed: Because I saw you as a potential mate. Admittedly, there was a good degree of anger in the book that I was not entirely aware of (at the time of the writing); like I said, while I wrote it, it was either pick up the razor blade again or write the book. It had taken four months to complete the manuscript, and I thought: I feel fine. I'll be okay now.

It's over, the pain is over. I can do without April; I really can. The book is over and so is my pain. She never loved me and that's why she never bothered to call, why I had never mattered to her.

And then I had a relapse, got it bad (at about the eighth month of being on my own), just as fierce as before; all the aches were back. *All of it*: the begging to the ceiling, the pleading to the walls, everything. So it was not over, far from it. I had hoped to fool myself into believing that the book had cured me of April, that I had been healthy enough now to go on with my life; if only I had known that five years later I would still be mixed up, screwed up, a hopeless case, that I never would get over her, no matter what I said or did. If I had known all this right after the split I probably would have chucked it right there and then. I'd had no idea that the healing would take years and years. . . .

As I said, I was at the coffee shop, and this radiant woman, I guessed Kendall to be 24, was giving me attention I rarely, if ever, got from someone with her looks. Yes, April had been attractive, but that too had been another of those rare occasions.

And there was something about Kendall's face: *it was radiant.* There was a radiance, there truly was.

She looked like a woman in love. Have you ever seen a woman in love?—the way a woman's eyes can brighten and glow? Her face glowed, exuding that happiness that came from within.

I was looking at Kendall and her transformation was obvious to me and I wondered if it could have been this slim little book that I had written?

Was it possible?

I did not know how to take it. *Was she actually interested in me?—the loser cabby with no future in sight?—the loser sinking lower and lower, who lived in that dark hole full of dying senior citizens? Me?*

She kept asking about the book, kept asking about me. Was I going with anybody? I let on that I did write it. She had guessed that much. Every chance this woman got she made the effort to be at my end of the counter; at one point even planted both of her elbows on the counter directly in front of me, resting her chin in her palms and saying dreamily:

"You know something? *You really are special.* I'd like a chance to get to know you."

If she were blushing—I had to be doubly so.

Was this really happening? She wanted to get to know me?

I was at a loss for words, and sipped at the tea I had ordered. We made small talk at every opportunity (as the place was busy and she had to keep working). Kendall said: "I'm working all night. Would you like to get together in the morning at the end of my shift for coffee or breakfast?"

I'd never had a woman that looked like her come on to me this way.

"I'd really like that," said I, and left.

At 4:30 a.m. I got another message from the dispatcher.

"Call Kendall," he said.

I phoned her.

"Would six o'clock be all right with you, Chance?" she wondered. "I really would like to talk to you."

"I'll be there," I told her.

"I can't believe there's still guys like you around here. You're special. I really mean it."

"Thank you, Kendall. You're pretty special yourself. I'll be there."

And I was.

We ordered two cups of coffee to go, and I walked her to the parking lot in back of the building. Kendall was driving an old Volkswagen Beetle that had seen better days; it was rusty and beat-up looking, a dune buggy of sorts, a real mess, just out of place in Beverly Hills; so I thought: *a good sign*. I was impressed. She doesn't care about cars and things that are not important anyway. She's got a good heart, and that's all that matters and that is all *that should matter*.

"What would you like to do? Where would you like to go?" she asked.

I shrugged, and thought Roxbury Park might be appropriate.

"We can park our cars and just talk."

She liked the idea. I would drive my cab and she would follow behind in her Volks. "That way you'll be able to drive home directly from there," I explained: "and I'll be able to go back to work."

She was agreeable to anything I said. *I had the magic formula: Chance Register*.

Can you see how confused this had made me? What was so new and different about me all of a sudden? Did my face become handsome suddenly through some strange miracle? God had waved his hand and given me good looks? I glanced up in my rearview mirror, did it twice. No, I was still the same average-looking guy: longish brown hair, tired blue eyes, tired features in general; a cab driver with no money in the bank, no car, and I still owed my buddy Angus Gladwyn that two hundred and fifty bucks I had borrowed from him, money that had made the move into that one-room apartment on Hauser possible. That loan had been a Godsend. I was still Chance Register, and this attention made me suspicious.

What now? *Why now? How real could all this be?—all this affection she was lavishing me with*? (This woman that really did not know me—nor I her.)

We reached the park, and it was decided we would sit in my cab and sip our coffee and talk. That was all I had wanted. Talk. Let's get to know one another. I was physically attracted to this blond-haired, well-built lady, there was no doubt about that; but I had learned—to have love there had to be more. You had to take the time to know one another. Right? *Right*.

She got real close, sipped her coffee; her eyes dreamy and focused on my own, and she was looking, more like *gazing*, deeply into my eyes this way. God, how I had wanted to fall in love with her, just a man aching for love, and how much I had wanted to hold her in my arms and kiss her. But I said to myself: No, you would feel awkward and uncomfortable about it, because you know you are not in love. This isn't love; it couldn't be this soon. It might happen, but only if it is given the proper chance to flourish. This is what went on inside my head, while Kendall pressed herself up against my torso and revealed her life story. It poured out of her, the men she had known over the years and fallen for, and the lies she had been fed by these men so they could get to her and use her; the professor who had lied to her and gotten her pregnant (and later turned out to be married with three kids), the subsequent abortion; and there had been other love affairs gone bad: a rape even, at gunpoint. It seemed she had had nothing but bad luck with the opposite sex, just as I had. My heart went out to her. It was easy to relate to the pain, loneliness, of having been used and later conveniently discarded.

I was beginning to feel that there might be a chance for us. God was smiling down on Chance Register this time, and had sent me someone decent to fall in love with.

I had attempted to explain my life to so many so often in my cab in the past that I was weary of hearing myself express another word about it, and this time would make sure to let this woman do most of the talking. I was no longer interested in the Chance Register story. More often than not, when someone got in your cab, and if the ride was of any length at all, in order not to appear rude, you gave them (if they inquired) a capsulized version of your background. Where you from? How long have you been in L.A.?

How do you like it? What brought you out here? Ever miss the seasons? How about them Lakers? Ever go back to Chicago? Where are you from originally? (That one in those days I considered a bit personal—and would answer around it; on the other hand, if the person asking was a genuine human being, I might say Sarajevo.) If people were friendly, and I did get some passengers that genuinely were decent and interested, I opened up a bit. It made the job easier to take, the rides smoother.

This time I would allow the other person to do most of the talking; I wanted to know about Kendall, and I listened intently while she spoke. And when two hours later it was decided it would be best for her to go home and get some rest—after all, she had been on her feet all night—we hugged, and agreed to get together at a later date. We would go out, a dinner or something. Her face was still glowing, and she needed, desired me to kiss her—*and I could not bring myself to do it*. That's too intimate. I felt awkward; it was too soon. Not now, not yet, I reminded myself. Once, years before, while sitting in my car with a date at a drive-in movie, our first date, I had attempted to be romantic, had moved in for that first kiss, missed the woman's lips and our teeth had locked!

Talk about your embarrassments. She had cut the date short, and had never wanted to see me after that. Some guys were cut out to be Romeos, quick with the moves, slick and smooth and all those things. I simply could not move that fast. Kissing someone on the mouth was a lot more intimate than having sex with them. That's the way I was—and couldn't change it. So be it.

Instead, I hugged Kendall; gave her a good squeeze with all my heart and soul behind it, and we broke.

But I remained suspicious—about all of it.

Love did not happen this easily. It never did, even when it appears to be love at first sight—not that I was looking at this experience here with this woman as anything near that; I hoped that it could be, would be. I remained suspicious, scared.

I had learned.

She let me know again how glad she was to have met me, and walked to her Volks. We waved goodbye, and drove off in different directions.

For the next ten days or so a day did not go by that she did not phone at least once, either the cab office or my place. She often phoned two or three times a day, leaving plenty of messages on my answering machine: "*I want to get together with you, Chance. I want to see you; just to talk to. Please call me.*"

My lovesick heart was easily opening up to her and doing its darnedest to convince my mind that it would be okay to go along, it would be all right to give in to her—but my mind knew better. Still, *my heart would not listen.*

Love did not happen this easily.

Look how long you've gone without somebody to love, my heart insisted; and my mind kept countering with: *It's too soon. How can it be love this quickly? It just does not happen this fast.* She does not appear to have stability.

She's interested in me now—just now—and she'll tire of me just as quickly. She's the type. How do I know she can go the distance—or would even want to? I don't know what she's like, and don't have a damn idea, as a person.

Character, man. Character. It was frustrating as hell.

And it all happened over that thin, one-hundred-page self-help book I had written on how to recover from a bad split. What a joke, I thought just then—look who's trying to hand out advice, when I couldn't even heal myself.

Forget it. Your heart was in the right place; that's all that matters—and people know it, see it, feel it.

Forget it.

I couldn't, stop thinking about Kendall, that is.

The phone rang one evening I happened to be in.

Kendall wanted to get together. I was petrified, down to my toes. Man, I wasn't even out of the woods with this thing with April, the one I had given my all to—and here I was with another possible mess looming overhead. I was scared shitless. By now I was certain nothing would come of this.

What I was looking for, desired and needed, this woman could not give me. I couldn't put my finger on it, as beautiful as she was, she just did not strike me as the type that would be able to stay with a guy, just one guy—all the way through. She would not be the soulmate I was looking for, and I was already falling for her.

Do you see my fate now? Do you see that I could not win, no matter how hard I tried?—how hard I scraped and struggled to get on without my girl, to live my own life, to find love and pick up the pieces of the puzzle again.

Kendall had wanted to come to my place and "talk," she said; "We can drink beer and just talk." This woman thought she was in love with me after only ten days. She was after sex, no doubt—which was fine, nothing wrong with that at all—only there was no way I would allow myself to go that route with this woman before we'd had a chance to know what was in our hearts and minds, before we could fall in love. I wanted love, dammit. First love, and then once we knew where we were going, once that was arrived at and understood, why then we could make love and stay together and, who knew, get married?

This is the way my mind worked. Was it strange? For L.A. perhaps—but people in other parts of this great nation thought this way, people out in Canada and South America thought this way, people in Europe and other countries thought this was normal—but not here in Tinseltown. This was considered strange and unusual behavior.

I explained that I was not proud of my small and messy room and that we ought to go out and maybe drive around a bit and we could talk and get something to eat.

The truth of it was I was not healthy enough to begin dreaming of love at this early stage of the game, did not feel safe and secure enough.

Kendall showed up in her Volks dressed in tight jeans, and a jacket that barely reached her waist, thus revealing a fine and sexy, if muscular rear end. She had all that golden hair done up and she had taken extra care with her makeup and what a breathtaking beauty she truly was, and I knew, as hard as I tried, I was a mess inside my head, the psyche throbbed with pain; it was too soon for me. I was still fighting off the dark, the blues, the past. It would not be long, I was certain, before Kendall got wind of that, how strangely I behaved, how strange and nervous, the silences; and she would walk like the rest.

But I had to try, had to keep trying. It is tough to accept defeat, tough to admit being a quitter. Quitters never got anywhere, and I would not be a quitter. I would keep reaching out to love any way I knew how, just keep reaching out to it and I would be saved. *Love was the answer, love was the only cure*. It was this same love that had cut my heart and mind to pieces, the same love that had screwed me all up, and it would be love again that would come in and save me, put me back together again—so to speak. Only love can mend a broken heart. That was a Gene Pitney song. It was.

Never mind.

I kept hoping this woman would understand and give me time, and would not expect *too much too soon*.

We got in her car and drove.

I did not have the money to take her anywhere, nor did I really feel like doing anything but drive around. I simply wanted to be with her. It would be a good way to get to know each other.

She drove us out to Veteran Ave., near Westwood, and showed me the third floor apartment where she had lived while attending UCLA a while back. She indicated the window of her room where she had spent many hours studying and learning how to do stained glass . . . and I thought: Thank God, another *loner*. And this renewed my hopes. A loner of the opposite sex. What a relief. A loner would understand me and give me a chance. Only could a loner relate to a loner; the pain of it, the lonely hours spent by yourself while desperately needing to accomplish something. Loners knew what it was like. This woman had spent many hours cooped up by herself, just as I had, trying to do things, trying to create something she believed in and could be proud of. She had waited all this time for someone who would be good to her, and understand her; all those years spent in tiny rooms, all those years of studying, taking classes, working hard, all that time spent alone. . . .

She knew about it. She could relate.

We drove south to Pico, and a bit west, and she showed me another house where she had lived with a guy prior to their breaking up. She'd had her share of heartache. Men don't really understand how a beautiful woman like this could have her heart broken, that women, no matter how sexy or good-looking they might be, have their share of misfortune, their good share of loneliness, of having had their hearts torn apart.

I was looking at Kendall and her perfect face, the nose, the green eyes, the high cheekbones, the kissable lips and the blond hair, and found it so tough to imagine. It did not matter how good-looking you happened to be in this world, you received your slice of pain as well. And really, I may have suspected, but I had been unaware of the extent.

The general consensus was that homely men and women were the ones who suffered the most; people with looks were privileged and used to being catered to—men went drooling after good-looking women; the beauties of the world had it made. And here was Kendall, proof that it was simply not so.

I'll be good to you, Kendall, I wanted to say; just give me the chance to prove myself. Give me that one chance to show you what a good man I really am. That's all I've wanted all this time. I have learned so much by now. *I know what not to do*. I have learned so much from all the mistakes I've made before. I need a chance.

But I could not get much out.

The blues kept my jaw clamped shut. Kendall was making every effort to keep up her end of the conversation. I did not say much the entire time—and could see this bit of good fortune as well slipping right through my fingers.

She must know that I am really not okay just yet. *The wounds have not yet healed, Kendall; I wish I could explain. . . .*

I said nothing.

At one point I suggested we get something to eat. There was a Norm's nearby. We went in. When I saw what a greasy spoon the place was, I decided against staying. To be well-mannered about it, I left a dollar bill on the table.

We rose, and I started for the exit. Kendall turned, scooped up the money and jammed it in my hand, explaining:

"There's no reason to leave a tip; we didn't order anything."

She had been right.

The wounds needed more time to heal. I was not thinking clearly. But do you see how hard I kept trying? My former girlfriend had no use for me, and I wished to understand and kept trying to find love and I was not well enough to get anywhere. Who would have patience for me?—to stick it out with me and give me that chance?

We drove east, through Beverly Hills. It was obvious we were not getting anywhere. What a *dud* the date had turned out to be for her, I kept thinking, wanting to apologize. Kendall, I wanted to say, I'm in awe of your beauty, and just too shy; I'm just off-kilter and so confused right now. . . . Do you realize how grateful I am for your company? The words faded before they reached my lips.

AND THIS HAPPENED ALMOST EVERY TIME. . . .

We ended up at Nibblers, near La Cienega and Wilshire. Kendall ordered a beer. My dwindling budget on my mind, I ordered for myself fries and a Coke—and it did escape me at the time that this move had made me appear as nothing more than a tight-wad. The truth of it is, I am far from a cheapskate—only I could not do anything right, not here, not with her.

We touched on the self-help book some more, with Kendall saying: "There's one thing that's in the book that I don't agree with—I don't think you should hate the person you split up with."

I couldn't argue the point, nor could I recall anywhere in the book that said hating your former spouse/lover was all right; in fact, the entire message in the book is just the opposite: forgive and forget—and move on.

She got up to buy a pack of cigarettes. I ate my fries in a daze, not quite knowing or understanding why I had ordered the damn French fries (that tasted like cardboard). Kendall was gone for quite some time. Limbo was back, my limbo; numbness. I wished I could have crawled under a rock.

April, April—you filled me with your love, gave me life—and then promptly yanked it all away from me. I thought about that phone call earlier in the evening from Kendall, she had been so eager at the prospect of being with me, so excited and ebullient . . . and now the change in her was more than evident. . . . She had written me off. As I had feared, I was not the right man for her. . . . I was too passive (not by nature, but the confusion and pain had rendered me into a walking mummy, lacking in energy or any sign of life). I hardly spoke at all. She was in control, all personality and charisma. What personality/color/self-assurance I might have possessed once had vanished into thin air; not a trace remained. Quite aware that I appeared lifeless, while at the same time rather helpless at being able to shed this invisible gag and straight jacket that clung to me in their relentless efforts to crush me into total and utter nonexistence.

It took Kendall quite a while to return to the table, fifteen, perhaps twenty minutes. She was puffing on her cigarette, and chuckling, shaking her head. "Did you see what happened back there at the cigarette machine?" she asked.

I had no idea what she was talking about.

"You didn't see what happened back there? Turned into quite a fiasco, had a pretty hard time getting my cigarettes out of the machine. One of the guys ended up kicking it; it was quite a scene."

Hell, did I give a damn about any of that? Kendall, Kendall, how could you have turned so quickly? I thought, hoped you'd be different. She was so sexy and attractive, killer looks, like a beauty pageant entrant—and yet she was too damn tough and cold inside for my taste. My heart sank lower and lower.

I said, in response to the bit about the cigarette machine:

"No, I didn't know a thing about it."

We stayed a while longer, and decided it was time to leave. Back at my building, we sat in her car for a couple of minutes. Kendall was telling me that she was about ready to return to Placerville, where she was from. "I can't take L.A. anymore. I don't like the people; I've never been happy here."

Don't know why, but I asked if I might be able to see her again, that I needed more time and I would be all right, I'd be myself again, that the breakup had left me a mess.

Kendall smoked her cigarette, looking cool and beautiful, an ice queen, in total command, detached; she felt nothing toward me and was no longer even remotely interested.

She said, blowing smoke and not even looking at me, but straight ahead: "I don't see how that would be possible, since I'm moving up north. It just wouldn't work."

Should have told her more about myself, where I was born, the childhood, the army, getting through the rice paddies and dodging bullets in the jungles of Nam, about always missing out when it came to love, about the struggles to make it in L.A., all of that—but I never got the chance, they didn't give you much of a chance these women—and would it have made any difference to her at all, I wondered?

I nodded.

I had been right. It had been too much to hope for. All the attention and affection she had initially showered me with had been but a passing fancy. I had suspected all along—I would not be her Mr. Right.

I hugged her, and we said goodbye.

Back in my room I pulled on a beer. Alone again. Alone.

Missed out again. . . . I kept trying, I kept trying. . . . Now I was going to have to turn off what I had begun to feel for her.

I phoned her place of residence three times the following week. Kendall was always out. I rode my bicycle to her place the week after that as she had said that's when she would be leaving Los Angeles. I had merely wished to say goodbye to her one final time. One of her roommates, a striking brunette, answered the door. The other roommate, also a looker, was sitting on the living room sofa. I was told that Kendall was out.

I phoned Kendall later that day from a pay phone in Westchester, as I was working. Kendall finally answered. "*Why do you keep calling*?" she said in a curt tone of voice. I was stunned, and did not know how to respond to that. She then revealed that she had been in her room when I had shown up at her place earlier that day and hadn't wanted to see me. "I don't appreciate you coming to my place, I don't like you calling here all the time. My home is my sanctuary."

"What did I do?"

"You just became unpopular, that's all."

". . . I don't understand, Kendall."

"You did exactly what that first guy I lived with did; he kept after me, wouldn't stop phoning."

"I didn't mean to, Kendall. . . . I didn't realize; I'm sorry."

I still didn't get what was going on with her. *What had I done? What had I said? What was it?*

"Forgive me. Was it something I said?"

"You're a nice guy." Her tone was softer now, at least.

"What is it, Kendall?"

"Please don't do this," she said.

"You can't even give a guy a chance? . . . I just wanted to see you. . . . I thought we might get to really know each other, and then maybe we could fall in love. . . ."

"I don't think so . . . ," Kendall said. "I'm sorry. . ."

"Can you at least tell me why?"

"I'm moving back to Placerville."

"I know you said you were moving back. . . . We can't even give it a try? The only reason I kept calling is because I just wanted to see you one more time."

"What for? We'd already said goodbye that night."

". . . I . . . I thought I might ride up there with you; it would give us a chance to get to know each other."

"I don't think so."

"I . . ." I wanted to convey that I was beginning to have feelings for her, that I was beginning to think along those lines, but I knew everything she had said to me, all those words and compliments: "I think you're that someone special I've been looking for to fall in love with. . . ." Words; empty; without meaning—like all the other words I'd heard before.

I hated to admit it, but she was another one that was lost, another ripped-off soul. I wished her luck. She said the last goodbye, and hung up. The sense of defeat when something like this happens to you can be overwhelming. I made it slowly back to the cab and sat there for a while. I didn't understand it, didn't get it.

Nothing added up. I would never learn, no matter how old I got to be, I would never learn anything. Stupid bastards like me were doomed to keep repeating their mistakes.

• • •

And How Are You This Evening?

It was after ten p.m., and it was raining again in L.A. and the streets were slicker than a shaved beaver, and I made an extra effort to really stay alert in that noisy old cab and was feeling like shit because I hadn't been able to make any money in over a week. I'd been breaking even, that's it. The cab cost me thirty bucks to lease (per night), plus about $15 for gas. I'd been breaking even; putting in twelve hours a night and only breaking even.

There was justice in this world, somewhere, I was sure of it, but not in the cab business. But money was the least of my worries. It was a woman, it's always a woman. She didn't care anymore. I hadn't seen her in close to two years, and I was living the life of an old man, someone that had given up, at 30, mind you. You bet it pissed me off, you bet it did. Living the life of an old fuck: I went home, I slept, I drove the hack, went home slept drove the hack. Didn't have any friends, wasn't looking for any either. What a way to live. Wasting it away, wasting it away. And I used to get on *her* for being so lifeless, without zip, gusto; used to tell her: "You don't know how to have a good time, you don't know how to live."

Hah!

What the hell would you call what I was doing? Stuck in a job I was sick and tired of, stuck in a room with a hot plate in a building full of senile old people, a building that used to be a retirement hotel. I was as close to being a Travis Bickle as you could possibly get, without actually going the full distance.

Maybe I was about to have a breakdown, I wasn't sure. I think I wanted it to happen, hoped it would—because that limbo-in-between-existence was nowhere, no fucking where.

I had driven a couple to a restaurant in Santa Monica and was working my way back toward Westwood, when the dispatcher called my cab number.

I responded.

"I got one up on Mulholland," she said; "want it?"

"Why not?" I said.

She gave me the address—a good three or four mile haul from where I was. I was pissed for having taken it. All that gas I'd be wasting, all that gas—and the cab I had got about 8.5 miles to the gallon. And I cursed and bitched and hit the freeway and got off on Mulholland. I know, I know—my own bitching was getting to me too. There is only one answer to bitching, only one: *action*. One did something about it, period. You acted, or you shut the hell up. But at that point, I didn't know any better, didn't want to perhaps. I was in a rut, the bitching, complaining, moody fucking rut. I was sinking fast, going under, and maybe it was what I was ultimately after. Destination: Camarillo State Hospital. I had always believed I was so goddamn tough mentally, physically; always believed I could handle anything, and hell, why not? I'd made it through Nam with flying colors, survived a rough childhood, getting shot at, beaten up; survived ten years of staring at spiders in tiny rooms all over L.A., survived paranoia, the humiliation of having to live on food stamps (for a few months during the early 70s; when and if the food stamps were available), the many nothing jobs, and of course: love—"true love"—the meanest, toughest blow of all, the deadliest crippler, meaner than the big C, than malaria, than a bullet; that most merciless muther of all: LOVE. *Yeah, maybe I was ready.*

She'd had me crawling, whimpering; turned me into a pathetic little worm of a man, not even a worm; total humiliation. You give your heart, and after all you've been through together, after two years, she throws your heart back at you as though it were a piece of shit, *a piece of shit*.

I headed east on Mulholland, taking it easy. It was night and the San Fernando Valley on my left was a sight to behold: green and red and yellow bright lights *glimmering* below. It was truly something. I continued to take in the lights until I reached the address—a house with a white 6-foot wall around it. Hollywood Jack's place. I reached for the phone at the gate, let them know I was there; waited for the gate to open and drove on through.

"She'll be right out," a male voice announced. I shook my head, amused at the procedure. It always worked that way, though—the door would open partly and a guy in a bathrobe would poke his head out and tell you that she (most always a prostitute) would be right out. People in L.A. were crazy, especially up there in Bel Air, Beverly Hills; fucking around with sleazy hookers and drag queens, beating them, etc.

I waited a couple of minutes and did not turn the meter on.

She came out. I didn't see what she looked like, not that I really cared or that it made any difference at this point.

I left the dome light on until she got in, turned the light off, turned the key in the ignition and made it down the driveway.

"*And how are you this evening*?" she asked. Now that was certainly unusual, believe me. She had put some genuine feeling behind it; the words meant something. Maybe she wasn't another hooker, hookers seldom said two words to you—other than maybe: "Can you *step on it*, honey? I got to get to such and such hotel, got an impatient trick waiting."

Anyway, I feel like I'm being buried alive, but I say, barely audible: "Not bad; and you?"

"Fine, thank you."

Definitely not a hooker, I conclude, and in a way a relief. I'm not bum-rapping hookers here—but the ones I've seen (for the most part) were slimy, sleazy and ugly. I'd had it with prostitutes. How about some women that aren't?

I don't rightly know why, but I mentioned the millions of mesmerizing lights down below in the Valley, how fantastic it all was; and she agreed.

And we got a conversation going. How it all got started I'm not entirely sure, but it did, which wasn't bad. I made a left on Beverly Glen, took it down to Ventura Bl.

She had been in L.A. only two years, and really loved it; was from Canada. I told her I had heard a lot of good things about Canada, and that the Canadians I had met were all right, and I meant that. She said that a lot of people who lived in L.A. hated it and were always bitching, instead of doing something about it.

She was right.

We talked about some other things. She had lived in New York, thought it was okay. We touched on the subject of money, that that was what most were into in L.A., fancy cars, expensive homes, showing off in general. She said the town she had grown up in in Canada wasn't anything like that—everyone knew each other, would help each other in need; no one was uptight or anything.

That's what I missed, I told her. I'd like to live in a place like that. Everyone was so impatient and angry in L.A., cutting each other off, cursing each other out.

And in a way it was funny, I was carrying on a conversation with a woman whose face I hadn't even caught a glimpse of, didn't know what she looked like—but it was nothing unusual; it often happened this way. It made me feel good to talk to her. She wasn't your usual L.A. bimbo with a chip on her shoulder, a man-hater.

I got her to the house in Studio City and I had $8.90 on the meter. She gave me $15.

It wasn't the money, the money had very little to do with it, it was the person, the woman, she had smiled when she got out, truly smiled.

I let her know I had enjoyed the chat. She said she had too. But that smile, that warm, radiating smile—I had forgotten what a smile could do to you, the power of a genuine smile. It more than made up for all the bullshit fares I'd encountered during the past two years, more than made up.

Thank you, Sue, for that smile that carried me for quite a while. Just a smile can do that to you now and then.

• • •

('82)

The Famous Person

"Pick up the famous person in front of Barney's Beanery," the dispatcher said.

I had just dropped off a fare in Hollywood and was heading back west on Santa Monica Bl., when I took this call. It was Sunday afternoon. Sunny Sunday. But to me it was just another day of barely hanging onto my sanity, struggling to keep from having a total breakdown and being sent away to the VA mental ward in a straight jacket (insanity, I was certain, was a dark pit from which there would be no bouncing back, not for me—if I dropped into it. So I fought, did my best to remain among "the sane.").

"Oh yeah?" I said. "What famous person is that?"

"You'll find out."

I hadn't liked the tone of that, but shrugged, and let my fare flag me down. She was a woman in her 30s, heavy-set, 5'6". I noticed the rouge on her cheeks; there was too much of it really. She was wearing a plain summer dress, sandals, and she carried a small purse.

Well, when I see a woman with this much rouge and lipstick on her face I know something is not right. I waited for her to get in the cab.

"Hello," she said merrily.

I greeted her with a nod; eyed her skeptically.

"To the airport."

"LAX?"

"Of course," she said.

I pulled away from the curb, stayed on Holloway Dr., taking it toward La Cienega. As we passed The International House of Pancakes on our left, I noticed a police car parked near the entrance. The pancake house was popular with the West Hollywood sheriffs who worked the area. Now, why I even bothered to notice the cop car at all I have no idea, but I sure am glad that I did, because I was going to need a badge in about a minute.

I got us to La Cienega, heading south.

"The dispatcher said you were a famous person . . ."

"Your dispatcher is right, honey. I am a famous person."

By this time I had developed a system for screening my passengers to determine whether they were safe or not, whether I ought to get my money up front and avoid getting "burned" at the other end. I liked to talk to my fares a bit; if they sounded okay, had all their marbles (meaning they were in better shape mentally than I was), then I could relax some and usually expect a relatively smooth ride.

Since she didn't look like any famous person that I knew of, I said, "May I ask whom?"

"Maria Callas."

"*Who*?"

"*Maria Callas.*"

I said: "Maria Callas died two months ago. It was in the paper." It just so happened I had read the obit myself in the *L.A. TIMES*.

"*What do you want*?" came from the backseat. "*Ya want proof? That what you want? Ya want to see my license? Ya need to look at I.D.? That what you're saying*?"

I had the cab going a lot slower than the posted speed limit.

"I need my money up front," I told her.

"*You gonna bother me with that bullshit now? Whatsa matter? You don't believe me?!*"

We were two blocks south of Santa Monica Bl. I pulled over to the curb, turned my head to face her.

"Ma'am, the company policy is that we get our money up front for trips like this—" I was being polite, courteous about it, I thought.

"*I am Maria Callas, I tell you, the world-famous opera star! Why are we sitting here? I have to get to the airport*!"

Why is this happening to me? I wondered. Why me? What did I do to get passengers like this? Wished I could have said to my ex: Do you see now why it often took me upwards of two hours to unwind after a night of dealing with sad cases like this? Do you understand the depression? The blues that wouldn't lift? The blues that kept me down, even when all I ever wanted was to be up for you and for me—up and happy and full of life? I just wanted a chance to do something meaningful with my life.

"I'm sorry," I said calmly. "I need the money up front—"

"*How much*?"

"Fifteen bucks."

"*Fifteen dollars*? All right, you'll get your fifteen dollars when we get there. I am in a hurry. NOW, CAN WE GET A MOVE ON IT?!"

I shook my head. "Sorry," I said.

"*What is the matter with you?! I have to get back to New York. Take me to the airport!*"

I turned away. I couldn't take looking at the red lipstick mouth and all that rouge. How do I get myself into these messes? How? And how do I get out of this one? I remembered having passed the cop car in the IHOP parking lot moments earlier. I wondered if I was going to have to go back there in order to get rid of this woman now.

I could hear her digging around inside her purse for something.

"Where in the hell is that goddamn picture?!"

Finally, she came up with a faded, dog-eared, black-and-white photo of a guy in his 40s, hair greased back. I didn't know what any of it was supposed to mean. I just wanted to get paid in advance, or else figure out a way to unload her, get her out of my life. Period. I didn't need this. I wasn't in any shape to handle scenes like this. I felt empathy for people like her, I truly did, but my own state was pretty damn shaky at best.

"Here," she said. "Isn't he handsome? That's my sweetheart." Then she started kissing the photograph. "I love you, Manny honey. I love you so much. I luvvvyoouuuu! I'll soon be at your side, Manny honey."

Then she looked up. "*We're still sitting here—why? Why aren't we moving?*"

"Because I need that money."

"*You what? How dare you insult me like this?! Do you realize who I am?!*"

I was shaking my head hopelessly. "Yes," I said. "You're Maria Callas. But I still need my money up front—or else we're not going anywhere. We're not moving; in fact, if I don't get my money you'll have to get out of my cab."

"You're strange," she said. "I knew it. I knew there was something strange about you the minute I laid eyes on you."

It takes one to know one, I guess—something to that effect.

It took a nut to see that I was as batty as she was—only, for the Grace of God, I was able to keep it in check somehow (and for how long? Fares like this made it impossible).

"*Please*," I begged, "*I don't want any trouble. I'll be glad to take you anywhere you want—just pay me first.*"

"You don't believe anything I say, do you?" she screamed, then suddenly started singing arias at the top of her voice, just belting it out right there in broad daylight on La Cienega Boulevard. It was probable that she'd had voice training somewhere along the way—only that did not make things any easier for me. I was trapped with a psychotic. It didn't make any sense for me to keep talking because she didn't want to hear a word of it. Nothing. So I kept my mouth shut, thought about that cop car back there. I'd never done this sort of thing before—but I was trapped—no other way around it. If I went back to the IHOP she would get handcuffed, arrested, and hauled off to jail for not paying the fare.

When at last she stopped singing to catch her breath she was raising the hem of her dress, revealing those heavy, sunburned thighs. There was a queer smile on her face. I kept looking at all that rouge, the smeared lipstick, and it did things to my stomach, tightened my guts.

Why me? Why couldn't I get a break? I was just trying to make ends meet, playing by the rules; just another poor schmuck stuck in the mire—and now this.

She rubbed her inner thighs. "How about it?" she whispered. "Would you accept a little love instead? Would you?"

I found myself sighing. "*Please don't do this to me, lady. Please?*"

". . . my God," she undertoned, "a rapist. You're a rapist. *You want to rape me.*" And her voice increased in volume as she continued: "*You just want to use my body and discard me as if I'd never existed. My Dear God, how could you? How could you?*"

"Please, lady; don't do this—"

"A SEX FIEND! I KNOW YOUR KIND. SEX—THAT'S WHAT YOU'RE AFTER!" And then she started yelling at the top of her voice: "*RAPE! RAPE! I'M BEING RAPED! HELP ME! RAYYPPE!!!*"

I had no choice now; I turned the key in the ignition, and pulled away from the curb. I made a U-turn right in the middle of La Cienega Boulevard. I was one desperate cab driver.

She stopped screaming long enough to say: "*What are you doing now? Where are you taking me? I demand an answer!*"

"Taking you back where I found you. Forget what you owe me."

I had just under four bucks on the meter—most of it Waiting Time. As we pulled into the IHOP parking lot I was relieved to see the police car still sitting there, the ace up my sleeve, even though the last thing I wanted was to bring cops into it.

I said: "*I want you out of my cab.*"

She would not budge. "*Why are you doing this?!*" she yelled. "*Why are you being so rude?! Why do people have to be such assholes?!*"

"I'm just trying to make a living," I explained in an exasperated tone of voice. "Please understand that, if you can—"

"*YOU* UNDERSTAND *THIS*—IF YOU WANT ME OUT OF THIS CAB YOU'LL HAVE TO *DRAG* ME OUT! THAT IS THE ONLY WAY I WILL GET OUT OF THIS FUCKING CAB! YOU GOT THAT?!"

"See the sheriff over there?" I said, indicating the vehicle—actually there was no one in the car itself.

"What do I care about the sheriff?"

I sighed, got out of the cab. "You pushed me into this. I know you've got problems; I didn't want to bring the sheriff into this—" I looked up just then—two county sheriffs were emerging from the pancake house and could easily pick up on the commotion coming from my cab.

"*YOU BASTARD*!" she shouted. "*YOU ROTTEN BASTARD*!"

"Look, I don't care about the money; just get out of my cab."

She noticed the sheriffs looking our way and suddenly decided to leave my backseat, slamming the door behind her.

"You satisfied, you bastard?! All you care about is *money! MONEY, MONEY, MONEY*!!!"

"Did she pay you?" the taller of the cops asked. The guy had reddish blond hair, a full mustache. The other cop's mustache was dark, perfectly trimmed, as always. L.A. cops looked like TV soap actors. Still, I was not unhappy to see them.

"No," I answered. "But it's okay. I'm just relieved to be rid of her. She's been screaming ever since she got in the cab. I don't know what's going on."

Maria Callas started to walk away. "Hold it right there, Miss," the taller cop said. When the woman refused to do as asked the cops grabbed her arms.

"LET GO OF ME, YOU COCKSUCKERS! LET GO! LET ME GO!"

They suggested she settle down, but she wouldn't hear of it.

"What does she owe you?" the tall cop asked.

"It's really not that important officer," I said. I just wanted to erase the entire incident from my mind, forget it had ever happened. "If she doesn't have it, that's fine. I don't care about the money." And I didn't. Let me go off somewhere and *collect myself*, let me go about my business. Let someone else handle "the famous persons" of the world.

"What's on the meter?"

"$4.10."

"Where'd you pick her up?"

"In front of Barney's Beanery," I told him.

"How far did you get?"

When I answered that one, he said: "That's kind of high, ain't it, cabbie?"

"There was Waiting Time involved," I explained. "She wanted to go to LAX initially. When I asked to be paid up front she gave me a hard time, wouldn't get out of my cab."

"That's against the law, you know?" he said to her.

"*FUCK OFF!*" she shouted. "*HE TRIED TO MOLEST ME, AND ALL YOU CAN THINK ABOUT IS FOUR DOLLARS AND TEN CENTS!*"

"Do you have money to pay the man?" the tall one's partner asked her. She was nodding and spitting. "How can you stand there when I'm being molested?!" she was saying to me now. "I'm being molested by these animals, and you stand there with your thumb up your ass! WHAT KIND OF MAN ARE YOU?!"

The tall cop had been holding her purse while all this was going on. He extracted her wallet, handed it to her. The woman withdrew a five dollar bill and flung it at my feet.

"There's your fucking money!" she snarled, spitting at the ground. "You make me sick! ALL OF YOU—MAKE ME SICK!" Reluctantly, I reached for the five dollar bill. "*Thank you*," I said, and started for my cab. I wanted to get out of there.

"GO TO HELL!" was her message to me, to all of us, I guess.

Handcuffs were placed on the woman's wrists, and she was shoved into the backseat of the cop car.

"Hold on a second, cabbie," the reddish-haired cop called after me. "We'll need some information from you."

"YOU'LL PAY FOR THIS! YOU'LL PAY FOR THIS!" she kept screaming from the backseat.

"I really should be getting back to work, officer," I said to the cop.

"I understand that. It'll only take a minute."

I nodded. I didn't want to, but I would stick around.

"We'll need to know where you picked her up. We'll need to know your name, address, etc., what exactly happened. All that. She hurt you?"

"No, sir."

I was handed a piece of paper, a pen. And as I started writing I could hear the woman singing again, sotto voce now. She wanted us to know she had control, that she could sing at that. Cops in this area were used to scenes like this. It happened all too often. It was a typical Hollywood occurrence. Both were grinning now, their sense of humor returning, as the tall cop said to his partner: "She's not bad, you know?"

His partner was nodding his head, agreeing. "Not bad at all."

As long as she was singing in their cop car and not in my cab, that's all that mattered to me. She could sing all she wanted—and I didn't even have anything against opera at all.

Over the years I had learned to appreciate the greats, the masters—Pavarotti, Placido Domingo, and some others with names too tough to pronounce or remember.

I jotted down the information requested of me in a hurry, handed the piece of paper over to them.

I was free to go.

As I got in my cab and slowly pulled out of the IHOP parking lot I could hear "the famous person" singing her arias back there, opening up all the way, wanting us to hear what powerful lungs she had—full blast. Maybe she was trying to tell me something—what I would be missing out on now, all that fine singing, now that she was no longer sitting in my backseat, but in theirs.

I rejoined the traffic on Santa Monica Boulevard. I understood, I really did. It was not her fault. Sometimes the old melon had a way of malfunctioning, but to have a "Maria Callas" happen to a guy who was hanging on by a mere thread himself. . . .

The gods couldn't be this cruel—or could they?

I turned south on La Cienega, followed that up with a left at Holloway. A while later I was on Sunset, holding the mike in my hand.

"She flipped out on me," I told the dispatcher. "You knew it was going to happen, too, didn't you, Palmer?"

It was easy enough to detect the dispatcher doing his best to suppress a chuckle.

"Yeah," he finally conceded; "I half-suspected."

"*She claimed she was Maria Callas.*"

"What's your present location?" he asked.

"Sunset Boulevard."

"Got another call on the Strip. Want it?"

"I don't think so," I told him. "I need a break after that last one."

A year later, I was sitting at the Beverly Hills Hotel along with several other drivers one afternoon waiting for a fare. There were two Beverly Hills cop cars parked in the driveway under the world-famous canopy. The cabbies wondered what was going on. Why were the cops here?

Twenty minutes passed and a couple of the police officers stepped out of the main lobby entrance, turned right, walked down the driveway past our cabs. They made another right, reentering the hotel through this side entrance.

What the hell was going on?—we all wondered. The carhops were always "too busy" either parking cars or else retrieving them for the famous guests who frequently stayed at this hotel to bother with cab drivers like us and let us know what the commotion was about.

Another twenty minutes elapsed, and a fire truck drove up.

Two firemen entered the lobby. The cabbies cranked their necks. The carhops were not offering any information. We weren't good enough to even bother with. Most of these guys had the attitude. They drove late model cars and lived in comfortable homes in the Valley. For the most part they remained indifferent to the celebrities who favored this hotel when in town, but always managed to shine that professional smile at just the right time, and say: no, sir, or yes, sir; no, ma'am, yes, ma'am. Their timing was impeccable. They were paid to be ass-kissers and they were the best at it—even though they didn't care for the two-bit phonies any more than we did.

Was this another bomb threat? I asked myself. There had been several over the years. Nothing had come of these threats. Overzealous fans got rebuffed by their favorite star and suddenly that fan was no longer a fan and was busy phoning the desk to warn the hotel of a hidden bomb somewhere on the premises.

Like I said, it happened from time to time. Finally, Jimmy Vance (black, 45), the former chain smoker who owned and operated his own shoeshine stand inside the lobby, sauntered over to chat with us.

"What's all the excitement, Jimmy?" Big Pedro asked.

Big Pedro/aka Big Pendejo was a Mexican who stood a good 6'3" and weighed two hundred and sixty pounds—but Big Pendejo liked to claim he was half Hawaiian every chance he got, when he wasn't busy changing his background and nationality to suit the moment. It was his way of endearing himself to the other drivers, thus making it easier to steal the better fares, the longer rides, and made this M.O. a lot smoother and easier by greasing the palms of various doormen here at the hotel. Big Pendejo was well known for his fabrications. If he thought you had Native Indian in you Big Pendejo suddenly became part Indian. If Big Pendejo thought you were Jewish, Big Pendejo's father was suddenly Jewish. In his thick south-of-the-border accent Big Pendejo would insist (laying on the earnestness):

"No kidding, man—my father got Jewish blood. I wouldn't lie to ju, man. I'm part Jewish." Or if he thought you were French, suddenly his mother had French blood; or if he knew you to be Puerto Rican or from Spain, from the Philippines, Big Pendejo would alter his story to accommodate the occasion. "I never tol' ju, my mother is part Filipino; no kidding, man; I got Filipino blood."

The purpose behind it? Big Pendejo liked to tell tales, Big Pendejo wanted you to think he was your buddy, he wanted you to relax in order to be able to stab you in the back by taking those good fares, the money-making trips that came out of the hotel—the Disneyland rides, the Newport Beach rides, the LAX rides. . . . And if you were under the impression that Big Pendejo was your buddy it made it that much tougher for you to confront him and accuse him of dirty pool, to accuse him of paying off the doormen for the choice trips, while you were stuck with three dollar fares down to the shops on Rodeo Drive. This was Big Pedro Morales, aka: "the biggest *maricon* of them all." And now his curiosity was eating him up and he was doing his best to be buddy-buddy with Jimmy Vance, the shoeshine man. Big Pendejo was itching to figure out what was going on—so were the rest of us, only we weren't frantic about it.

"*Why so many cops? Why the fire engine, Jimmy?*" Morales kept asking. Jimmy Vance was grinning about something. Happy to be alive. He'd had a close call months earlier, heart surgery. The bypass operation had given this former cocaine user a second chance and he was grateful to be breathing, grateful to be alive and kicking, enjoying the Southern California sunshine. Jimmy Vance liked to step outside and spend his breaks with us, chat a bit. Jimmy was giving Morales "the smile" now.

"Come on, Jimmy," Big Pendejo insisted. "The hotel got a bomb threat again? That's it, ain't it? Bomb threat? How come the fire truck is here? What's going on, Jimmy?"

"Had a woman hidin' in the elevator," Jimmy Vance said at last; "claimed she had a bomb in her briefcase. Been in there for hours;

wouldn't come out."

"No kidding?" Big Pendejo said.

"Finally she come out, then run off someplace else inside the hotel. She's hiding out, man; won't come out. Front desk told her to check out. She wouldn't hear of it, didn't want to leave. So now, she's hiding out somewhere in the hotel with the briefcase. They can't find her. Called the po-leece on her, the bomb squad."

"Ju kidding me, man?" Big Pendejo said. "She won't come out? She's gotta be some kind of crazy bitch then, right?—if she won't come out. That's what chu said, right Jimmy? She won't check out?"

Jimmy Vance was grinning, nodding his head. He turned his light-skinned face upwards, toward the sun. "They been in there damn near three hours trying to get her to leave the hotel," he said.

Just then there was some shouting, a woman screamed. We all turned, looked in the direction of the hotel entrance.

For a second I thought I recognized the woman's voice, the one doing all the cursing and shouting, but I couldn't be sure. I strained to get a better look, and could not get anywhere. Two other cop cars had pulled up and there were too many policemen around her. It wasn't until after the heavy-set woman was half-carried, half-dragged to the front seat of one of the cop cars that it dawned on me who she was: "*Maria Callas*".

She stopped struggling, stopped cursing and screaming and, like before, started singing arias—at the top of her voice.

A cop got in on either side of her, and they slowly drove past us. I looked in and could see the handcuffs on her wrists. Her face, that face I wouldn't forget for quite some time, was covered with rouge, blood-red lipstick overlapped those opera-singing lips. Yes, it was she all right—that passenger I had picked up in front of Barney's Beanery that Sunday afternoon, the lady that had started screaming at me simply because I had asked to be paid up front for a ride to L.A. International. And she sang loud enough now to just about crack glass.

Then Big Pendejo pointed his finger at the cop car with the singing passenger that slowly made its way down the winding driveway toward Sunset Boulevard: "I know that crazy lady," said he, recalling: "*She's a crazy bitch, I tell ju, man. Got money up the ass. She's from New Jork. Got big money*. She do the same thing at the

Beverly Hillcrest, man, six months ago. They told her to check out; she refused to check out. The man at the desk ordered her out. I was her cab. She wouldn't come out for two hours, man. I know that crazy broad. She's a rich bitch, but she's a mental case."

I said nothing.

The BHPD squad car with the opera singer was gone. "That's show business," Jimmy Vance said. His break over, he walked back inside. "I'm not kidding about it, ju guys," Big Pendejo insisted; "I had that crazy bitch in my cab six months ago." One of the valets blew his whistle at that moment.

"Personal for Morales," the blond-haired valet yelled our way. And Big Pendejo eagerly backed up his station wagon to the lobby entrance, even though it was not his turn. But the people had "requested" Big Pedro (according to the valet). The huge Mexican was salivating. Another good fare. I no longer cared. My thoughts were with "Maria Callas." I felt sorry, I felt something, a kinship. Something had gone wrong in her life, so terribly wrong. . . . The truth of it was it could have been any one of us being carted away in a squad car like that, it could have been me. I knew it all too well. I knew it as much as I knew anything. This is what I feared most—that insanity would finally move in, that all rational thought would abandon me—and that there would be no way back, no way of ever again connecting with the one that I loved on any level.

• • •

Sheila

She was a jogger, and I'd see her from time to time jogging in the Fairfax District, along Beverly Boulevard, other times along Burton Way in Beverly Hills. This time right there in front of CBS TV Center on Beverly, east, past the post office. Her jog over and done with she was walking, crossed Beverly, made it north up Curson. I was on my bicycle, having just returned from the high school track where I'd had a pretty good run myself—it kept me alive; exhaustion sometimes kept me from thinking about suicide. I kept a P.O. box there at the post office on Beverly and routinely checked it for orders and/or checks for that self-help book I was selling as a mail-order item; the only trouble was the few checks I received I never had the heart to cash, guilt or something kept me from doing it. The book had been written to help others and I did not even have enough business savvy, better yet fortitude, to recoup the bucks it had cost me to publish. I won't lay it on the fact I had been born in a communist country or say that no one in our family had an inkling what business was about—I will simply state I had no business being in business. But none of that mattered much as I continued to stare at this woman's well-developed and tanned legs. *You have to make your move. Say hello, at least. It won't kill you. She'll turn me down, like all the others. She'll see how much pain I'm in and she'll tell me to get lost.*

I swallowed hard, my palms clammy, forehead beaded with sweat. My scalp always itched when this happened. Dammit, you're a man and she's a woman. Go after her. Make the effort. You have to get on with your life. You need someone to love. Give it a try. She may not be the right one for you, but if you don't try you'll never know.

I'd gone through this so many times, and always to have it thrown back in my face. I just was not the pro my buddy Red Gunderson was. I didn't have the confidence, the witty lines, the flamboyance. Low-key, that's what I was, although once past this initial stage-fright, if I ever got past it with someone, I did fine, did what was required of me in the sack department. I didn't think I had anything to be ashamed of. I wasn't small down there. I wasn't large, but seven and one-quarter inches is not tiny.

There were a lot of guys who didn't even have that much.

I approached her from behind, walked up. Said hi. She smiled; said hello.

"I notice you jogging all the time," I said. "My God, you look fit."

"Thank you," said she; "you're not bad yourself."

Ironically, just then, what I found quite embarrassing about myself she found rather encouraging—I could not conceal or do anything about the rising, enormous erection that was happening right there inside my blue sweatpants, my cotton sweatpants—and there was no denying it, no way to camouflage it. I think my face flushed, in fact, I know it did, but I noticed this woman's eyes darting down there to the general area, taking it in and liking what she was seeing. It showed in her eyes. My face remained flushed. I stammered with a couple more lines, gave her my name, told her a bit about myself. I found out she was a maternity nurse, lived just up the street, said her name was Sheila Overland, and the following just about floored me—offered her phone number. "Call me sometime," she said; "I'd like to make you lunch."

"Really?" I said, finding it difficult to accept. Women around these parts did not give out their phone numbers that easily; maybe one in a thousand, maybe this was that one.

"Would you like me to call you?" I needed the assurance.

"Sure."

"Well, it was real nice meeting you," said I.

"Call me," said Sheila Overland, the nurse.

I promised I would. We said our goodbyes, and parted.

I thought about Sheila for the next two days, and finally phoned her one midmorning. She seemed genuinely happy to hear from me.

"Is that invitation still open?"

"Why don't you come over."

I showered, shaved; got into clean shorts, T-shirt, socks, combed my hair and rode my bicycle over to her place.

It was a gray, two-story building that she lived in. Probably eight units, well-tended lawn. On the corner.

I walked up the flight of stairs, carrying my bike with me.

Sheila's greeting was cheerful, as was her apartment. I saw polished hardwood floors, spacious rooms; potted plants hung from the ceiling; a jazz album collection on a shelf below a fine stereo and speakers. Her apartment was sunny, clean, projected life, a far contrast from the gloomy one-room cell I was stuck in.

After lunch we sat on her couch in the living room and sipped on our beers. We touched on jazz.

I'd just been getting into it; what little knowledge I had acquired had been via the courtesy of an FM jazz station and their fine D.J. and jazz expert C. Niles that I often tuned to while working nights.

Sheila had Keith Jerrod on and explained how she'd gotten into jazz through a black guy she had dated for a while some time back. I listened. There we were, on the sofa, sitting next to each other sipping our beers and talking. Then we got on the topic of sex, relationships; how difficult it was to find a relationship, all that. She was seeing a guy from Canada, on and off, a house painter; but he didn't want to settle down, didn't seem to want to marry her. Sheila gave every indication she was hungry for sex (about the best way to describe it)—and I kept thinking: What are you going to do now, Chance? Are you going to allow your stupid shyness, at your age, to ruin it for you? Here's your one chance to make love to a woman who appears to truly like you, who appears to find you attractive, desirable even. Maybe April didn't want me, perhaps I was no longer worthwhile or needed by her—but here was a woman who obviously did. What are you going to do about it?

Get over your shyness. Forget the Goddamn shyness. Make love to her. If she wants it—just do it. *Fuck her.*

"That doesn't mean that I think it's right for people to jump into bed on their first date," Sheila clarified the point succinctly enough. I was getting mixed signals now.

Forget it then, I thought: just drop it. You only *thought* she was interested in you. Look what she's saying now.

"I like you," I said. "I don't want you to think I came up here just to go to bed with you right away. I think love is so important, true love, the real thing. I wanted to marry my girl, but . . ." I would blow it again. Did April have any idea the kind of hold she had on me? Did she know? Could she see it? I was nothing to the woman I had split up with, a bug not worth bothering with—and I found it difficult to go on.

"Don't get me wrong," Sheila corrected just then: "I like sex, I really do." What now? She was changing her tune again. What was going on? Does she want to have sex or not? If not, that's fine too; I'll just leave.

"I like to *fuck* as much as the next person," she said.

I did a double-take. "That turns me on," I said; "but if you don't think it's right, we don't have to do anything . . ."

"Now wait a minute," she implored; "you don't have to be so complacent about it."

"I didn't come here for sex alone," I stressed again.

"Don't agree so quickly."

That's when I said to myself: now or never. To hell with it. We either do it, or we don't. She either wants it, or not. And if not, she can always stop it. I don't give a damn. I reached under her dress, got my hand in there, inside her panties; got my finger in and probed—found her pussy and slid it in. I stroked it. She feigned resistance, then sighed: "Ooohh, you don't waste any time. . . ."

I simply grinned, and stayed with the finger, rubbed her clit, kept sliding my finger inside her and felt her grow moist. I bit her ear and neck and heard her squeal.

I lifted her dress, and got a good look at the pink panties with the embroidered white flower patterns; her juices had soaked through the fabric. I could see her pubic hair through the thin, wet fabric of her panties. I pulled her panties off, got on my knees and kissed her patch. I was licking her pubic hair, got the tip of my tongue just inside her pussy. This is what I had needed for so long now, what I craved, lusted after, needed so desperately.

A man needed it from time to time in order to go on, to keep from drying up. Somebody had made us this way. The laws of nature could only be ignored for so long. If my heart wasn't into it, but my groin would be. I would force myself to make it with this woman! That's right, goddammit!

I would have sex with this woman! Finally! I would be alive for the moment. I'd be getting mine finally, FINALLY, just like April was getting hers out there. I stood up, unzipped my pants and pulled my groin out. There it was—stiff; seven and one-quarter inches of hard Slavic salami, The Yugo Cucumber. She gripped it, liked what she was holding, seeing.

"You're hard," she cooed. No shit, I nearly said. What an understatement; instead, I said: "Good and hard. It's been a while, that's why."

"I want to suck you off," she said; "but not here. Let's go in the bedroom."

"Why not right here? So what if the neighbors see us? I don't care; I really don't." Not that there appeared to be neighbors in the immediate vicinity of her apartment. Her front windows faced the street and all her other windows overlooked the alley.

She giggled, rose, wouldn't take her eyes off my erection.

"It'll be more comfortable in the bedroom," was her eager response. She walked to a bedroom in the back and I could easily see her undress through the open bedroom door. I followed her lead, got as far as the hallway and could hear Sheila saying: "Now, I don't want you to think I do this with every guy I meet. I'm really not like that."

"Don't worry," I said; "I'm not thinking that at all."

I got out of my clothes where I stood in the hallway. By the time I reached the bedroom she had her dress off and was waiting for me in her slip. My cock throbbed, kept waving.

There it was, right in front of me—hungry for pussy.

Sheila couldn't take her eyes off of it, grinning.

She was stretched out across her bed, and I came on board.

She dove down with her head, wrapping her lips around my cock. She made a lot of noise, but she wasn't very good at it after all. I kept my head buried between her legs for a while, then came up for air. I decided to slide it in, stroked. Sheila liked that, her body shaking, quivering as she reached orgasm after orgasm. I did my best to get off, but I couldn't make it. She made too much noise, flailed about; it wasn't genuine and it was more distracting than she ever knew. I didn't mind it when a woman screamed and howled and jerked about during lovemaking, it could even add to it—make it more fun, exciting, when it was real. It had to be real. I didn't care for the ruckus Sheila was making.

I felt like telling her to calm down, close her mouth for a second, but wouldn't. It was frustrating as hell. Couldn't do it, wouldn't do it this time. The price I kept paying for having fallen in love with the other one. It was easy enough for me to pound-off to photos of naked women, but here I was with this real live woman and although I stayed hard, I could not get off. It wasn't right. Sheila lacked a full, well-rounded rear end that I liked a woman to have; maybe that had something to do with it.

After all, she was a jogger, she should have had a womanly ass, but didn't. She had no ass. No butt. Flat as a board.

I didn't get any satisfaction. It wasn't right. Where was the justice? Was April having the same trouble with her bed-partners? In her carnal encounters?—I wondered. I bet not. I'd have bet anything that she wasn't.

Sweat poured from my body, and Sheila's overplayed yelps and screams were about to give me a headache. I needed a break, and asked why she wouldn't take her slip off. Then it came out. She told me about the scars.

She'd had her breasts reduced as well as reshaped. The plastic surgeon who had performed the initial operation had left the nipples lopsided, unaligned—and she'd had to go to a second surgeon to do some rearranging with the nipples.

And the scars were there, readily visible. It bothered me more than it did Sheila. I couldn't help it. The way Sheila told it it didn't seem to phase her at all. She was a nurse, I suppose, and saw it on a daily basis: scalpels, blood, people being cut open. She thought nothing of it.

For me it was a bit too much. Even when she reached down to do her best to get me off orally and insisted: "Don't come in my mouth; let me know before you do, okay?" I kept seeing in my mind's eye a doc's scalpel cutting her open, the blood pouring; sewing her back up. Hell, it bothered me plenty. I had her stop whatever it was she was doing down there. Kissed her. She wondered if anything was the matter? "It takes time for me, that's all," I did my best to explain. "I like to be emotionally involved. Without love . . . it's just . . ."

"I'm sorry."

"No, you did fine. It's me . . . it was good, really. . . . We'll be seeing each other. It took a long time for me to fall in love with her . . . and it'll take a lot longer even to fall out of love, to get over it. That's all it is. I need time. But I like you, Sheila. I'd like to see you again." To myself, I said: *The scars are not her fault. I'll do my best to deal with it, accept it.*

"Oh yeah," sighed Sheila, planting kisses all over my face. "You're a sweetheart . . . ," she whispered, and rested her head back against the pillow, smiling. I looked at her, amused in a way (by this attention and affection). To this woman I was "a sweetheart"—and to my ex I was what? Creep? Loser? Asshole? Liar? No good? I had revealed to Sheila that I'd had my name changed legally while serving in Uncle Sam's Army. You could say I'd learned my lesson. Hold anything back (for whatever reason), and they're quick to label you a liar, being secretive, trying to hide something, covering your past. Only when Sheila asked what name I'd been born with, I refused to reveal that to her.

I explained: "I prefer to stick with one name, the name I'd chosen to be known by the rest of my life." She accepted the explanation easily enough, as her own father had changed his last name as well many years ago. It hadn't always been Overland. Sheila's father was Jewish, and to avoid having to deal with anti-Semitism in New York's garment district he had legally changed his name. I would have said to my former girl: So you see, April, it is not so rare, it is not a criminal act. I am not Jewish, not that I have anything against anybody, anyone's race or religion, but Sheila's father had had his name changed for his reasons, and I did for mine. I wanted no part of my childhood, my old man, the beatings, the brutality, the humiliation endured all through grade school, high school, and then the army; being an outcast: "*that fucking foreigner.*" I had been running from myself lo these many years—and we all know—that is one impossible illusion to pull off.

But Sheila Overland accepted me, the cab, the writing, the struggle. She didn't look for reasons to cut me down, instead praised my efforts at every opportunity.

I found out Sheila's parents had been divorced for a number of years. Her mother was Catholic, her dad, as I said, Jewish. The old man had dumped the mother for a woman half her age (not unlike what April's dad did to her mom). Sheila's mother had never quite recovered from the blow, even though the old man had left her with a million or so. The money hadn't mattered to the woman; all Sheila's mother had wanted was her husband back. The pain goes on for so many of us. Life.

Sheila was showing me the family photo album one day: pictures of her mom, an attractive woman in her early 50s, Sheila's brother, two years younger than Sheila, who had a peculiar habit of attending East-Coast orgies and had lots of photos taken and would then mail them to his sister.

She laughed as she told me about all this. Even when they were living at home in New York her brother would do these nutty things, leave explicit photos lying around for either the mother or Sheila to come across.

"It was pretty embarrassing," she said; "but my brother didn't seem bothered by it." I wondered what kind of family this woman came from. Yes, I was discovering that Sheila Overland was a bit on the kooky side, especially when she told me about the time a man she did not know introduced himself in front of her building and talked her into letting him come up for a glass of water and forced her to fellate him and swallow his load. Sheila did not seem perturbed by any of this as she recounted it—life in the big city. I wondered if Sheila was playing with a full deck. And then there were the other signs: she liked to jog in those skimpy shorts up and down Beverly Boulevard and into Beverly Hills, shorts so tight and skimpy that a good deal of her ass-cheeks could be seen hanging out (the shorts did get progressively shorter after I stopped seeing her).

But she had qualities I could appreciate. She was a good-hearted person, a happy person; never moody or vindictive, never down on people or life in general. In this respect she was doing better than I.

Sheila kept talking about marriage, about settling down.

She wanted me to move in with her. Would I consider it?

She had a job that netted her forty grand a year (with substantial raises coming) as a maternity nurse at Kaiser, not to mention the money she stood to inherit (both her parents being millionaires). When I told Red Gunderson and Angus Gladwyn about this, when I mentioned it to several others—they all responded in the same way: "*Go for it. Marry her. You'll be on Easy Street.*" One regular Beverly Hills fare of mine, a partially senile Jewish gent in his 80s I used to drive out to a restaurant he owned in Encino twice a week was quick to admonish: "*Don't be stupid; marry this gal. Don't wait. Love will come later.*"

"*You think so*?"

He shrugged. "Sure." Then added: "What's love anyway?"

I don't know why I even bothered to listen to it because that was something I could not do. I could not marry for money. It would have been out of character for me, against the grain—to marry for money. I did not want it. People ought to marry for love. You go around only once in life—marry only once, should marry only once, and that one time ought to be for love, true love. They all laughed at me. Shook their heads. I was a hopeless case.

But again, I was out-of-step with the rest of them, all those others out there, the opportunists. They married for money, career moves, fame, stability. I couldn't do it.

I wanted to keep seeing Sheila, to stay friends with her. I wanted to give this a fair shot. I did not want to walk away, cut her off without giving it a real chance.

We decided we would go to San Francisco one weekend, drive up in her car. I'd never seen the city, or taken a good look at that part of California, other than a glimpse or two at Monterey that time I'd taken a fare out there, the drive April and I made out to Santa Barbara one afternoon, not withstanding. A week before the agreed-upon trip to Northern California, I was on my bicycle in front of the post office on Beverly Bl.—and there she was—I easily recognized her from the photos Sheila had shown me—Sheila's mother, even more attractive than in her photos, well-kept, classy. Better looking than Sheila. She was twice her daughter's age, but much better looking. I tried not to stare: Should I go up and introduce myself? Say hello? Did I have the nerve?

Just then I noticed her turn her head, gazing at me (I don't know, could have been due to my height I had reminded the woman of her ex-husband; could have been the shorts I had on that revealed my tanned legs). I didn't know what it was, but her eyes had lit up when she noticed me.

I never considered myself a pretty boy, never dressed to impress, never much cared how I looked to myself or others—I stayed clean and my clothes fit, but that was about it.

As mentioned, my primary reason for staying fit by jogging, playing racquetball with Red, weightlifting, riding my bicycle as often as possible, was exhaustion. This was my objective: a constant state of utter exhaustion through which I hoped, believed would keep my weak and feeble mind from considering suicide as the only reasonable way out of my dilemma. Man, I just wanted to forget about the one I'd lived with, needed to shake it, thoughts of her that refused to be shook. I know, yes, true—my ex was just another female with big tits, just another lost-cause confused female who didn't know her elbow from her asshole—and there were millions of others out there just like her—but that did not keep us from falling in love with them.

I didn't invent the screwy game, I didn't create the way we existed and went on about this idiocy between men and women. I was just another fool stuck in the mire.

So where was I? Sheila's mother. She's looking, she's interested. Probably in as much pain as I am. And Sheila had also told me about some bald-headed 50-year-old type with slick lines that had made the moves on her mom, was clearly after the big bucks—and her mom hadn't cared for the guy, but a good man was hard to find. I had been shown the photos. I had no answers for anybody. All I was doing is searching for a rope, a branch, something to pull myself out of my own trap of quicksand (I had dug myself in).

There was Sheila's mother, a looker, great legs and a rear end. What had happened to Sheila?

She hadn't retained any of her mother's good looks. I turned away, reasoning: You can't do that. Forget it.

You're seeing Sheila. It would be wrong to drop her for the mother—and not only that, they might both be of the opinion that you're after the money. So don't even think about it. Fine. All I did was look. Forget it.

I said nothing. Kept on pedaling.

The trip to San Francisco had gone over quite well. This is exactly the kind of trip April and I should have made while we were together but we never did. This is where April had taken part of her training as a clothes designer, then moved down to L.A. to further her studies at that college downtown. But I was here with Sheila now. We rented a motel room, visited the shops in the Embarcadero, bought white chocolate, even a couple of prison-gray T-shirts with the Alcatraz emblem and bogus cell numbers, like typical tourists. The fog and the wind felt like being back home in Chicago. It was great; a beautiful city. Being away from L.A. gave you that instant sense of being reborn. I knew finally what that Tony Bennett song truly meant. It was a city worthy of the tune named after it, written in honor of it.

The one other thing I noticed, that I could not quite figure out, that was a bit off-putting to me, even though I was with Sheila everywhere we went, the looks I got from all the homosexuals. I didn't get it. No matter where we went, coffee shops, art galleries—the eyes were there. Men ogling, not her, but me. No, I wasn't being paranoid or too sensitive or even imagining things—these guys were staring at me. What gives, I thought? Hell, I'm but 5'11" (in my shoes), got long hair, average looking, medium build. What was it these guys were looking at? All right, I wasn't ugly, but I wasn't Robert Redford either (and as my buddy Toby Silverman once said: Even Robert Redford isn't Robert Redford. True, but beside the point here). What goes? I wished I'd gotten this much attention from women.

That night in the motel room was much better than the first time in her apartment. We'd both just taken a shower together, soaped each other's back, stepped out, dried one another off—and she reached down, grabbed my groin, squeezed.

Well, it grew. She was down there, lips wrapped around it, pulling like a vacuum cleaner. "Don't come in my mouth," Sheila reminded me once again. I promised I wouldn't; of course at a time like this you are going to promise the world, from fear she's going to stop mid-explosion. This time she was better, or maybe it was simply because I'd gone without masturbating for a while and I was horny. I needed the release, I needed it. She kept at it, worked it, would look up from time to time with a big smile on her face. I had to lean against the shower door for support, enjoying the moment. I watched it slide inside her mouth, and back out again. The head was sensitive. It had been a while.

The next time her eyes looked up, I said: "Wait; let's fuck."

She rose. "Come on," she said, leading me to the bed.

Then she let on it was that time of the month for her.

"We can still do it," she assured me.

"Are you sure it's okay?" I asked. "I mean—"

"Oh yeah," she said.

"You don't care? It doesn't bother you?"

"Why should it?"

"What if we leave a mess for the maid?"

She shrugged, laughed: "It's her job to clean up." I wanted to laugh along with her at the cavalier way she had responded. Sheila was on the bed spread out, arms open, waving. "I want you to fuck me," she sighed. I got on top, gave her a few strokes. It felt good in there, wet and warm.

Snug. *Hell, yeah.* "Your pussy is nice and juicy," I sighed in her ear.

"You like it?"

I didn't say anything; grunted with the explosion. It was good. "That made up for the other time," I said afterwards.

We visited the Golden Gate Bridge. I had to see the bridge—and what a sight to behold. Manmade. Incredible.

I stood there in awe, gazing at the damn thing. Human beings, those tiny grains of sand, scurrying little ants that they were, lost and frustrated, at times spiteful, at times loving, at times bloodthirsty and evil—human beings, those hopeless little ants, had it in them to create from time to time some mind-boggling, incredible things. We sat on a hill overlooking Marin County, admired the clean air and the breathtaking view of the sailboats floating on the water.

I did not, *did not* look forward to returning to that smoggy hades on earth known as L.A.

Alas, it was time to drive back.

A quality I admired about Sheila was her seeming candor and lack of guile. The bit she revealed about her brother and the photos of the orgies he'd attended back in New York, about her allowing that stranger up to her apartment and then having to perform fellatio on him, and other things—made her appear vulnerable to me, human—and a bit dingy at the same time. I could never be interested in anything long-term with this woman. The chemistry simply was not there.

I didn't find her attractive; the hair frizzy (although professionally highlighted), too close cropped. April had been 5'9"; Sheila, although not short, was several inches under that. And there were the chest scars that I could not ignore. The idea that a woman could allow herself to be scarred in this fashion, for no logical reason that I could think of that justified it, worked against this thing going anywhere—and of course the no-ass. How could a woman, that jogged as often as she did, not have a womanly rear end? I found it impossible to conceive. A woman needed to have a womanly butt, or else I could not be interested. I wasn't into anal sex, not that I had anything against it—if a woman wanted it this way, it was no big deal to me—to me just the sight of a big womanly rear end was plenty to get worked up about, the sight of a larger-than-average, firm, and well-rounded female ass got me plenty worked up, desiring to taste that luscious beaver that peeked at you just underneath the fine buttocks (while the woman positioned herself on all fours just so). Doggy style was my favorite of all positions, as this way while driving it home, while sliding it in the woman's wet and hairy cunt there was that rear end to admire, to kiss and worship. Some were tit-men, some (like Elvis) liked the woman to have small feet, some liked short women, some liked thin women, some liked them flat-chested even, some liked them to weigh three hundred pounds or more. For it to work for me the woman had to have a great ass (preferably be my height), with meat on her bones; legs and ass—of course before all that, I needed to like the face, the eyes; I wanted kind eyes, compassion, a degree of intelligence—but yes, physically, it came down to well-developed calves and firm thighs and a healthy butt. Something Sheila did not have.

Some men would find her attractive, I was sure of it—only I didn't.

What I needed was someone who was built like the woman I had been living with, only with better shaped, larger calves and with a preferably tighter cunt; some hip action would have also helped, a sense of rhythm. That's all. Was I asking for too much?

Also, in our discussions about sex Sheila liked to tell me how she wished somebody would just grab her and fuck her real hard, almost rape her, rip her clothes off and give it to her. Did this explain why she always did her jogging in those skimpy shorts? Maybe she was trying to live out some type of fantasy. She craved male attention obviously. Did it explain her particular as well as peculiar mentality? I had no answers.

I didn't think women had fantasies like this, not with so many actual rapes going on all the time, but there she was, Sheila going on about it.

"Don't get me wrong," she said to me one day, "I wouldn't want somebody to hurt me, but I wonder what it would be like to have my clothes torn off by a man I didn't know, and be given a thorough fuck like that."

Was I hearing right? I'd never heard a woman say this to me—then again, Sheila was a bit different from the norm, and yet this woman worked in a hospital as a maternity nurse, of all things. I didn't know what to make of it, didn't get it, didn't understand it.

Finally one day she was coming over to pick me up and take me to brunch at a popular deli on Westwood Bl. I waited for her. As soon as she entered my small apt. I grabbed her from behind and threw her on my bed, face first, so that she was lying on her stomach. I parted her legs, pushed her panties to the side and thrust my throbbing groin in there and started stroking. It felt good for me, it was happening; a reasonably good fit. I pumped. She made sounds I couldn't discern, didn't care. She may have been excessively noisy and lousy that first time, she wasn't making much noise this time and I worked it. She was all right.

Although Sheila did not know what the hell was going on, it had all happened so fast for her, saying she didn't want it, but I didn't listen to any of that, and just stroked long, hard strokes and filled her wet cunt with hot cream.

After I was through, grinning by then, she rose to her feet, pulled her skirt down, and said, not accusingly, but rather in an observing tone: "You know what you just did? You raped me."

I couldn't shake my grin, pleased with myself. She was a much better lay when she didn't pour on all that fake wailing.

I said: "You don't mean that?"

"You just raped me; that's what that was."

"You always talked about wanting to get it like that. I thought I'd do it."

"It's still rape."

"It sure felt good. How was it for you?"

"Oh, no, I'm dripping. There's cum running down my leg. I need something to wipe with."

I handed her some toilet paper. She wiped her inner thighs. I wrapped my arms around Sheila, kissed her, and rubbed her pussy again. "You know, it was kind of fun," she said; "the way you grabbed me and just threw me on the bed."

"You said you wanted to be raped."

I lifted her in my arms, laid her out on the bed. I pushed her skirt back and pulled her panties down, all the way, got them off, and that pussy was staring right at me and I slid my erect cock in there and she liked it. I stroked for a while, suddenly thought I'd like to go at it with her doggy-style, had her walk over to the weight bench; helped her position herself on all fours on the bench, her head at the other end, away from me, while her ass stuck up in the air facing me. I got it in there again and went at it, pumped for a while and she started in with the exaggerated moans and that turned me off right away. Women don't seem to get it, but contrived grunts and moans and gasps and screams are the quickest turnoff.

And then there was the no-ass staring at me, the ass that didn't interest me. Sheila had a flat rear end—and she wanted me to keep going, and I simply didn't feel like it, and withdrew, said to her: "We'll be late for brunch." Zipped up. Disappointed, clearly she was, Sheila shook her head, and sighed: "*Men.*"

I smiled, amused by all of it: me, her, men and women—love, sex, the no-win situation of it all. Nobody ever won. We got nowhere—and were all headed down that same road to nowhere. . . .

Well, I hugged her again, had nothing against her truly, and held the door open for her.

I'd been helping Sheila sharpen her chess game. The new apartment manager of the building I lived in, a guy who had also split up with his old lady, had taught me how to play chess and I thought it would improve my game as well by playing other people.

It was a sunny, clear day in L.A.

Sheila felt like driving out to the beach. We'd get some sun, play chess, and then go for a bite to eat. Okay, we'll go to the beach. Sheila did have a nice chess set.

We'll go to the beach and play chess.

"Okay, we can do that."

She'd been doing all the calling. I hadn't been holding up my end at all. Disinterested, I didn't know how to break it to her. There was no need for cruelty, no need to hurt her feelings—I'd had it done to me so often by now. Being cruel, unfeeling, callous was easy—the other way was a bit harder, took some patience, class. I wasn't in love with her, and I couldn't see or understand what use she could have for a brokenhearted shell of a man. I had the dark blues and suicide was on my mind constantly. But Sheila liked having me around. I was a lay, I suppose. Men did it to women all the time, so why shouldn't this woman have the right to want a man around for that same reason? And I thought: If I am to survive it, if I am to get over April and get on with my life I ought to at least give it a decent try.

We drove to the beach in Sheila's Pacer, that is she did the driving—it was her car, and it felt good to be driven by someone, for a change. We drove way out there, Will Rogers Beach. And miracle of miracles—it was one of those million to one shots—that powder blue Volks owned by April's bodybuilding buddy, the gym owner she had been hired by at that downtown gym, the blue Volks with the white trim and white convertible top that I had spotted my ex tooling around town in from time to time was parked there in the lot. There was no mistaking it; it had to be it, the immaculate blue VW bug with the particular white designs along both front and rear fenders. And I still thought:

No, it couldn't be. She can't be out here. I easily felt my heart pounding inside my chest, the adrenalin surging. Of all the times I had merely attempted to say hello to her as she drove past me in her car while I worked the streets in my cab in Hollywood, Century City and Beverly Hills, and other places, the times I wished I could have embraced her and conveyed to her how much I had missed her, and April frantically doing her best to put distance between us, saying to the effect: "*Can't you understand that it's over?*" And me needing, aching to say nothing more than: "Yes, April; please, sweetheart, I get it—but these feelings I find so impossible to turn off. My heart aches for you. I can't help it. I'll do as you say—just let me look at you once, let my eyes take in that wonderful face I cannot stop being in love with. . . ."

I never got that chance. The message was there: you did not go up to someone and embrace them if they did not wish to be touched by you. It was that simple, sounded simple—was far from it.

What if she's not by herself? What if the iron-pumping muscleheads were with her? What then? It wouldn't have mattered. This was a public beach. I would keep a lid on my feelings and emotions; wouldn't be easy, but I would force myself to. I would respect her wish to be left alone.

I looked up, out toward the beach, to the right—and there she was in that brown bikini I helped her pick out at a bathing suit shop on La Cienega; in fact, it had been custom-made by a three-hundred-pound bearded character who'd had a tough time controlling himself as he measured April's 38 double D chest. I remembered it well. She was lying on a beach blanket by herself, on her stomach, reading.

I mentioned nothing about it to Sheila as we walked across the sand in the opposite direction, maybe two hundred yards from my former girl. We lowered our things in the sand, Sheila and I, spread the blanket, opened the chess set. I glanced back in April's direction from time to time and was not even sure that she had noticed us. She was preoccupied with whatever she had been reading—perhaps one of my pathetically long (and just plain pathetic) letters and/or please not to throw what we'd had away, to give our love a chance, a true chance; but I had lost my cool and the body-builders were much happier people and had spending cash and could take her places.

God, I thought, *forget it. Don't go over there. Say nothing.* You'll only manage to upset her and she'll start running away from you again, screaming: "Leave me alone! Please leave me alone! It's over! I DON'T LOVE YOU ANYMORE!"

It was clearly impossible to concentrate on Sheila and our chess game, although she had no inkling what was the matter with me, or that anything was. The pain amounted to being pricked with needles over every inch of my screaming, howling, raw body, and worse. If I could have only been allowed to hug my baby, if I could have said to her, without her getting uptight and nasty, angry and so damn defensive: I just want to wish you the best, April. It's from the heart, sweetheart. Don't you have any idea how much I love you and always will?

I stayed put, and did nothing. I had no right. I fought off every impulse to call her name, wave to her, just that much—but I had no right. . . .

An hour and a half later, Sheila and I rose to our feet: we'd had enough of the sun, folded the chess set, and walked back to the Pacer. April still had her head down, reading, and never once looked up—and there I was with someone I did not love, with someone to whom I was nothing more than an erection. Bottom line. I wished I could have been in love with Sheila just a degree, but there was nothing there. She had wanted to settle down with me, start a family. She was not a bad sort, but there was nothing there for me. I'd fallen for April so damn bad. . . . You did not fall in and out of love at the drop of a hat. When you loved someone you stayed with that person, your coupling was supposed to mean something; you hung in there, as a duo, all the way through.

Man, my ideas were dated. Fuck it. And I looked back one final time as we got into Sheila's car. I could not help it, and uttered, to no one in particular: "That's the girl I broke-up with. . . ."

Sheila looked up, taken aback by this sudden revelation.

"Really?" she asked. "Why don't you go over and say hello?"

I shook my head.

"You should at least say hello."

I wanted to, I wanted to more than anything in the world, but I had no right to bother her. I had no idea what April's reaction would be. Would she be angry? Would she see me with this woman and get the wrong picture? Would I be accused of following her? Would I be accused of pulling nothing but a cheap trick simply to make her jealous by appearing with another woman this way? I didn't dare make a move of any sort. No more than eighty yards was the distance between the woman that I loved and I—but we were worlds apart just then—and she had stated in that letter to me, as well as verbally, that she wished to keep it that way.

We drove out of the parking lot, headed back to town. It had taken all that I had in me to push back the tears, the Goddamn tears, the burning pain, to keep it all in check.

I had my face turned away from Sheila.

"You all right?" Sheila asked.

I looked up, managed a smile: "Yeah."

"You're thinking about her again. . . ." She had said it with empathy and some degree of hurt. If I were thinking of the other one, I'd be offending *her*.

"Oh, no," I assured her, "I'm fine, really"; and began fiddling with the dial on the radio in a clumsy effort to conceal the shaky state I was in. There was an oldies station, oldies but goodies. I still liked those old rock and roll tunes. Orbison was singing his heart out. My favorite singer of all time. Elvis was great and I liked Sinatra and Springsteen and Streissand and Janis Joplin and Ray Charles, Stevie Wonder, Al Green, Merle Haggard, Patsy Cline and others, but Roy Orbison had the greatest voice I'd ever heard.

Nobody could hit high heaven the way Orbison did; gift of the Gods, no one had a way of conveying the depths of loneliness a life without love left you in, the bleak depths of loneliness and despair caused by a broken heart. Nobody.

"Let's get something to eat," Sheila said.

"Sure."

"My treat," Sheila offered.

Sheila Overland was a decent sort. Of the millions of women in L.A., she was one of the rare ones. Most women expected the male to foot the bill, to pay for the movie, dinner, drinks, concerts, and all else; most did. But here, sitting beside me in this Pacer owned by her as we zipped along a sunny Southern Cal. beach I had a woman willing to carry some of the load. It was refreshing. Sheila was not bothered by the fact I was financially strapped, she was happy to have me around, more than happy, it seemed—and for me it was no good.

I was hopeless.

I had fallen for the other woman three years before Sheila and could not, as hard as I tried, shake the hurt. I could not, did not know how to stop thinking of the other one, did not know how to stop being in love with April.

We saw each other for a couple of months, Sheila usually phoning me, and not the other way around. She complained that I never bothered to call her, that she was the one who always had to call *me*.

What could I tell her? She was a friend, nothing more. I liked her, but that's as far as it went. She started dating the house painter from Canada again, and asked me what she should do about it.

"Should I stay with him? He doesn't want to settle down; and I'm ready, ripe and ready to get married and start a family."

We were tooling down Robertson this afternoon in her car, south of Wilshire, headed I'm not sure where.

I said: "The truth is, Sheila, nobody can answer that for you; you're the only one who can make that decision."

She thought about it for a moment, let it sink in, then said: "You know, that's a good answer."

It was the only answer I could have given her. Yes, I realized I could have been a heel and given her bad advice, not unlike what McDill and the others had been giving my girl. Sheila was gullible, would have done as I asked. I could easily have kept her dangling on a string, kept using her, kept her around for the occasional lay when and if I were interested, for the occasional date when and if I were willing and ready; I could have done all that and more.

I refused to be that way. And I was proud of myself for it.

I didn't want it that way. If I hadn't been treated with a modicum of decency by others in the past, at least I would be decent here with Sheila.

It was not long after that I allowed this friendship to dissipate. Sheila stopped trying, saw it was useless.

Last I heard she was engaged to the house painter. As I headed up Rodeo Drive one afternoon in my Eager Beaver Cab I happened to look to my left and was pleasantly surprised: there was Sheila in a white chiffon dress, high heels, hair fashionably restyled; all done up, with a dark-haired guy in a suit. They were holding hands, window shopping. Sheila looked contented. I was happy for her. She never noticed me as I drove past.

I wished her luck.

• • •

Working the Hard Side of the Street

3:00 a.m. Sitting in my cab at the Beverly Hills Hotel. Dozing off. It's been a slow weekend, a bad weekend. Close to forty hours invested and not much to show for it. Dozing off; no business. The new dispatcher with the Australian accent says he's got one at Laurel and Sunset.

I take it.

It's a Kirkwood address.

I whip the cab down the driveway, go left on Sunset, drive over to Laurel Canyon. Turn left on Kirkwood. It's pitch black. No lights. I near the address, look up—a woman in some kind of white dress waves to me. She'd been waiting outside. And right away I know she's a prostitute. The dress has that wrinkled, slept-in, lived-in soiled look to it. The girl is probably in her early 20s, but looks ten years older, easy. Dishwater-blond hair. Bad complexion. Too much makeup. She's got her little purse like all hookers.

"Hi," I say.

"Hi," she says.

"Been waiting long?"

"It seemed like it in this cold."

It's been a cool January for L.A. I ask her where she's going.

"Marina del Rey," she says. A good trip. "Do you know where Via Marina is?" she asks.

I tell her I have a pretty good idea where it is. I take it down Laurel to Sunset, make a right and take Sunset Bl. all the way out to the 405.

Not much is said.

Things are going through my head: another sad story, one of many. *Why is this one doing it*? Needs the money? Too lazy (unable?) to get a real job? Needs the money for junk? Should I feel sorry for this one? I'm not sure. I do anyway. Nobody should have to live like this.

I try to shrug it off.

Sunset Bl. is just about deserted.

3:10 a.m.

A Mercedes passes us.

There is small talk. She asks if I work the airport. She says she has been taking cabs a long time but has never had me before, just small talk. I tell her I've been with the company over five years; the reason she never got me is because I've been driving weekends a long time now.

I can smell her perfume: a cheap, strong perfume that does not agree with me. Most prostitutes seem to smell this way, usually something cheap and strong.

I crack my window open.

Her beeper goes off.

I turn up the volume just a bit on the jazz station I've got on. I've got nothing to say.

We get on the 405 south. I ask if she is going to need a cab later on (the beeper is a signal for them to call "home").

"No," she says; "I'm through for the night." Sounding relieved about it too. I find out she's sharing an apartment in the Marina with another girl and would like to find a place of her own—and that apartments are really expensive.

I agree.

We get on the Marina Freeway, take it on in. She tells me all she has is a hundred-dollar bill and apologizes for not telling me earlier. She asks if I wouldn't mind stopping somewhere to get change. No sweat, I tell her, and suggest the Marriott, since there is no way they would even look at a hundred-dollar bill at a 7-11.

She agrees.

She's in a soiled dress, a hooker with a bad complexion, hair a mess, and not really pretty to look at; she lets men she does not know do things to her for money—and yet there is something tender about this human being sitting in the backseat of my cab, something naive and maybe innocent.

She's not hard (not yet), like so many hookers that I get (she'd had her share of hell, for sure, and the profession she was in was aging her fast and hard), and shit, there's something in my belly or heart, a goddamn teardrop or two, wanting to weep for this woman. HELL—sometimes it's a fucked-up world and not much to be done—nothing—SHIT, NOTHING. It just goes on. And my own life wasn't any better.

I live in a single with a dirty orange carpet, a room that reeks of roach spray, of decay, of death. I was always convinced the previous tenant—an old woman or man—had died there; and the pain goes on.

Who was right?

Who was wrong?

I judge no one these days. Never had a right to judge anyone anyway. Life is sad. Her life was marking her and maybe preparing her for an early fall—and the other way, "the right way," the loving way, being in love with someone and wanting to see it last, only to see it crumble instead, had left me just as marked as this hooker, just as scarred and hopeless. Life is a dead-end.

Tell me different, show me I'm wrong. I have worked these hard streets for ten years now; I've seen it all. Show me different, let me see. The tears are there for all the pain, all that pain that never goes away.

We reach the Marriott. I get out with her hundred-dollar bill, get change from the desk clerk. "I'm a cab driver and this hundred-dollar bill is all my fare has on her."

He gets me change, then indicates another tired (even her artificial tan looked tired) woman in a green miniskirt of sorts in her mid-40s, wearing high heels with sparkle on them. Needs a cab.

"Sure," I tell her; "where are you going?"

"Beverly Hills," she says. "You have a passenger, don't you?"

"She's just going two blocks from here," I explain upon hearing Beverly Hills—it would be nice to get paid for going back there as this is my turf. She decides fine, but is not interested in being charged extra for this. "No," I explain; "you won't be charged extra at all. I just have to drop this lady off, and then I can drive you to Beverly Hills. I have to go back that way anyway, you see—"

A woman passes us, compliments her on her shoes—and I'm thinking: They've got to be kidding. Nobody wears shoes like this, *nobody*; except maybe some young punk rocker, some teeny-bopper.

The woman with sparkle on her shoes gets in the front seat, lights a cigarette, is clearly upset about something. My passengers say hi to each other.

"People can be such assholes," the one in the green dress says. "If there is one thing I cannot stand it's being with people sitting around waiting for their dealer to show up."

She's been with a group of people waiting for their coke to arrive—it never did.

"*I tried to tell those assholes that the dealer was not showing up.*"

I drive the hooker to an apartment complex on Via Marina. The fare is $31.70. She hands me two twenties and asks for seven back. I give her change, thank her.

"*Thank you*," she says.

"Take care," I say.

And she's gone. Another one of many that I would never see again, another nameless, faceless blur, somebody I would not remember ever seeing in less than a week. They come, they go. So many, so many. You see them once, and they're gone—but maybe this one will not be forgotten so easily, maybe this one will not be nameless and faceless and just a blur; maybe this one, at least here and now, for me and for you—and if she ever comes across this—for her as well.

She'll be a little more than just another nothing victim prostitute *working the hard side of the street.*

The woman with the rhinestones on her shoes is still pissed at the "assholes" back there at the hotel, still pissed at the fact people cannot try to have fun without their cocaine.

"I can understand getting high," she says; "Christ, I've done it myself often enough. But goddamn, it just pisses me off the way our whole evening was ruined. Why does cocaine always have to enter the fucking picture? I've seen a friend *ruined, totally ruined* by that *shit*."

This is another one that has had her share of life's beaners. She'd been there.

I ask what she does for a living.

"I'm an interior decorator," she tells me.

I like her.

A heavy boozer, it's easy enough to see: the slight paunch—and just not my type. I like her company nonetheless.

I want to talk but know my mouth by now is like the breath of a dog. Poor diet, eating junk food, the ulcer acting up; so I can't really talk as much as I would like to, to this woman, just talk. She is almost like a breath of fresh air compared to getting all those spoiled rich little bastards of Beverly Hills, spoiled and stupid and ill-mannered.

So she decides it would be best if I drove her to the Marina City Club instead.

"The guy—my date—I was with is really not bad. I've known him a while now. It's those other assholes with him. I'm sorry," she says. "That's life, I guess."

I nod my head. I understand.

"I'll call him from the Marina City Club. I know someone who lives there and I can get a drink. I'll just call my friend to pick me up."

She wants my cab number so she can ask for me in the future.

"Sure," I tell her, and give her my number and let her know I only drive weekends.

We chat some more—me not opening my mouth too wide—the goddamn breath and that one tooth way in the back chipped and full of food particles and I know I've got breath coming out of my mouth like an elephant. What the hell can you do?

I give her my card.

And I can see that by talking with her, just talking with her, it has made her feel better—and she even smiles as she gets out, offers to give me some money. I don't take anything for the short run.

She tries again.

I refuse to take anything.

Money, money—the source of my problems all these years.

I lost my love because of money—*or lack of*. If I didn't have to eat, or pay rent for that room of mine that smells of death I wouldn't go near money.

She walks away with a cheery thank you. "*You're a sweetheart*," she says; waves to me.

And is gone inside the office.

Driving the hack down a lonely Marina del Rey street, getting on the Marina Freeway, taking it to the 405, taking it back to town. The weekend had not ended soon enough for me.

Tired, just exhausted, needing to get back to that bed in that room on Burnside that reeks of something terminal, needing to fall asleep—and forget about everything.

• • •

People Can Be Cruel

Tossing in my bed, I sat up, rubbing my eyes. I walked to the refrigerator, reached for a beer, sat on the edge of my bed staring in the semi-darkness, staring at nothing . . . at my former lover's photograph . . . at the phone . . . back down at the rug. . . . The phone was ringing and it startled me.

"Yeah?" said I.

My sister Emina, two years my junior, was at the other end.

"Chance, is that you? Oh God, I don't believe it."

Pausing, I said: "Yeah, it's me. . . ."

"Are you okay?"

"Yeah, I'm okay."

"Are you all right? Did I wake you?"

"I'm okay. How's things with you and Jemila?"

"We're fine. I can't believe I'm talking to you—I tried so many times before."

"I was living with this girl; the phone was in her name."

"God, it's been a long time."

"It sure has. I almost got married, only it didn't work out. . . . I thought this one was it. It's a long story." Then I asked: "Are you calling long distance?"

"Oh no," said Emina; "I'm here in L.A.—matter of fact, I'm staying at that same place Jemila and I stayed the last time we were here—on Sycamore, near Beverly Boulevard—"

"That dump? Are you serious?"

"I had no choice. It's only temporary."

I believe I sighed. "I just don't understand you two. You keep coming back to this sewer—and for what? What do you expect to find here?"

"You don't understand—"

"The last time you were here you hated it, kept crying and complaining—and now you're back again."

"You don't understand; there's nothing back there for us. It just got too cold. I figure my family's here. . . ." Here's where I rolled my eyes upon hearing "*family*" mentioned. She continued. "I've been meeting nothing but creeps back there. I want to start over. . ."

"You picked the wrong place to start over."

"Let me be the judge of that—"

"Yeah, well, I ought to know. I've been here long enough. It's a sewer—nothing but dopeheads and psychos. This place draws them, man; believe me, Mina. Don't expect to find anything decent in this place. The decent ones don't stick around too long—"

"There's you—and there's other guys like you. That's just negative thinking."

"I'm giving you the facts. Look, the only reason I'm still here is because of what I'm trying to do—otherwise I'd be gone, I'd be gone so damn fast! This place should be retitled Scum City—"

"You're being negative—"

"Listen to me—there's something about this place that just destroys anything that's decent. It corrupts. And I don't care how good and decent you are when you get here—a year, two, three years later and you're a different person! You get *hard* and you get *desperate*. Decency goes right out the window. You learn not to trust anybody! Nobody! I've been here ten years now—how many friends do I have? After having met hundreds of people, and I mean hundreds, maybe over a thousand—they're dirt. *They're dirt, Mina*! *Users and con-artists*! I'm telling you the truth, Mina. I'm not exaggerating, dammit; I'm not! The ones I consider friends I can count on the fingers of one hand. And I feel fortunate at that."

"Any big city is like that," said my sister. "You just have to be careful who you deal with—"

"I had a production office. Spent a year trying to put a movie together. Do you realize how many people I met? How many actors and actresses, agents, production people I met? Do you realize how many? And all the people I met on the job while driving the cab—and do you know how many I stayed in touch with? None. That's it. *None*! Toward the end when I could no longer keep the office going, the place was broken into and robbed by the very same person that worked with me on the production! My so-called right-hand man. How about them apples?" I had to pause. "L.A. . . . that's what it's all about. . . . A great place to live. . . ."

Mina said: "My belief is there's good people out here . . . they're just not easy to find. Anyway, I thought I'd just call to see how you're doing. I kept having these dreams. . . . I thought you were in some kind of trouble. . . ."

"I was for a while . . . the breakup and all. . . . I'm doing better now. . . ."

"How long were you together?"

"Two years. We were going to get married. I didn't want anyone else. But we kept having financial problems and stuff . . . and then her so-called friends kept giving her 'advice,' putting ideas in her head; these so-called party animals." Then I said: "L.A. Swingers; yeah, baby. She was a good lady—but they got to her. . . ."

I was fighting tears at this point.

"I know what you mean," said Mina. "They were jealous. I know what friends like that are like." She paused, then said:

"Do you ever talk to her?"

"Huh? No, I see her now and then in her car when I'm out there driving my cab. Sometimes she's with another guy. We had a pretty bad fight at the end there. She doesn't want anything to do with me. I wish we could just talk, just sit down and talk. I screwed it all up. I . . . I'll just have to forget I ever knew her."

"You never know, she might change her mind. Those things take time."

"Not her. I know the way she is. I got ugly, said some things . . . I needed her so desperately . . . I just . . . I didn't know how to let go. I wanted her to know that I would let go if only she would help me with it, if she would show me how. . . . I didn't want to make her do anything . . . I just loved her so much . . . but I keep thinking: She's like the others now, she's like the rest, like her L.A.

friends—hard; *no good*. I kept things from her, about the folks; the way we were treated. . . . I didn't know how to deal with it myself. And when I finally did try to explain, it was too late. It just made things worse, anyway. She said I lied to her, didn't tell her the truth—"

"You can't expect someone like that to understand if she's never been through it herself—"

"I realize that; but, Mina, she's been through enough herself. She loved her dad so much and now she seldom hears from him, ever since he remarried. Her mom and dad divorced when April was 13. She used to get along with her dad so well. He used to love her so much; she used to tell me about it. I never really understood, I couldn't relate because I had learned to do without all that. I knew we had a couple of real nut cases for parents—but with April it was different—she had a halfway normal upbringing. I don't know anything about anything anymore. The whole world is screwed up. Why do they allow wackos to have kids? They should have been locked up for what they did, they should have been put away for twenty years."

Mina said: "Sure, but look at them now. Try and say something negative about them in front of Emir and Zuleika. Just try. The last time I saw Zuleika I tried to explain to her why Jemila and me had to run away—and she said to me, get this, she said, she was angry: '*Don't you dare talk about my mom and dad like that! Don't you dare!*'"

"I know; they love them. The folks were easier on them and I'm happy about that. I believe they were raised with a bit more love and respect than we saw. I'm happy for them. I see Zuleika now and then walking past the high school track where I go to jog sometimes. She's grown so tall. Seems pretty happy." Then I added: "I'm going to let you go then. . ." I found myself pausing: "I do care about you two. It's my own hangup. I've always been a loner, I guess. . . . I've got a couple of good friends I feel very fortunate to know. I've been very lucky. They've been supportive. Angus and Red, and Renny—one or two others. They put up with my bullshit. Take good care of yourselves. . . ." I hung up the phone, and thought: April cut you off the way her father cut her off, the same way you cut Jemila and Emina and Emir and Zuleika off. People, people . . . they know how to be cruel, don't they? Don't they . . . ?

• • •

Looking for a Ho' in the Rain

"Go to — Loma Vista," the dispatcher says. 11:30 on a Sunday night. Sunday night Beverly Hills shuts down early; in fact, the whole city of L.A. shuts down. I pull away from the Beverly Hills Hotel, take Sunset east to Foothill, take Foothill on over to Trousdale Estates.

This is where the big money is; motion picture composers, expensive lawyers; the big wheels with the big cons. I take it up Loma Vista, being careful not to make any wrong moves in the light drizzle. It's been raining all day and into the night. It's dark, the pavement slippery.

I reach my address.

A chunky guy in a suit holding an umbrella comes out. He's got dark hair, curly, a perm job.

"Hi-ya doin'?" he says.

"How's it going?" I say.

He's in.

"Here's the story," he says. "I got this friend staying with me. And the thing is—he wants me to go out there—let's take a ride down to the Strip—he wants me to go out there and find a girl. You know, a hooker? Something nice. Is that okay with you?" he asks. "Is that all right?"

"Sure," I say. "I'll do whatever you want, as long as I get paid for my time."

"Oh, you'll get paid. My friend just wants me to bring him a girl."

"We can try," I say.

"Sure, we can try. Why not? There's girls out there. It shouldn't be a problem."

I take him on over to the Strip. We pass a bony, ugly black hooker standing on the corner of La Cienega and Sunset. I slow down, glance at him.

"Christ, no way," he sighs. "No way. My friend wouldn't like that. Shit, no."

I want to chuckle.

"That wouldn't be his cup of tea," I say.

"Shit, no. She was ugly. Christ." Then he says, "White. He wants a white chick."

We stay on Sunset, going east, passing another black hooker.

"Don't slow down," he says. I keep going.

"Shit, where the hell are they?"

"It's Sunday night, you know?" I tell him. "This town shuts down early Sunday night. Besides, ever since the cops started to crack down they chased all the hookers out of the area. They work farther east now—down around Western."

"Western is too far," he says.

"Or else they're up in the Valley, Studio City now, up and down Ventura Boulevard."

"Christ, that's too far to go for a piece of ass."

We pass Fairfax, and see a figure standing in the dark by a bus bench, waving at us.

"Could be a cop, you know . . . ," I tell him. "Some of the hookers are policewomen, wired and all that."

"You think so?" he asks. "They're doing that now? Christ. Who needs it?"

"Some of these hookers look so damn good they just can't be hookers. They slap on a lot of makeup, wear the skimpy outfits and all that—try to act like hookers, but they're not. They're policewomen."

"It's all right," he says. "Get closer. I'm a lawyer, I know about the entrapment law. Let's get a better look."

I do like he says. It is so damn dark by the bus bench as there is a huge tree directly behind it that we almost have to pull up to the sidewalk. It is a white hooker this time, worn, nothing really left to sell, just as hopeless as the other two—and we can see a black pimp standing in the background, too.

"Keep going," the lawyer tells me. We roll east. "Where the hell are they? This town is changing."

I shrug. "They used to be lined up all up and down the street," I tell him.

"Yeah?" he says. "When was this?"

"About two years ago. Cops are cracking down. People started to put the pressure on, about hookers and pimps ruining their neighborhood. It was getting really bad. Nothing but hookers, all up and down the street. I'm not kidding, man. Nothing but hookers."

"All we need to do is find one—just one white hooker. She doesn't have to be great looking—I don't want to come back with a dog either," he says. "Know what I mean?"

I nod.

He's looking for a hooker for himself, but he doesn't want to admit it. But what do I care? I don't anymore, about anything.

My meter is ticking. That's all I care about. It'll help me pay my rent that is ten days overdue now. Being late with the rent is a bad habit to get into. I always liked to pay my rent on time. It eliminated problems. It kept the landlord and the apartment manager off your back.

We near the Sunset-Palms Motel. A white chick in a black dress and a beer belly starts waving at us. I honk my horn, just for the fun of it.

She walks up. "Hi, honey. What can I do for you?"

"Sorry, not interested . . . ," the lawyer in the backseat tells her. "Sorry. I'm looking for something else."

The hooker is riled. "*What chu stop for then*?" I pull away; can't help but chuckle, shaking my head. "You don't think your friend would like that?" I say rhetorically.

"What? *That*? No. That's *bad news*."

In the distance, at the gas station on the corner of Highland and Sunset, we spot a couple of girls moving around. We get closer.

"What's that over there?" he says.

"They look pretty young to me."

"Honk your horn," he says.

I honk my horn.

"Let's go over there."

We pull into the gas station. There's two of them—blond and a brunette. The blond is wearing skintight black cords. She could be anywhere from 14 to 18. Tough to determine. The brunette is a little taller, and prettier—although both are good-looking—wearing just as tight Levis. Maybe 17. The lawyer waves them over. The first thing the blond says is: "Are you a pig?" The lawyer says: "Who? Me? I'm not a pig."

"What do you want?"

"Let's go for a ride."

"Where are we going? To the Pig House where all the little pigs are?"

"Pig House?" the guy says. "You're kidding? Do I look like a pig? We're going to Trousdale."

"Where is that?"

"You don't know where Trousdale is? Sunset and Doheny. Right there."

"Why Trousdale?"

"That's where I live."

Both are chewing gum, trying to appear streetwise, street-tough. The brunette lights a cigarette. Both are looking around, like the older pros do. Somebody honks a horn and they wave or smile, or flip the guy off if he's driving anything less than a luxury car—all this while talking to the guy in my cab. For some reason they're not interested in him.

"For how long?" the blond says.

"Couple of hours."

"And you're not a pig?"

"Of course not."

"If you are, man—that's entrapment."

"I know that. I'm not a cop. Here—you want to see my card?"

He pulls out a card. She looks at it. The brunette at this point doesn't give a shit about the guy at all. "What do you think?" the blond asks her friend. The brunette shrugs. "I don't think so."

"Why not?" the guy says. "What do you got to lose? Just a couple of hours. . . ."

At this point no one has mentioned money—which is kind of

unusual, no mention of money or sex. A hardcore hooker, a pro will get right down to the nitty-gritty—first they want to know if you're a cop, then how long? and how much? And none of them are going back to your apartment with you. Most won't anyway.

The guy turns to me: "You don't mind, do you?"

"No, I don't mind," I tell him.

"Sure, you don't mind," he says. "You're getting paid for it. I'll take care of you."

The girls walk away from the cab and start talking to a couple of young guys in a maroon pickup that has just pulled up, bantering back and forth, exchanging one-liners. The brunette still smoking like a young, street-tough chick, but there is nothing tough about any of it. I don't like to see it. What do you do? They were too young and good-looking to be doing this. What can you do? You do nothing.

My passenger starts calling after them. To me, he says: "Give me five more minutes. I just want to talk to them."

"Take your time," I tell him. And mean it. I'm thinking about my rent. Take all night, I feel like saying. A cab pulls up from one of the other cab companies—a Checker cab. I know the driver. He's got his top light on, sitting there, his mike in his hand, waiting for a call. He walks over, grinning, taking in the scene. He knows what is going on. We shake hands.

The driver is in his 30s. Iranian. A nice sort. I get out, and we saunter to his cab so he can be within reach of his mike should a call come through for him. "What's going on with that guy?" he says. "Looking for pussy, huh?"

I nod. "I don't like to see it, man; not when they're this young. Shit. They should be at home or going to school, you know?—with a boyfriend; something decent, man; instead they're selling themselves like this. It's too fucking sad."

"I know what you mean," he says. "The shit gets to you after a while. What's he doing? Bargaining with them?"

"Yeah. They don't seem to want to go with him. I think they're scared or something. Hell, I don't blame them."

"They're good-looking, too," he says.

"Yeah. . . ."

"You making money? How's the business?"

"I used to make money. I make half of what I used to make. Just making the rent, rent and groceries. That's it."

"I know what chu mean."

The young hookers are back at the cab talking to my passenger. After five minutes of that, they walk away. I walk back, get in.

"What happened?" I ask.

"I can't figure them," the lawyer says. "The blond looks good. I like the blond. My friend would really like that. I think she's interested, only her friend doesn't want to go with her."

"That's too bad," I tell him.

"I can't figure them out. They don't act like pros."

"They're too young. Maybe you should forget about them."

"The blond is just right. I think she's interested. It's her friend, the brunette, that doesn't want to go."

"Was there any mention of money?"

"No. Not at all. What I can't figure out."

A short white guy in worn Levi jeans and leather vest appears; dirty hair in a ponytail down to his ass, tattoos on both arms. The guy's got a bushy Fu Manchu, and he's lugging a gigantic ghetto blaster. He seems to know the young hookers and is talking to them, and looking at us from time to time; meanwhile, the lawyer keeps calling the hookers to return to the cab.

"*Hey, jack, hit the fucking road*!" the guy with the ghetto blaster yells.

"I just want to say something to them," the lawyer says.

"*HIT THE FUCKING ROAD, MAN! RIGHT NOW!*"

The whole thing is kind of funny, but I don't want any trouble.

Walrus Mustache is about 5'5", wearing cowboy boots with three-inch heels; the great protector/street preacher doesn't want my passenger to be bothering the girls anymore. I turn the key.

". . . Macho man . . . ," I hear the lawyer mutter to himself, in reference to pint-sized Midnight Cowboy.

"You want to try to find something else? These two chicks are just too young, man. They don't act like pros. They don't seem to know what the hell they're doing."

"I sure like that blond," he says. "Make the corner, just pull around by that pay phone." I don't really like the idea as the pay phone is still on the premises, but I do it anyway. The guy may or may not want to make a phone call—and I've decided the punk with the ponytail and the ghetto blaster can go fuck himself. Maybe he was genuinely interested in the chicks' welfare, and maybe, just maybe he was also getting laid for playing the role. Who gives a damn? The streets. The goddamn streets.

My black-haired, curly-haired, chunky lawyer walks over to the phone. I wait ten minutes. He's back.

"Let's go west," he says; then adding: "Go around the block, just once. Come up on the gas station side. Let's see if they're still there."

I take him around the block, come up on Highland, drive through the gas station. The young hookers are gone, and so is Ponytail.

"Let's go west on Sunset," he tells me. The meter is ticking. We go west on Sunset. He wants to know what my name is, what else I do, if I'm an actor and trying to break into show business. Everybody is an actor in Hollywood.

"No, I'm not an actor," I tell him.

We pass Famous Amos, and there by Ralphs, sitting on the curb, is a long-haired bum in a tattered duster, puking in the gutter.

"What do you think of that chick there?" I ask facetiously.

"*What chick*? You mean that wino? That's a wino, that's not a chick."

"I guess you're right. It looked like a chick from back there."

"That's a drunk puking in the gutter. Where the fuck are the hookers? What's happening to this town?" Then he looks back, cranking his neck, trying to spot the blond and her friend. We keep going and don't see anything until we reach Crescent Heights—on the corner of Laurel and Sunset, a long-legged, bony white hooker with a pockmarked face is ready and waiting. I pull a U-turn. He starts talking to her. She's just too damn ugly.

Christ. But he's talking to her. The same questions and answers: Are you a cop? No, I'm not a cop. How much? Where? How long?

She looks at me and then says to my passenger: "How do I know *he's* not a cop?"

"I'm just a cab driver," I say in response to her inquiry.

"I'd feel a lot better if just me and you could talk," she tells the guy in the back. I get out of the cab, standing outside, until they have finished discussing whatever it is they got to hash over. I look back and see her walk away. I get back in.

"What happened?"

"Too expensive. She didn't want to go back with me."

We see another hooker standing on the southwest corner, smoking a cigarette, talking to the one we had just left.

"Make a U-turn here," he says. "Go down Laurel." By the time we reach the corner the two hookers are busy talking to two fat guys in cowboy hats and don't want anything to do with the guy in my backseat.

We go west. See nothing.

"Let's go back."

We head east once again. By now I've got over 20 bucks on the meter. And that's the way it went for about three hours, up and down in the drizzling rain—and the meter ticking, and the guy having no luck and me thinking about making rent, thinking about what the gutter is doing to me. I may not be the guy in the backseat—how do you make it through the gutter without getting some of that stench on you? How?

I got fifty dollars on my meter by now. It is after one in the morning. A black-and-white is busting a black hooker in front of the burlesque club.

Not a soul in sight. No cars. Nothing. Just my cab and the flashing red lights of the cop car on the south side of the street.

We reach the corner of Sunset and Laurel—spot the blond in an '83 Ford Mustang with three other hookers parked there at the gas station. They pull out, go north on a side street. The guy in the backseat wants me to follow them. I do—get close enough to honk my horn. They're making a U-turn, heading back down to Sunset, but stop to check us over. The blond recognizes me and my fare, says to the other hookers: "That's the asshole I told you about."

"YEAH, THAT'S THAT ASSHOLE," the brunette who is sitting in the back says.

"Fuck off, creep!" they yell at us, and pull out, heading east.

We make it down to the corner. A car passes with two girls in it. The lawyer waves. They smile. He wants to follow *them* now. We stay on their tail down to Beverly Glen, and lose them.

"Take me back to the house," he says. And I'm glad. The meter is ticking, close to sixty now, but I'm getting tired of the whole thing. I'm getting tired of this guy, tired of the small talk, tired of looking for hookers, tired of the sleaze.

I want to go home and take a hot shower, maybe soak in a tub full of hot water.

I take him back to the house. He gives me $70 to cover my troubles.

"I did try," he says. "Got to admit that. We did our best."

"We sure did," I say.

"That's all you can do; do your best."

"Thanks," I tell him.

"You bet," he says, walking to his door. And I'm relieved it's over. I pull away, drive down Loma Vista, reach Doheny, and notice the umbrella in the backseat. Shit! Now I have to drive back up Loma Vista, a good quarter of a mile (or more) uphill all the way; it's a steep climb; leave the guy's umbrella at his door, hurry back down to the AM/PM mini-market at the corner of San Vicente and Sunset, say a weary hello to the sleepy-eyed Arab behind the counter, give him money for gas.

I jam the nozzle in my tank and a faded red Volks pulls up to the pumps across from me as I look up. The woman driving hasn't noticed me yet, but I recognize her. Janet P.

Janet was one of the decent ones. Goodhearted Janet of West Hollywood. Had dated her once or twice after a devastating breakup with the one I had given everything I had to (and I don't mean money or anything material).

To be fair to Janet, sweetheart that she was, I had stopped dating her, being on the rebound that I was. It's a crying shame, but true—a bad female ruined you for many of the good ones you met afterwards. And I was running scared even now, close to three years later, a whipped dog too beaten-down to try again with anyone else. And I do recall the words that came out of that teenage, spoiled Beverly Hills female brat sitting in the backseat of my cab saying to me that time: "How could anyone love *you*?"

Beverly Hills bred guttersnipes with fake nose-jobs, face-jobs, tit-jobs and ass-jobs—lacking in brains and heart. After all, what had I expected? But the spoiled B.H. teen's words spoken to me two years prior reverberated inside my head as I stood at my pump filling my tank and glancing at Janet, patient, intelligent Janet; someone I could have easily fallen for, someone I could have easily considered getting down on one knee for and asked to marry me—but that other female, the shallow man-hater I had given my heart and soul to, had left this psyche scarred pretty good and I quickly turn my head away so that Janet won't notice me.

She enters the AM/PM. I continue to jam the nozzle in my tank, wanting to escape, desperate to flee, avoid a possible tete-a-tete with this lovely woman I had nothing against.

Perhaps the Beverly Hills brat had been right after all: I wasn't worthy of anyone's love.

I can hear Janet emerging, walk to her car and reach for one of the nozzle pumps. By now I am relieved—my gas tank topped off, only my nozzle is leaking and some of the gas drips on my sneakers and pants, my left hand. *Man, it's been a long night.* At least I'm ready to flee, get away—steal a final glance at this woman I had once held in my arms, kissed various parts of her luscious and voluptuous anatomy, drunker than a skunk I was back then (my safety net that was *neither safe, nor a net*, as booze, we know by now, induces far more pain than it relieves) and detect a forlorn look to her eyes, a sadness. She has lost a bit of weight. Has some slick and heartless L.A. S.O.B. put her through the mill in the same tortuous manner as my former unfeeling bimbo had put me through? I wonder about it for a second. Just then, sensing my presence, she happens to turn in my direction, lifting her head. She looks at me.

Our eyes lock, if for a split moment—but I avert my gaze without so much as a blink. I can't even face someone as nice as her. Just a *whipped dog* not worthy of anyone, *a whipped dog running scared, forever running scared.*

I turn the key in the ignition, and pull out in a hurry.

A numb zombie is what I am, running away, running for shelter.

Man, have you ever felt this way? Gone through it? Have you ever?

Now my hand smells of gasoline. Like I said: It's been a long night, my friend—*one hell of a long night*.

• • •

On the Subject of Invisible Scars

"I'll be with you in spirit," I explained to my sister Emina at the other end. "Okay? I don't hate you guys. I don't. I just have to be left alone. You're crowding me. Every time I talk to you two it brings back the past. I can't handle it anymore. I know it's not your fault. I know that. And I'm not blaming you two. I'm not. I do care about you. I know I don't act like it sometimes. I don't want to think about the past. All it does is make me angry. I'm trying to start a new life."

I could tell Emina was crying.

"Don't cry. Please. Forget about me. You can't get attached to people. Look at what happened to me. I gave this woman my heart and it meant nothing to her—"

"This is not the same thing."

"I know that. Please, live your own life."

"I am. You're our brother. . . . "

"God, I wish I could make you see. It's just the way I am. I don't want to hurt you. You're good people. I have to be on my own. I think I'm going nuts. I had a breakdown when April and I . . . only I didn't even know it. Don't get attached to people. They will always let you down. *Always*. I never loved anyone as much as I loved April. . . . I don't think I will ever be able to love anyone again like that. It ruined me. . . . You two should just take good care of yourselves. Don't worry about me. Find a career that you like and stay with it. Love just doesn't work. Forget about love. Love is a lie. Nobody wants to love all the way anymore. They can't. They haven't got a clue."

Then I added:

"It seems to me every time I talk to you and Jemila we end up discussing the old man and the old lady. I can't handle it anymore. I get so angry when I start thinking about what they put us through. Sometimes I just want to go out and find him and beat his cowardly ass for him. He's a coward. That's all a motherfucker like that could ever be—a coward. A real man doesn't go around beating up little kids. He couldn't even stand up to her, the little bastard. I get so worked up when I talk to you—and it's no good, it's no good to go on this way. I don't want to hate—and I don't. I don't hate them anymore for what they did to us. They just didn't know any better. They just didn't know. But we're lucky. We still have our health. We're lucky. Just think—stuff like that goes on all the time—kids being put down, beaten and brutalized. Some never make it. We're very lucky. But I got him that time—smacked him when he was beating on Jemila—just before I went in the army. And the coward never fought back. He's pathetic. There's no other word for someone like that. Pathetic."

• • •

Burned Alive

Taking your love away was like striking a match and setting me on fire. I have been burning alive these years now, burning. . . . Life for me has been a series of tortures. We, every one of us, naturally wish to give, to reach out and love. All of us. I believe this to include the bad as well as the not-so-bad and the decent. All of us. Born and started out wanting to love people, all people, all things, life, everything, bees, flowers, trees, cats, dogs, goats, cows, horses, elephants, tigers, lions, turtles, and even snakes and skunks.

This is how we all start out and wish to go on this way—and then life reaches out with its claws and rakes you across the face for being so naive and sentimental and warmhearted, for wanting to love.

Life has been a torture chamber. From A to Z.

Do you know that once in Basic Training while waiting in the chow line a drill sergeant (Maddock) hauled off and punched me in the stomach and knocked me down for no reason at all, simply because my name had been Alićahaić? Maddock, always on the juice, had merely looked down at the roster before him, noticed what looked like a foreign name to him, a name he could not even begin to pronounce—the man was xenophobic, a Southern bigot—decided he was going to take his problems out on an unsuspecting 18-year-old kid who was obviously not a born American. And did—the only way ignorant, hate-filled types like him know how to do. If only I could have explained my situation to him.

Listen, Maddock, I never wanted to move to this country. You can blame my folks for that one. I was happy in Brussels and didn't want to leave. But I was only ten at the time and had no say in these matters, you see? And if I had been able to get the words out to Maddock, would it have made any difference? Would it have quelled his hatred?

All I know is I was down on the mess hall floor gasping for air; the blow had knocked the wind out of me completely because I had not seen it coming. Not to overdramatize, but this is the same type of punch to the stomach that had caused Houdini's death.

How easily I could have retaliated, not right then of course, but later, the next day or the day after, as I was in top physical shape back then, either by sheer brute force or through the proper legal channels. But I did not. I had no desire to do to him what he did to me, and I was not about to be a snitch either. He had a wife and a kid—and a bad drinking problem.

This was a redneck who did not know any better, a racist redneck who was too ignorant to know any better and I think I even felt sorry for the poor fool.

But what would this mean to you, if anything? I had blown my cool at the end with you. I had taken so much by then that I could not deal with it any longer. My last hope for anything good, the last thing I clung to, believed in, *love*, was being taken away from me. I knew I was nearing a breakdown and needed to embrace the only thing that could save me: You. I was clinging to a mirage; dying of thirst and a used-up, wasted body and mind too sore to keep it together. The breakdown was coming on, the breakdown. There was no postponing it. And you laughed in my face for the fool that I was, and I knew you were right.

You were.

I was a fool and have been since the day I was born, since the day at that tender young age I dreamt of finding you someday and being the perfect man for you, the perfect partner and soulmate. I have been a fool all this time, a lost cause who did not fit in.

Never could, never would.

• • •

Wishful Thinking

A dream I have from time to time—and this is why I call it wishful thinking—the split, that ugly split never happened. This is right after my visit to Chippendale's with Red Gunderson and Renny. It's late at night and I walk into the house drunk out of my mind, in pain, forever in pain due to our impending breakup—and there you are awake on the mattress in the living room (no longer did you want to sleep in the bedroom with me).

"All right," I say to you, nodding. "If that's what you want—fine. I understand . . . I do. We'll act grownup about it. . . . I'll just go my way, Bunny—if that's what you want. . . . I love you so much. . . . I hope I can make it without you, that's all. . . . "

I go to the closet to try to pack some of my things, avoiding your eyes, from fear of breaking down in front of you.

"Just don't let anybody abuse your kindness, honey . . . ," I say to you. "Don't let them use you . . . don't let them use you . . . "

There is a long pause. Then I hear you say: "Come here. I want hugs."

"Bunny . . . you mean it? You don't hate me anymore?"

"I never hated you. Come here."

I go over to you. We hug.

"I never, never hated you," you say. "We're not going to end up like everybody else. This is one team that's staying together."

"Bunny, I love you . . . I love you, sweetheart." And I have to pause to take in the moment, this unbelievable moment. I say: "I knew it, I knew it . . . if I prayed long enough and hard enough everything would be okay . . . I just knew it . . . and we wouldn't be arguing . . . none of that stuff. . . . " And then I ask you: "Do you think we could get married, honey?"

You say: "Sure—why not?"

"We'll have to figure out a way to get some money—"

"No sweat, hubby. We take out a loan—and we go to Vegas."

"Vegas? I like Vegas. But is Vegas okay with you?"

"Sure."

"I thought you always wanted a big church wedding, honey, you know, like you said—so that your family and friends could be there?"

You're shrugging. "The important thing is that we get married—"

"My God, I can't believe this is happening—"

"Yep. I was confused for a while there. I didn't know what I had until I went out with a couple of creeps—went to a couple of bars. They're pathetic. The last date I had—"

And here you chuckle.

"Took me to a pub in Santa Monica—and all the jerks in there kept staring. I didn't know what was going on. I hated it. Just kept staring at me. And I mentioned it to my date and he laughed, explaining: 'Eye-contact. They're letting you know they're interested.'"

"I'll be a good husband to you, Bunny. I'll get out of the cab business—I'll get a good job. We could get out of L.A., Bunny. We don't have to stay here." Here's where I take pause to make sure the following comes out right, to make sure that you know that it is from the heart. " . . . I said some pretty nasty things to you, Bunny . . . I'm sorry. . . . "

"Honey, it's okay. I got pretty nasty myself."

"I just want you to know I deliberately did it to make you cry—that's all. Just to hurt you. I didn't mean any of it, Bunny. . . . "

"I didn't either, honey." Then you add happily: "*We're going to make it.*"

"*We will make it, honey. We will.*"

Your eyes are welling up.

"What is it?" I ask.

"To think we almost ended it. . . . "

"We just didn't realize how much we needed each other, that's all. We just couldn't see it right away. But now we know, honey. . . . Now we know."

In tandem, we say: "*I need you. . . .* "

This is my fantasy, a dream I keep wishing would happen more often than not. Wishful thinking. That's what they call it—what you might call it. Wishful thinking.

• • •

Back to the Slicks

The slicks. That's what some call them. Fuck magazines. And hardly much more. And the women, when there was a woman, were either too hopeless or too good and me too far down to expect better than hopeless—so I stayed clear of them all, kept to myself. But "*the slicks*" were always there during the greater part of the '70s. I'd buy two or three, pound off to them until I got tired of looking at the same pictures, go out buy some more. I'd hop on my dying Yamaha dirt cycle in the middle of the night, find an open bookstore, a newsstand in Hollywood, and go through the slicks, buy a couple, and back to the room for more masturbating and fantasizing. When the typewriter did talk it hardly ever said anything right, and so it would be "the tomb" (what I referred to the various small rooms I lived in in different parts of this sun-bleached, smog-soaked hades on earth known as City of Lost Angels), the slicks, for who knew how many more years? And there were the nights spent in porno houses. I'd hurry back to my room afterwards, pound-off, work myself into a state of utter exhaustion and fall asleep.

What a way to live.

It wasn't living (by any stretch of the imagination), then again it was hardly existing; looking for a way, *my way*, my own road to take, a sign, a bit of luck, a bit of happiness to come my way—not in L.A., pal. And a man in his mid-20s was doing this to himself. *What was I suffering for?*

In the name of what? A dream? Art? A goal or two I'd set for myself? All this was costing me my sanity (what little remained, what little I was able to hold onto, hardly at that). I could have been anything but a starving nobody living by himself, doing himself in. And as much as (I thought) I wanted to climb up out of it—*I couldn't. I just knew I couldn't.* The chains were invisible—but they were there! They were there!

The slicks, the porno houses, the gloom and the doom disappeared for a while shortly after I turned twenty-seven. There were, at the time, *as silly as it sounds* (and it *do* sound plenty silly) *butterflies* in my guts, a song in my heart when I met her. She understood my struggle, acted like she could relate (perhaps even tried there for a while), but she had an agenda of her own (that did not ultimately include me). The song quit playing two years later, and the butterflies and laughter were gone as well.

Give her credit for jumping ship. No need to spend a lifetime to know there's no hope with a loser (although deep down, *deep, deep down*—I never considered myself a loser. Get this: there may have been a few suicidal days and years there, some bleak, bleak times; loneliness and despair may have had me in tears plenty of times—screaming out and praying to the one up in the heavens, all that—but I refused to accept myself as a lost-cause-loser.

That tiniest, teensiest bit of optimism remained way, *way* down there that refused to accept defeat. I refused to stick the label of loser on myself. Others were doing it, and a good job of it—so why help them?)

To get back to the jumping-ship-type—yes, do you kick a dog when it's down?—and can use your help? You do not kick a dog when it's down. You stick around, offer kindness, a helping hand, understanding. This made for a bonding, a special kind of bonding—and you became pals for life. *Soulmates.*

What else is there?

What else do we really have?

But what do I know? That's old-fashioned thinking, out of style these days. She drank those protein drinks at the gym she worked at, ate health foods, lifted weights, and even appeared, a year later—to my mild surprise—I should not have been mildly surprised or otherwise—on the cover of one of those slicks in a leotard so minuscule and pulled up tight between the cheeks of her great big, muscular butt (facing the camera and hanging out). She had no brains to speak of, no big ambitious and/or passions, although everything else was big about her: big tits, big ass, big feet and, tragically, a big vagina (that she never knew what to do with).

But around here all a woman needs is big tits, and like I said, at 38 DD she had that. The attention went to her head, you see? She had been chubby and plain with not much going, no presence or personality, when I first met her and fell for that deceptively shy, albeit contrived little smile: I'm-so-sweet-and-nice-and-oh-so-shy-bit. But at her core all that was missing. There was a touch of cruelty to the eyes, I suspected at the very beginning, but chose to overlook. Never, *but never* disregard your instincts—for you will pay a heavy toll eventually—you see?

When a person is truly good and decent at their center there is never that need to go around smiling and acting sweet to make sure everyone is convinced of your generous and kind nature. There's no need for pretense, as you know who you are. You might curse now and then at life (at whatever; you're human, I hope)—seldom hold back—there's no reason to conceal a thing, nothing to conceal: *you are good at your core.*

And I can recall (during '78-'80) riding my bicycle home in the early mornings (the Yamaha junked by then; we had a used and battered Toyota that worked when it felt like working) after a hard night of hacking and seeing these broken-down, sex-starved guys standing around the sex magazines at the Pico-Robertson newsstand, and I was glad I was not one of them, that I had someone waiting at home for me, someone who cared, who loved me at that duplex on Flores in West Hollywood.

But it was back to that, *the slicks*, the tiny room, the gloom; back among the hopeless, the lonely, desperation, pulling at my hair because of what I'd lost (never had it to own, lost it just the same. We own nothing in this world, *we own nothing*), in a rage at the injustice of it all. What had I done to deserve it? Why was I being punished? *For working long hours? For pursuing a dream?* (A trait that is looked upon favorably and with respect by women in other countries, as it should. When you worked your ass off, put in those long hours—if nothing else, it showed that you weren't a lazy-good-for-nothing.)

Did the hours I worked justify being emasculated and nailed to the cross? Hell no! No way! It was enough to the L.A. (even though she was originally from the Sacramento area) female though. It didn't take much for some of these male-bashers to do just that to you. And we allowed them to get away with plenty—these man-hating lezbo-cunts from hell whom you can never please no matter what; their warped minds cannot comprehend reason; bile and bitterness must be a way of life.

Anyway, angry at myself I was, because I had created those chains, created the shackles myself and no freedom in sight, no sign that anything would change.

And it's no way to live.

And I noticed her the other day riding in an expensive new car with a dark-haired and mustachioed Romeo at the wheel. They were laughing about something. The car was lemon yellow. The Romeo was in a suit, good haircut.

And me? I was on my old bicycle (purchased for $5 from a guy named Red) with the wobbly wheels and defective brakes, bald tires and a missing pedal.

It was okay.

I was resigned to it, you see. Life seldom made sense.

People around here often opted for the short-cut. I rode the bicycle back to my room, to my own kind of short-cut: the ladies in the slick porno mags.

• • •

The Miracle Woman

She was from out of town. Chicago. My adopted hometown. A decent lady. And I must not forget this lady, this good woman, this miracle I got to meet. And what a coincidence in the way it had happened, too. Saturday night. I was at the Beverly Hilton, 1st up, and it was moving. I was having a decent week, only because I'd gone without sleep, had stayed in that cab since the previous Friday evening, had only gone home Saturday afternoon to shower, shave, change clothes, etc. So that loud taxi bell went off in the Hilton driveway, the bright red light flashing.

They needed a cab. I pulled off the stand and drove up to the entrance.

"They need a cab around the corner at Trader Vic's," the doorman said. I was disappointed, because Trader Vic's is always, ALWAYS a short ride not worth bothering with. What to do? I really did not feel like picking up the fare. Reluctantly, I pulled out of the Hilton driveway, went around on the Wilshire side, made the right turn on Santa Monica Boulevard and pulled up in front of the restaurant's entrance.

A white woman in beige slacks, beige sweater, matching heels and frosted hair of medium length appeared, walked down the steps with a smile. Well, to begin with the smile alone was worth noting. She was smiling. But I was suspicious.

Was this the real thing? A genuine human being? Or another Beverly Hills bimbo?

I was out and had the back door open for her, as I often liked to do.

"Hi," she said, as she got in.

Please don't blame me when I tell you exactly what my next thought was. I thought, honestly, here's another empty-headed Beverly Hills bitch, another shallow rich bitch, either that or some prostitute. In any case, I was not too happy to see her get in my cab, as 9 times out of 10 this is true, the way it happens—empty-headed people get in your cab and make you wonder what the world is coming to.

"Your cab is very clean," she said. "That's unusual."

It was cause enough for me to raise an eyebrow. I appreciated the fact she appreciated the cleanliness of my cab.

We started talking.

She was saying things that made her stand out right away, things that revealed a degree of class, intelligence. She was from Evanston, Illinois, to be exact. Married, with two daughters. She was 37, and get this—this is why I found her so beautiful and rare and miraculous—SHE HAS LOVED HER HUSBAND SINCE THE FIRST TIME SHE LAID EYES ON HIM AT THE AGE OF 13! (Her husband is the same age.)

BRAVO!!! WONDERFUL LADY!

There was nothing derogatory about men, about marriage, about kids, about people from her. There was nothing like that coming out of this woman sitting in my backseat.

And if she had some frank and less-than-favorable observations to make about L.A. she did so without malice, but her words rang true.

One of her neighbors back in Evanston had been a man from L.A. whose marriage had busted up. My passenger's husband had helped this guy out financially—and the man from L.A. had not so much as said thank you. Hey, that's typical, I felt like saying: the L.A. way.

I hardly spoke about breaking up with my lady at this point; after all, this was four years later, and the heart mending nicely—thank God. And I had to mention the split to this wonderful woman now as we were discussing relationships, love, all that stuff. And she understood.

"Love can be the greatest thing when it's right," she said, "and so painful when it's not."

She had so much goodness in her, this attractive, sexy woman, that she made me feel good. They just don't come along that often.

"How old are your daughters?" I asked, "because I want to marry one of them."

We both laughed.

"Tracy is 10," she said. "And Amanda is 13."

"I could wait a few years," I said. "I wouldn't mind."

She had fortune cookies in her bag to take home to the kids.

She was too good to be true. She was sweet, but genuine about it. Why couldn't I have fallen in love with someone like this? Why were they so rare? Why so hard to find?—and, really, already taken.

I had mentioned the writing to her, and she said: "You're a gem trapped in a rut." She understood. She truly understood.

"Things will work out for you," she said. And meant it. *And meant it*, for crying out loud! The words meant something, words from the heart from this woman, this total stranger sitting in the backseat of my cab. I wanted to wrap my arms around her just for the heck of it, wrap my arms around her and thank her and tell her how grateful I was to be in her presence, how wonderful and unbelievable it was to have someone like her in my cab.

"If you're available tomorrow morning," she said, "I'd like you to come by and drive me to the airport."

"I'm your man," said I. "I'll be there. Just give me the time and room number."

I dropped her off at the Westwood Holiday Inn. "It has been a real pleasure talking with you," I said.

I felt good all night, thought about her, wondered how it was possible for someone like this to exist. I have met a few that were phony at it, a successful put-on, when in fact, they had black hearts. They were cold-blooded and conceited and could not care about anyone but themselves; professional bitches, in fact. So many, so many. But this woman was a saint, an angel. When she had spoken of the love she had for her husband and kids—*her eyes had misted*.

I worked the rest of the night up until 1:30 in the morning, when I dozed off in my cab up at the Beverly Hills Hotel. I was awakened at 6:00 a.m. by the desk clerk, a man in his 40s. He was holding out a small plate with a slice of apple pie on it and a plastic fork. He was either being a nice guy or he was homosexual. I did not care what it meant, took the apple pie, thanked the man. This is the only time something like this happened to me at this hotel. Even though none of the bellhops and/or desk clerks went out of their way to be friendly with the cabbies, we did greet one another as a matter of common courtesy. To receive a hunk of pie from one of these guys, however, was indeed out of the ordinary.

Yes, it was. And I was hungry and the pie went down and hit the spot and I did not care what any of it meant. I had that special lady on my mind.

At 6:15 I got a fare to the airport and several other trips prior to going over to the Westwood Holiday Inn.

I made sure I did not look too grubby, pulled into the Jack-In-The-Box parking lot at the corner of Veteran and Santa Monica, washed my face in the men's room, brushed my teeth. I made sure I had enough chewing gum for the breath.

I just could not go home and do it properly (from fear of collapsing on my bed and not being able to get back out there again). One could not make a living that way. So I drove on over to the Holiday Inn at 9:30. Went to the desk to have her paged. Soon she appeared. She had been in the hotel coffee shop having breakfast. Smiling.

"I wonder if you wouldn't mind waiting for five minutes?" she asked. "I just ordered eggs for breakfast."

"Not at all," I told her. "I can wait. Take your time."

Then she laid what should have been a bomb on me: "Instead of taking me to the airport," she said, "would you mind dropping me off at the Flyaway Bus Service?"

Here's exactly what that meant to this cabbie: instead of making 23 bucks, I would make only four dollars, or less, as the Flyaway Bus was just down the street on Sepulveda. To tell you honestly, it did not bother me. Not one bit.

"I want to wait," I told her.

"You really don't have to, you know?" she pointed out.

"It's all right," I said. "I'll wait. I want to."

She went in to have her breakfast. I walked outside to the cab stand and told Fletcher about her. Fletcher was in his 50s, a film editor by profession who was now driving a cab because he could not find work in his field. Fletcher was one of the good guys I talked to now and then. His own marriage was in the process of collapsing after 27 years.

"I've decided to take her to the airport for free," I told him. "No charge. I'll just charge her for the distance to the Flyaway."

"I don't know," Fletcher said. "She must be pretty special."

"She is," I said. "There's nothing I want out of this or hope to get, Fletch. It's just that she's so damn decent, has so much class . . . I just want to spend some time with her, just to talk to her. You just don't see women like this, not around here. You know what I'm talking about."

He nodded his head.

She came out. Three pieces of luggage, all matching red leather; a large suitcase, and two other bags. She was wearing a tan sweater, a green-gray suede jacket, gray leather pants, matching heels. All exuding style, class. She was smiling, apologized for having kept me waiting.

I put her luggage in the trunk, and said: "I'm taking you to the airport. No charge at all. It's on me. You've made such an impression on me that I had to tell a couple of the other drivers about you."

She laughed. "Thank you," she said. "But you don't need to do that. You have to make a living."

"Oh, I'm okay," I told her. "I want to do this one thing. I'm just thrilled to have met you."

She kept saying that it wouldn't be right. So I said: "Okay, you can pay me four bucks; that's what it would cost you to go to the Flyaway."

She got in, and we headed west on Wilshire, got on the 405, south.

"How did it go for you the night before?" she asked.

"Just fine," said I. I found out that the visit to L.A. had been a business trip.

"We buy and sell jewelry," she said. Sometimes she made these trips alone, sometimes with her husband. We talked about books. She told me about Shirley McLain's *OUT ON A LIMB*, enough actually to get my interest up. "I'll make it a point to get a copy and read it," I promised.

"As a result of having read that book," she said, "I'm getting more and more into the *BIBLE*. I'm more interested in reincarnation, things like that."

Well, I never believed in reincarnation or anything of the sort. I believed we got our one chance, one time around—that's it. Good, bad, indifferent—that's it.

"I'm going to hang-in there until I meet someone like you," I told her. "Then I'm going to marry that lady."

We got to the airport. And I hated to see it end, hated to see her go.

I had her bags out.

"I don't want any more than four dollars," I told her. She held out fifteen.

"I can't take it," I said. "It's on me. Really. I'm just grateful that I had this chance to meet someone like you and spend some time with you."

"That's sweet," she said, still holding out the money. "It's yours. I want you to have this."

What could I do? I didn't want the money. Finally accepted it. "God, you really are something," I said to her, and then I hugged her.

"Best of luck," she said. "Have a good life." She was smiling that warm, genuine smile. And me feeling good as a result, and hating to see her go. She had an inner glow. I had come across something pure finally, finally, and it takes such a long while and if the world had more men and women like her what a great place this would be. What great kids she must have to be raising them with this kind of love.

I think my eyes even misted on me; but you know, they would have been tears of joy and sheer appreciation.

I waved to her, and drove off.

And that is what I call A MIRACLE WOMAN.

• • •

City of Angels

"The hell happened to you?" the woman asked. Charlie Sweet sipped his beer and didn't look up as the woman took the barstool next to his.

"You get mugged or something?" She was chuckling when she said: "You look like something the cat drug in, if you don't mind my saying so."

Charlie Sweet lit a filterless Camel and took another pull from the bottle. Out of the corner of his eye he could make out the woman lighting up as well.

"Why don't you be a sport and buy me a drink?" she said.

Charlie Sweet reached for his bottle and relocated himself to the far end of the bar, away from the woman.

"Well, screw you, buddy. *Hear*? Screw you," the woman said loud enough for the handful of rummies in the Hollywood Bl. dive to hear. "Shit!" she muttered underbreath. "You're too good, ain't you? Fucking creeps. Town's fulla creeps. L.A.—shit!" And she ordered a double shot of something strong. "You decide," she instructed the barkeep. "You make it, I'll drink it. Got it, buddy? Long as it tastes good. Mix me up something with some kick to it. You got that?"

"Yes, ma'am," answered the bored bartender. He was pushing 50, with a gray ponytail pulled back tight. An aging hippy. Domestic shit, no doubt, he thought to himself; that's what's troubling this unhappy broad. *People and their problems*. It never changes. He would stay out of it this time; furthermore, she wasn't his type: overweight, short, with huge tits, between 35 and 40. The tits he went for, come to think of it, but he liked them younger. And neither did he care for the tangled, lifeless, dark-brown hair that desperately cried out for a shampoo and a hair stylist's touch—a typical, over-the-hill, troubled L.A. female. He would stay clear of that. And while he prepared a drink for her, a concoction of his own design that tasted sweet enough and yet packed the wallop of a mule, he could easily see the woman continue to eye the guy she had just called a creep. Better him than me, thought the barkeep. I'm staying out of it.

The guy she was hassling had his own troubles, and plenty of them, like the weight of the world was on the man's shoulders. I best stay clear of it, he said to himself, although he had to admit, he found it a bit puzzling that a guy like that, obviously not a rummy, would even be in a nowhere, dead-end Tinseltown bar like this. Even though the guy's appearance was clearly disheveled and the tan suit needed dry cleaning as did the white shirt and the guy clearly needed a shave, it was obvious to the bartender that this man of about 30, if that, did not belong in this dump of a booze joint—but the woman had called him a creep, and maybe he was.

The woman stared at the creep as he sipped his beer and smoked his cigarette, not looking at anybody or anything as he did this. The woman looked away, irritated as hell, twisted her lower body on the stool, then glanced once again at the silent smoker.

"The hell is the matter with you anyway? Ya think I'm gonna rape you? Think I'm gonna grab your balls or something? Not on your life. I don't have to do shit like that—not this gal—not Charleen Johnstone."

When her drink arrived she poured it down her throat swiftly enough, wiped her mouth with the back of her hand, and resumed staring at Charlie Sweet. Then she turned to the chunky barkeep behind the counter. "T' hell is eatin' him anyway?" The barkeep shrugged, hustled his nuts with his left hand while popping a handful of roasted cashews in his mouth with his right and then walked over to the color TV set hanging from the ceiling at the far end of the bar to turn the volume up. Wrestling was on. Charleen Johnstone shook her head and puffed on her cigarette.

"*Men*. There are no real men left in this world. Hell. . . . I'm wasting my breath. They like sucking each other off; that's what's wrong or not wrong. I don't know. They like cock. What're ya gonna do? Huh? What're ya gonna do? They want cock; they all want that cock. . . . So what's a woman to do? How's a woman to get any satisfaction anymore? Hell . . . ."

The barkeep was back at her end of the bar. "You'll have to keep it down, Miss."

"Right," Charleen Johnstone said. "You got it, buddy. Are you queer, too?"

"Please"

"All right. I'll keep it down. How about a beer this time? And one for the gent down there."

The barkeep did as asked. He placed a bottle of beer in front of her and Charleen Johnstone watched as he proceeded to do the same at Charlie Sweet's end of the bar. Charlie Sweet, just then startled from his deep reverie, looked up at the barkeep quizzically. The barkeep simply nodded in Charleen Johnstone's direction. Charlie Sweet's head turned, and to her utter surprise, offered her a slight nod. There was a throbbing inside Charlie Sweet's skull, a throbbing and a numbness that made him feel as though he were moving in slow motion, moving and even seeing everything in slow motion. His surroundings had a surreal quality to him, a surrealism he was lost in, trapped in, and could not shake. Seeing this strange, angry woman and not seeing her, while looking at her, he felt an obligation of decency—he ought to at least thank her for the gesture of kindness—and hopefully he would be left alone. Charlie Sweet gave her a semi-nod, a vague motion of his chin in her direction and was back staring at the countertop before him, staring at nothing, deep space, back in his own world and thoughts that preoccupied him and he was hardly aware as Charleen Johnstone returned his nod with a smile, a nervous smile that cried out for attention.

She waited a moment and slowly made her way down toward him.

"I'm sorry. I didn't mean what I said. I had no right."

"Forget it," Charlie Sweet said without looking at her and lighting the last of the cigarettes in his pack.

"Well, I just wanted you to know. I feel awful about it. I'm usually not like this. I had no right. . . . I was just pissed. . . . My old man . . . I'm married to a real son-of-a-bitch. . . . " And her eyes welled up. "I caught the bastard with another woman. . . ."

"It's okay . . . ," said he, staring straight ahead, wishing she would go away, leave him be.

"I just thought I'd explain. Been together ten years. . . . I never stepped out on the bastard once, not once. He comes home late at night and he tells me about the tramps he's fucked. . . . Gave me VD twice. . . . It wouldn't be so bad if I didn't love him. . . . "

They drank their beers, and Charlie Sweet bought the next round.

"I don't go to bars, you know," said she. "It's just that . . . this time . . . I wanted to kill him . . . I could have killed him. If I'd have been able to get my hands on a gun I would have killed him."

"I know what you mean . . . ," Charlie Sweet said; a soft-spoken, quiet man who projected a natural class and dignity in spite of the state he was in. It was his nature to be polite and personable with people, even though all he wanted desperately was to be left alone. But this poor creature's aches and pains were no doubt agonizing to her and he refrained from asking her to just give him some peace and quiet. He continued that stare at the beer in front of him, while the woman unburdened herself.

"I wanted to buy a gun and shoot him. He's no good. . . . Why is it always that way? I never wanted nobody else. . . . All I ever wanted was him, you know. Just him. That's all I wanted out of life . . . maybe have a kid by him . . . but the bastard won't permit it. I'm 37, and he won't let me have a kid . . . doesn't want kids, he says. When you hit the Lotto jackpot we'll have a kid, he says—so we can hire a full-time domestic to change the kid's diapers, 'cause I ain't doin' it. That's what he said to me. Can you believe it? That kind of talk. A real man wouldn't say something like that to his wife, not a real man." She cleared her throat, grabbed a paper napkin to wipe her eyes with. "If I don't have a kid pretty soon . . . it'll be too late for me."

"Maybe it's a blessing in disguise,"Charlie Sweet finally offered.

"Huh? Yeah, could be. Yeah. . . . Who'd want a kid by a self-centered creep like that anyway?"

She called the barkeep over and bought a couple of packs of cigarettes, handed one of the packs to Charlie Sweet.

"Thanks," Charlie Sweet said.

"My pleasure," the woman said, and lit up. And in spite of all the pain she felt just now, in spite of the agony her husband Beal was putting her through, she could not help but notice that this man had plenty of troubles of his own. He looked as though he hadn't slept in days and his eyes were red-rimmed and conveyed a deep hurt. She did not know how to broach it exactly. We all needed a shoulder to cry on now and then, all of us, and Charleen Johnstone just then could not deny the embarrassment she felt at the way she had unthinkingly unloaded on this poor man.

"Listen," she said, "if you'd like to talk about what's troubling you, I'm all ears. Sorry for going on about my own problems like that . . . but if you need someone to talk to. . . . It just seems to me that you're hurting real bad inside. . . . Am I right? I'm right, ain't I?"

Charlie Sweet shrugged, lit a butt fresh from the pack. He dragged on the cigarette deeply filling his lungs and belly with smoke in a futile effort to drown his demons perhaps, thoughts and demons that pelted away at his aching brain with the relentlessness of a hailstorm. It was that bad. He was numb from the pain, but not so numb that he could entirely ignore the throbbing prickliness of it inside his head. It felt as though his skull was about to explode into a thousand little pieces. He truly wished the woman would let him be. She could never be of any help to him, not that he felt anyone ever could be.

After a pause full of thought, she said: "Would you make love to me?"

Charlie Sweet looked at her. The woman was obviously uncomfortable.

"Would you?"

"I'm married," Charlie Sweet said, indicating the wedding band on his finger. "Well, estranged, as they say. We're estranged."

"It's okay by me—if it's okay by you."

"You want to get back at your old man, that it?"

The woman nodded. "Partly . . . and partly because . . . partly because I just want to. I feel like it. That is, if you don't mind?"

"I don't have a car," Charlie Sweet said. "I'm down to my last dollar."

"No sweat," Charleen Johnstone said. "I got a car; nothing fancy;

it runs. Where do you live?"

"West Hollywood," Charlie Sweet said, and they walked outside into the night. The barkeep was shoving more cashews in his mouth and shaking his head incredulously. Who would have figured that the guy in the tan suit would even remotely be interested in a loud, filthy-mouthed broad like that? Who? Who the hell cared? Better him than me. Up on the color set Hulk Hogan was pounding hell out of some three-hundred-pound, out-of-shape hillbilly in coveralls and bare feet. "Yeah!" urged the barkeep. "Kick the shit out of the redneck! Stomp his ass!"

• •

Twenty minutes later, Charleen Johnstone and Charlie Sweet were pulling up to an apartment complex on Kings Road in West Hollywood. They boarded the elevator, taking it on up to the second floor and Charlie Sweet's one-bedroom apartment. The minute he let them into the apartment the woman was asking where the refrigerator was and if he had anything to drink.

He gave her a half-hearted wave in the direction of the kitchen as he walked over to the sofa, lowered his weary body down on it. There was a framed photo on the coffee table in front of him that he could not take his eyes off of; the photo consisted of Charlie Sweet, his wife Claudia and their young daughter Amy. Charlie Sweet found himself staring at the photo and his eyes watered.

The woman was back with two cans of Bud. Charlie Sweet lit a cigarette and wiped his eyes with the back of his sleeve.

Charleen Johnstone cracked open her beer, pulled on it, then she placed her arms around his neck, turned his head gently so that he would be facing her and gave him a peck on the cheek, kissed his neck just below the left earlobe. She kissed him lightly on the lips and sat back, dropping her arms. She hadn't felt right about any of it, and it was clearly obvious to her that neither did this man she had somehow talked into doing this.

"You have no real desire to do this, do you?" she asked.

"Sorry, no. . . . "

" . . . I understand."

His eyes watered again, tears rolled down. They embraced one another, held on tight. Charlie Sweet gently broke free, wiped his eyes. Sex would not deliver them from what ailed the man and the woman. They could not get it together, wished not to. Charleen Johnstone loved her husband too much, too damn much, and Charlie Sweet let on that the same bothered him as well. He just could not quit thinking about his wife and told the woman of their trek out to L.A., from Denver nine months back, about his job as an attorney for a production company in Century City, how he hadn't been able to get used to fast-paced L.A. and the so-called party scene, but that his wife had been pulled in by it and had taken to it like a bird to flight. "Now she wants a divorce," said he.

"I know what you mean," Charleen Johnstone said. "I know exactly what you mean. *City of Lost Assholes, that's what L.A. should be retitled*. It's a sewer, a fucking sewer . . . " And she began to sob again. "It wasn't always like it is now. If you got values, want to believe in virtue, you haven't got a chance in this town. . . . There's just too many creeps . . . everywhere you go . . . garbage . . . I love my husband so much. . . . "

She reached for the framed color photograph, studied it.

"Your wife and daughter."

Charlie Sweet nodded.

"They're both quite pretty," Charleen Johnstone said. "What's your daughter's name?"

" . . . Amy," Charlie Sweet said. "Just had her eighth birthday a couple of months back. She's in Denver with my mother-in-law. You see, we left our girl behind back there as this was only going to be a trial run for us, my wife and I, this trip out here. We had planned on going back all along, you see? L.A. is just not a good place to raise a child. . . . " and his mind drifted off, back in his own shell. He was quiet.

Charleen Johnstone said: "I want to have a little girl like that. I want so badly to be a mother, to have a family. . . . What's so terrible about that? We had six kids in our family. We weren't rich, but we had love. We had wonderful, caring parents—and they're still together and in love even after forty years." She felt the tears doing their best to surge forth all over again and she did her damndest to contain it this time.

"I wanted what they had, what we had, the same kind of stable, happy home life. . . . I wanted trust, true love, but I made a mistake when I picked a playboy, a goddamn skirt-chasing Casanova, to fall in love with."

After a while, after she had regained her composure and wiped her eyes, she said: "So where's your wife now?"

Charlie Sweet extracted a fresh cigarette from the pack and lit it with the half-smoked butt, taking the usual deep drag and letting the smoke out; he waved his hand then, indicating the closed bedroom door.

Charleen Johnstone was taken aback by the casual gesture. "*Your wife's been here all along*?"

Charlie Sweet nodded, not looking at her at all, puffing on his cigarette as he did this. She did not know what to make of it, hadn't liked it—then thought: Well, they're splitting up, no doubt; and hoped in spite of everything her old man Beal had put her through, that somehow they would still be able to salvage it. She did not want what this man sitting next to her on the sofa and his wife were going through. She would do her best to keep her own marriage together, do everything in her power to salvage it, because in her heart of hearts she believed it was worth salvaging. It wasn't that Beal was such a bad guy, it's just that Beal behaved like a real dog sometimes. She would threaten divorce, threaten to leave that two-timing lout if he did not change his act and grow up. She would straighten him out, or else. . . . She would put her foot down this time for sure, but first she would do what she could to help this poor man out here; she would have a talk with his wife and do what she could to prevent their breakup. It was clearly tearing the man up. He appeared suicidal to her.

She said: "Charlie, do you mind if I go in there and have a chat with your wife?"

He said nothing right away, smoked his cigarette in deep thought, eyes glazed over, lost, lost, his mind floating, a million miles away somewhere, not here.

" . . . I worry about Amy," he said. "I worry about her all the time. What do I say to my little girl? What do I tell her? . . . I don't know that I can face her. . . . " He wiped tears with the back of his hand, then said:

"Yes, do that. I'd like you to do that. You see, that's why I needed you to come up here . . . to talk to my wife. . . . Tell her, you explain to Claudia, my wife, that we really should return to Denver as planned; tell her it's best that way . . . for Amy, for the sake of our family. . . . L.A. is going to destroy our marriage. . . . Tell her love is all that matters, being true and good to each other, tell her . . . tell her I'm so sorry for all of it. Tell her, tell her . . . please talk to her. . . . I can't reach her. . . . "

"Hush now," she said to him softly, "before you have me in tears all over again." She patted him on the shoulder. "You're a decent man, Charlie Sweet—a Sweet man. Your wife just doesn't see it, doesn't know it. Women, some women, can be pretty stupid that way."

He said nothing. Charlie Sweet stared at the carpet.

Charleen Johnstone rose from the sofa. She thought: Here's a guy obviously monogamous and still being dumped on—and in my case, that S.O.B. I'm married to doesn't even understand what monogamy means and I'm trying to hold on to him. Did any of it make any sense?

She walked in the direction of the bedroom, knocked lightly on the bedroom door.

"Mrs. Sweet, may I come in?"

She waited for a response and got none. She turned her head to see Charlie Sweet seated still, on the sofa, staring at nothing. Then she saw him slowly reach for the framed wedding photo hanging on the wall above his head. She saw him hold it in both hands and stare at it that way. She knocked again, got nothing, wrapped her fingers around the doorknob and slowly turned it. She pushed in gently and allowed the door to swing open.

Her eyes first caught sight of a handgun lying in the yellow shag carpet at the foot of the bed and then her eyes darted up to the bed and the sight in it, and her body suddenly shook and she felt her guts tighten up on her and she could easily taste a bitter sourness winding its way up her throat from her belly and the need to vomit could not be suppressed. By clamping her hand over her mouth firmly like that and forcing her body to stop quaking was she able to keep from vomiting, although what her eyes remained focused on did not help much: there were two naked bodies lying in the blood-soaked bed—a man and a woman—riddled with bullet holes. It was easy enough to discern that the woman was Mrs. Sweet, the smiling blond in all those wedding photos that adorned the apartment. And then Charleen Johnstone heard a sharp whack, a noise like glass breaking. It did take her a good second or two to break out of this self-imposed stiffness, for she was well aware that if she moved too quickly she would be surely vomiting, but she turned in the direction of the living room as the noise seemed to be coming from there, hand still clamped over her mouth, while she sighed: "Dear Lord, Dear God . . . ," in time to see Charlie Sweet slit his throat with a jagged piece of glass.

• • •

eating wood/spitting blood

i had enough beer in me
and i had just finished
another letter to her,
and it had taken me
all afternoon to get it right
and then i just sat there
stared at it, stared, cramps
in my guts, as though i'd swallowed a
handful of hot gravel,
the brew pouring out of me
through the eyes,
and i knew the letter wouldn't do
any good—
she might read it, and she
might not—
chances were slim that she would
and even then,
in all probability,
would shrug
and toss it in the trash.

how do you explain?
how do you say the right thing
to someone who would like to think
that you do not exist and never did?
that what you once had, no matter
how true, is no more, and never
will be again?

i got up, staggered about the
room, rammed my head into the closet
door, contemplated flinging the

tablelamp at the wall,
made it to the bathroom, stared at the
pitiful son-of-a-bitch in the mirror:
bloodshot eyes,
a haggard-looking nothing,
a nobody
in pain,
a nobody wanting to
die, afraid to die.
afraid.
what if she needs me
someday?
what if she calls?
i clung to the mirrored bathroom door,
my face slid down.
there's no help for me.
there's no help.
i straightened out
and started chewing on
the door,
tasting the wood, digging
my teeth into it, cutting
my lower lip open,
spitting blood . . .

did you ever love like
this?
did it ever hurt like
this?
did you want to
die?
just curl up and fade
away?

and i recall that sunny afternoon
so clearly
the afternoon we sat in my

used toyota corolla 2 years ago
in front of the brick building
she was living in at the
time at gramercy pl. & 2nd st.,
the sunny afternoon
we decided to find a place
of our own, move in together
and live together,
to be together forever,
to stand by each other
no matter what.

nothing would come between us.
nothing.
NOTHING.

and i have never in my life
had the urge to
taste wood
and i know, deep down in my
soul, in spite of what has
happened, in spite of
every damn thing that
has happened
i will go on worrying about her
even though i never see her again
i hope no one ever puts her
through this hell.

i hope she never ends up
eating wood and spitting blood.

i hope she never wakes up
in a cold sweat
in the middle of the night
tossing in her bed, weeping,
quietly praying for help,

some kind of sign
that it will eventually end,
that the pain will go away.

(May 1980)

Two Cancellations, and a Brief Chat With a Male Hustler

3rd up on the Beverly-Wilshire Hotel.
Doc says: "Got one on Walden—wanna go?"
"I'll go."
"Honk three times."
"Check."
I make it to the 8 hundred block
of Walden,
honk three times (like the song).
No response —
I honk three more times
and don't feel all that comfortable
doing it.
Honking your horn in Beverly Hills
at 10:00 p.m. (or any time, for that matter)
is like honking your horn in a cemetery.
Dead.
Dead.
Million dollar mansions.
No people.
Some lights.

I press a button by the gate.
"Who is it?" a female voice says.
"Taxi."
The gate opens.

I make it up the winding driveway
past the guest house (the guest house
alone is probably worth half-a-mil—but so
what? I got my $250 a month room;
I'm happy, I guess).
 The main house is big.
  Three cars in the driveway,

a German shepherd walking around
looking to kick ass.
I roll my window up.
A 14-year-old chick with
a lot of makeup, wearing the
tightest red sweatsuit
appears.
"What happens if we don't want a cab?"
she says.
"What?" I don't understand what she's
trying to say.
"You mean you changed your mind—you don't
want a cab now?"
She nods, giggles: "Right."
"That's two bucks."
"What for?"
"Service charge," I say.
She goes back in, returns with a $20. I break
the bill, cut a U, make it
back down the driveway.
Beverly Hills, baby; how do you like the
way they throw it away? No, they're not spoiled,
they got rocks for brains.

Doc's got one up on Rosscomare:
"Call me approaching."
We do it that way to keep other
cab companies from stealing our fares.
I call him approaching. It's way
up there on Rosscomare.
Two women, and a guy.
The guy is stone drunk.
He's so drunk he can barely walk.
They're trying to convince him to get in the cab.
He won't hear of it.
Finally one of the women says: "Jerry, will you please
get in the *fucking* cab?"
He gets in the back.

I don't like drunks sitting in the back.
I like 'em where I can keep a good eye on 'em.
I tell him to sit in the front.
He gets out. The woman's got to help the stupid bastard
in again.
"Why don't you be a gentleman and get in the goddamn cab?" I
tell him.
He gets in.

The guy's got gray hair, premature gray, glasses.
Ninety feet later he says:
"Can you please pull over to the right?"
Ok; I don't want him puking in my cab.
I pull over.
"In front of that car," he says.
I park in front of the Datsun.
"What if I give you five bucks and you follow me in your
cab down to Sunset?"
The guy is nuts. He's slurring his words, can't talk and he's
talking about wanting to drive his car to Santa Monica (the
City of—that's where he lives.)
I'm trying to talk him out of it and I don't know
why—the guy's a jerk. And maybe I do know why.
"What if you kill somebody, man? Don't you know there's a
new law? They're really cracking down."
"How old are you?"
"30," I tell him.
"I'm 33," he says.
There's no hope for the son-of-a-bitch. "You'll never
grow up," I tell him.
"I know—the big asshole. Please, do me this one favor, ok?"
Fuck it. He gives me ten. I give him all the singles
I got on me. Four. He takes it, gets out, walks
to his car, gets in, takes it down the hill.
I stay with him for about a mile. There's no traffic around.
Maybe luck's on his side.

Doc's got one for me on Oak Pass
and Oak Pass is a good four mile haul.

I shoot up Rosscomare to Mulholland, take Mulholland to Benedict, Benedict to Hutton, Hutton to Oak Pass.

Another million dollar mansion. There's a hustler standing in
front of the gate. I know he's a hustler I've seen
enough of them: worn jeans, the lumberjack shirt, the short
hair, the mustache, the lumberjack boots—the standard
West Hollywood faggot uniform.
He gets in —
looks macho, but when he opens his mouth to speak the voice
doesn't match the appearance.
Soft voiced, too soft — and he says: "Do you know
who lives in that house?"
"No, I don't," I answer.
And he names a top, a very in, *a very in*, physical fitness guru, got
his own TV show, got a book out on "how to shed
those ugly pounds," owns a fitness salon in Beverly Hills
(of course.)
He tells me the place is equipped with security cameras, that it's an
incredible place, really incredible.
"You think the guy is happy?" I ask.
"No, no, I don't. He lives all by his lonesome in that
huge place. All by himself. All he does is work work work,
no time for a relationship, just quickies." The guy wants
to go to Santa Monica and Highland, later on changes his
mind and makes it Gardner and Fountain. "Where I started," he
says.
"Right," I say.

We were both
working the night shift.

It Wasn't Our Fault

(to J.M.I.)

it isn't you I'm screaming at,
it isn't you I'm angry at,
it isn't because of you
that I am losing my mind now;
it isn't because of you
that I walk around now
talking to myself,
making hand gestures and shouting
and sometimes catching myself at it
and sometimes not.
like I said,
it isn't because of you;
it's the forces
that caused it!
the Gods that did it!!!
the brutal Gods!
the whores of the universe
that split us apart,
that sprinkled our once
true love with a bitter dust,
with a spell that confused us,
that caused anger
and tears,
with a good dollop of agony.
it wasn't our fault, sweetheart,
it wasn't us—
the demons put a spell on us.
can't you see now?
the demons are scared to death
of anything as pure as what we'd had
that time.

it wasn't you, girl,
and it wasn't me;
we tried so hard
and were so good
and the demons were at first enraged
at how much we cared
and something had to be done
about it,
and soon,
and it was,
and if we had only been able
to withstand that
initial onslaught
we would have been
just fine;

if only, sweetheart,
if only . . .

Chocolate Chip Cookies

haven't done anything in several weeks now;
step outside once or twice a week
to move the car from one side of the
street to the other
for the street cleaner,
take a ride on the ten speed
to 3rd street to buy chicken
from the Kentucky Fried Colonel,
four times now,
to the small library on Gardner,
several times now,
to read a magazine or two,
just to get out of the
apartment,
to the liquor store for chocolate chip
cookies, maybe a doughnut,
but my money's running low
and lower,
agoraphobia creeping in,
got me by the throat and
slowly squeezing
and squeezing,
and many times I will put on the
clothes, get dressed with thoughts
of just getting out there to buy a
newspaper, maybe a candy bar
and then sit in my apt.
for hours
looking for excuses why I shouldn't venture
outside.
agoraphobia (they call it)
no balls, I call it, no guts, I call it

will be 36 in two months;
no pity, because then you'll just
piss me off—
but I don't understand what is going on
almost 36, survived the rice paddies,
survived the battle of the sexes,
survived quite a bit, at least
it seems like quite a bit, and then will turn around
and ask myself: just what the hell did I survive?
huh?
what was it?
anything?
made it through the split?
so what?
can deal with her wanting somebody else,
maybe even now wanting a kid by that same somebody else;
she did better;
and have to give her credit—
found somebody happier (I truly hope)
somebody normal (I truly hope)
somebody who doesn't sing the blues,
somebody who's got it together,
somebody her family really likes,
somebody even her best friend Carla really likes,
somebody who never wakes up screaming in the
middle of the night
clutching his skull,
licking cold sweat,
wishing he were never born;
somebody who doesn't get dressed
on a Wednesday afternoon
to go out to buy chocolate chip cookies
and then sits around for hours
staring at the door,
afraid to open it,
afraid to go outside;
somebody better (I truly hope)

somebody sane (I truly hope)
a good man (I truly hope)
somebody who's truly made her happy (I truly hope);
and you were right to do what you did, kiddo;
you made the right move.

the light in the room getting dimmer (one of the
bulbs went out)
and I got my sweater on,
still afraid to go out
to get those chocolate chip cookies.

a lonely business

i do as i please now
seem to be better off financially
now
(as opposed to before when i was
with her)
i answer to no one now
can read late into the night
and/or masturbate as often
as i feel like it
or go to a movie when i feel like it
maybe even a porno
i buy the skin mags
have a date now and then
i do the laundry and do the dishes
when the whim strikes me
i have the money now
to spend on records, books,
clothes, (little things i could
never afford before because i was
living with her)

i don't have to spend time with people
i don't like or don't understand
or care to understand, as they are
taking up my time
(for example: some of her friends, some of
her relatives, etc.)
i'm finally getting used to
living alone again
and i think i like it
most of the time i do like it
but, Jesus, the blues do strike now and then
but . . . being a loner is a lonely business
i should know that by now.

fear

under the covers,
wide awake.
it's 2 in the afternoon;
the sun is out,
Wilshire is busy
with the sounds of the city,
people walking about
out there,
reading the paper,
drinking coffee or tea or booze,
eating lunch.
some guys are so lucky
as to have a beautiful face to
look at across the
table from them.

i can hear a jackhammer going
full bore in the distance,
cars
and car horns,
trucks,
sounds of the city;
but i'm under the covers
where it's safe,
hiding,
shelter.
i know i should get up
but can't;
there is nothing wrong with me
but i can't get up,
too scared,
too weary,

my body is made of lead.
i only work weekends,
but i'm deader
than a dead man.
why?
i don't know why/and i do
know why:
fear;
the fear is back.
i should go out there
and catch a glimpse of the
sun,
i know i should, i really
should;
but i can't make it,
can't get up—

it's safer
under the covers . . .

Platoon

Saw *PLATOON*
and kept thinking
yeah, that's it!
That's it, man!
The truth!
THAT'S IT!
Choked on tears in the lobby, hurried
outside
to get to the ten speed, hurried to
unchain it,
hurried so's not to break down
in front of the line of people
outside the theatre on La Brea.
Got the bike unchained, rode it on home
in a hurry.
Shit! I should have died over there.
I can't shake it, man,
I can't shake it!
My woman didn't understand the
blues; saw something she'd
written in her notepad
just before we parted
(in '80; we'd met in '78):
wish Chance was the
way he used to be;
meaning cheerful, upbeat, (due to
beer, which she didn't know at the
time) but happiness is a tough act to
maintain—and toward the end of those
two years, the act caught up with me,
the blues hit, depression kicking my
ass
and my baby wanted out.

Okay, I said, I don't blame you,
and tried to keep my cool,
but the raging volcano within I could not contain.
Hell, man, I should have died over there!

I should have been blown to bits.
Fuck it, just plain fuck it.
What so many of us don't know
is that we did die over there.
We never came back.
We never got back.

On that plane on my way back to "the
world"
a pretty stewardess paused at my seat,
showing interest in me, waiting
for some kind of conversation, a word,
a nod
and I was too scared, too shook up, fighting
to conceal the nightmare
that ravaged my brain, that continued
relentlessly inside my
head,
wanting so desperately to be able to
smile at this pretty woman,
wanting to embrace her, to have her put her
arms around me,
and I just sat there,
stiff, frozen with fear,
fighting to keep the tears
from showing up, from bursting
forth;
finally, disappointed, she gave a shrug
and walked off.
God, what is the matter with me? I
thought on that plane, Dear Lord,
what is wrong?
This isn't right, this isn't normal;

put me in front of a firing squad and
fill me with lead.
Jesus, these are not just words,
but a plea.
Chop me to bits,
stick fifty bayonets in my guts,
do whatever the hell you like;

you see, you can't hurt a
dead man.

(Jan. '87)

can't get started

ate an apple,
ate a banana,
a box of dates,
drank two glasses of Arrowhead water,
pulled on the hammer,
another glass of water,
lowered my head
against the table top.
can't get started.
had more water,
rode the bicycle up to 3rd Street
for a haircut at Super Cuts,
rode the bicycle back,
sighted that rarest of rarities:
an available parking space
in front of my building,
chained the bicycle to a handrail,
ran up to 6th Street
where my Dodge Colt sat,
swung it around the block,
saw a woman in shorts great legs great ass
walking west on Wilshire;
hurried, parked the car,
jumped on the ten speed,
hurried out after the woman
wanting to take another look
at that fine ass, those long shapely legs;
caught up with her,
rode on past her,
rode the bike up to 3rd
bought a box of Kentucky Fried Chicken,
rode the bike back to the apt.
chained the bike outside,

hurried up the steps,
thought about the woman and
masturbated again,
ate the chicken,
had more water,
stared at the typewriter
shaking my head,
the novel waiting to be finished,
wishing I had a woman like the one
I saw on Wilshire,
needing to feel better.

just could not get started.

put on Aretha's Greatest Hits.

I have more days like this
than any other kind.

Fading Memory

there might just come that day
when they let me out of my rubber room
because I have a visitor
and that visitor might just be you
coming to see what has happened with me,
if I really have gone crazy.
you might want to take a real close
look at my eyes,
but you probably won't want to be alone
because you are not so sure
that I might not snap at any minute,
but when you see the way I've been kicked
around by the forces,
when you see me just stand there
not say anything, no expression on my face,
silent, forever silent,
maybe my eyes, just something in my
eyes wanting, trying to say to you
how grateful I am that you came to see me,
trying to tell you how much you mean
to me still & always will,
you might feel a teardrop in your heart somewhere
for me,
you might even embrace me;
I often wonder;
but you show no sign of
having missed me,
had come out of *curiosity*;
no teardrops, no arms to
hold me, no words are spoken,
as they lead me quietly
back to something that is
but a fading memory
to you.

the smell of death

it's an orange-colored rug
old and dirty and it smells
i walk into the bathroom and the ceiling
is cracked and water dripping from above
every time the guy upstairs takes a shower
i keep wondering when that ceiling will come
crashing down on top of me
one of these days i'm sure
and the kitchen is just as filthy
the oven doesn't work
no complaints really
my one and only complaint is
there should be a sign of life around here
somewhere
a sign of life . . .
something had died before i moved in
and something is dying at this very moment
i have a feeling
that something is me . . .

i just don't know the way

you have a gentle heart,
i have seen you show kindness to so many;
you must be one of the rare ones—
and yet, i find it so hard to believe
that you would not bother turning around
taking a second look at me
and try to help and understand.

but your heart is good;
i have always believed you to be
a rare human being;
you have patience, a ready smile,
a generous nature, always wanting
to help those in need.

and my problem is
i don't even know what is the matter,
so what kind of help should i seek from you?
help me explain myself,
help me see—please, just give me
a moment, my head is full of
stuff i cannot understand;
i'm stuttering and fumbling, crying out
to you, not doing it the right way
and don't know if i ever will
be able to;
wishing i could connect with you
somehow, wishing i had the words,
the strength, the smile, the guts;
wishing i had the way,
so desperate to hold your hand, girl,
and not knowing how
to reach the kindness that i
know is there.

all i ever manage to do
is create more confusion, anger;
and all it does is take your smile
from your face.
all i have ever been able to do
in all my hopeless efforts
is create anger in you;
and i will never know what to do.
wishing i knew how to make you smile
just one more time,
wishing i had the way.

please don't be angry with me, girl;
i'm just so lost these days.

sad endings

(for J.M.I.)

sweetheart, please do not weep;
it really is no one's fault,
there is no one to blame.
even if you had come back
to me it would not have made that
much difference;
don't you see, girl?
it would not have erased the
ugliness, it would not have
erased the memory of it, the
bleakness, the way we parted
at the end,
it would not have mended any of it,
the malice, the bitter words
from me and from you.
instead of hugging and kissing
and standing together
hard and tight
we let them split us up,
we let them
get to us, sweetheart,
and we never should have allowed
anything to interfere with our
love
it would never be the way it was,
it could never again
be the pure kind of
love we'd had in the beginning . . .
it is just too sad for me to
accept . . . just too sad . . .
please, don't blame yourself
for any of it . . .
people just don't have the way,
they never did . . .

what a life

I sleep
these days
I sleep.
ever been there?
again, I say
no GD pity,
no sorrow, don't sing the blues!
shit!
boy, do I sleep
all the time, man!
SLEEP!
at night, during the day,
and when I get up
it's only to use the john,
to eat something,
boil some rice, open a can
of vegetables,
pull on the hammer
once, twice, maybe again a bit
later,
but only to drop back down
on the bed
and sleep.
it's safer that way.
nothing to face or worry about.
the TV is there, bought over a
year ago (through a friend's help
on the installment plan)
but TV makes me only sicker
and so it stays off
and it's usually sleep, brother,
just sleep.
too scared to go out

too scared to live,
getting beaten down, it seems,
by forces I can't even see,
surrounded by forces and voices
that are probably only real
to me.
hiding under the covers,
just hiding here
in the dark—
it has finally come to that.
it's 8:31
on a Wednesday night
8:31 in L.A.
on a Wednesday
in January '87.

the hooker with the pleasant French accent

3:15 A.M. Friday morning. A Coldwater Canyon call. I took it up there, way way up there, *greenback land*—pulled into the driveway. The prostitute came out, a tall blond in heels. She got in the front seat. "Cheap motherfuckers," she said. Then she asked for a cigarette. I didn't have any. "The motherfucker only gave me a hundred," she said. "Wanted me to go down on his old lady—ain't that some shit?" At first I couldn't place the accent. It was kind of cute the way she went on. I thought maybe she was from France, someplace like that. She said she was from New Orleans. "Wanted me to suck his wife," she said. "Perverted motherfucker. I told him no way, so he gave me a hundred dollars to suck him off. Isn't that some shit? Fucking people are sick. His wife sat there in the chair never said a word. I don't think it was her idea. He's the one who wanted it. Lot of sick people in this world. *A lousy hundred bucks*. I shouldn't have left the Strip. I lost a lot of money by leaving the Strip like that. Should have asked for it up front. Cheap motherfuckers."

She was a good-looking woman, a lot prettier than most prostitutes I see out here. She had me drive her to a rundown motel on Vine in Hollywood. It was highly unlikely that I would ever see her again, but as she got out I reached for one of my cab company cards and quickly jotted my cab number down. I extended the card to her. "What's this?" she asked. "In case you ever need a cab," I answered. "Oh," she said, and walked away. On that, I backed it slowly out of the motel driveway, stealing a final glance at all that golden hair, the long legs and the healthy behind, as she climbed the staircase to the second floor—and there was no denying the bit of sadness that I felt in the pit of my belly because I wished she was in love with me (and knowing really there was no chance of that happening).

mixed vegetables

a need for a six-pack or two or three
a need to compound that pain,
instead drinking weak tea 'cause
that's all that's left.

hell, got about two cups of rice left.
yeah, left Nam ages ago
and still can't seem to get away
from the rice.

hell, never ate it while I was there
but a cup of rice nowadays
with some butter on top
is a cheap meal, you see,
and a bag of rice costs
about two bucks and can last me
a good month.

sometimes I'll have a can of peas with
that, mixed vegetables, etc.

that's what life is like at
Wilshire and Burnside.
the whole neighborhood is undergoing
a transformation,
rents doubling, tripling;
chic restaurants going up
all along La Brea
where nothing really much
existed there before.

and the old folks, I hear, are on
some kind of government program

and don't care how much
the rent goes up,
and the money grubbers are
rubbing their hands together
pleased about it all,
and wouldn't it be nice
if somebody were to line
them all up in front of
a firing squad
and chop them down
like the predators
that they are,
give it to them
the way Gilmore got it
in Salt Lake City
which, by the way, the grubbers
deserve a lot more than he ever
did.

and I haven't got the bucks
for the six-packs I could use right
now,
and I haven't got the guts
to start playing with that
razor blade without it.

(Jan. '87)

Rent

well, better get some cardboard boxes
at the supermarket on Wilshire
to put all the paperbacks in,
better start looking for a job,
another apartment.
maybe I can get hired to manage a small
apartment building—
wouldn't have to worry about rent,
wouldn't have to worry about
much.
I could forget about women altogether;
one needed money before one could
have a chance at love
in this town.
just to have enough money for food
and a roof overhead
and my Charlie Parker albums, my
Springsteen albums, my Doors albums,
my Ray Charles albums, the theme from
A MAN AND A WOMAN
and my typewriter
and I could go on living
the life of a hermit.
rent is five days away.
they want five hundred this time
and I haven't got it—
and that's not all
I haven't got,
some would tell you
I never had my sanity,
some would tell you
I never had much of anything
at all.

20 dollars and change

maybe it won't be so bad when it finally happens,
when they come up to the second floor and start
banging on my door to let me know (with a deputy sheriff in tow)
that a lock will be placed on my doorknob in two days,
maybe it won't be so bad;
could be it's the waiting for it to happen that eats away at you
the waiting chipping away at your brain
and it seems like I've been at it for years
waiting for them to push me out in the street.
down to 20 bucks and change.
ate up all the hot dogs,
got one apple left, one tangelo,
and then there's that bag of rice in the
fridge and there's that box of sugar.
but the waiting is getting to me,
the waiting.
I don't sleep these days,
just pace and pace.
it's 2 A.M.
thinking about it all,
keep thinking about chucking it,
too cowardly to do anything about it;
but it's like this for quite a few of us,
quite a few out there are going through the same
thing,
and some are even past it,
they've graduated to the streets,
are sleeping on bus benches,
in parks, under bridges,
in dark doorways—
wherever a safe enough place can be found (if there is
such a place)
there is no more waiting for them,

only maybe just waiting to die,
for the sun to come up,
to keep warm long enough
wrapped in their
numerous rags,
long enough for the sun to come up.

maybe it won't be so bad when it finally happens for me,
when they finally put that lock on my door.
I can recall spending 18 hours a day in that cab,
18 hours a day
just to stay alive and barely did that
and driving past these bag ladies and others
sleeping in the gutter in doorways
driving past them at night
and taking it in
and thinking: Jesus, I feel so damn sad for these
people, for all of them, and knowing, really knowing
that I was not far away from it at all.
you pay your dues and you pay your dues
and the fat cat's going to put his foot down on
you no matter where your heart happens to be.
the rent went up one hundred and 25 bucks today,
but so what?
like I said: am down to 20 dollars and change.

until the rice runs out

I've got a five-pound bag of rice
sitting on the bottom shelf in the
refrigerator
that cost 2 bucks,
there's sugar
for flavor
to be sprinkled over the rice
after it has been boiled—
so, you see,
for the moment life is not bad,
but the TV preachers keep asking for money
and it angers me just a bit,
at down to 35 bucks
might as well be in Ethiopia somewhere
starving with all those people
or Russia,
what difference would it make?

I've got a novel by Susan Fromberg Schaeffer
sitting on the coffee table in front
of me,
a biography of Jack London by Andrew Sinclair,
SCALPEL by Horace McCoy,
THE BELL JAR by Sylvia Plath,
THE STRANGER by Albert Camus,
THEY DON'T DANCE MUCH by James Ross.

sometimes the written word
helps pass the time away.
I don't look for answers like I used to
hidden somewhere in the written word,
just to pass the time away.
it's not as bad as TV.

I've got hundreds of others sitting on the bookshelves,
some good, some awful,
piled high, sitting there,
collecting dust;
most of which I have read over the years,
some of which I never will,
sitting there.
and some have photos on the back with
wise-looking authors
trying to hide the fact that they are
demented.

but that's okay,
I don't look for answers in these books anymore,
nobody knows much,
they never did.
like I said, in case you're interested,
I've got that five-pound bag of rice
sitting in the fridge
that I paid two bucks for,
I boil a cup of it every day,
sprinkle sugar on it for flavor,
and won't worry about a thing
until the rice runs out.

A Kid in Love with Laurel and Hardy (or: Little Boy Black & Blue)

I must have been 9 or 10. We were living in Brussels at the time. I used to pass this movie theatre every day on my way to school. One day I stopped to look at the posters hanging by the box office. They were posters from a Laurel and Hardy movie currently in release. I had never known anything about Laurel and Hardy up until several months back when they happened to screen several of their silent films at school. And I had been taken in, had fallen in love with these two comical adults. There was a need, a desire to be a part of their fun-filled world, a need to be a part of all that joy and happiness. Their world was devoid of tears and pain, devoid of fear and beatings, yelling and berating (that was prevalent at home). So when I noticed the movie stills and posters outside this movie theatre naturally I wanted in, wanted to see it and be part of it, particularly since this movie happened to be a talkie. This was a new release. I studied the poster in front of me. This particular show seemed to be about the two of them in the foreign legion. They had funny haircuts, were in uniform—either washing a mountain of laundry or peeling huge kettles of potatoes. Both of these guys had much longer hair in these photos, silly looking at that; pageboy cuts, I believe. All of it had me smiling. I wanted to see the movie. I had made up my mind that I would see it—but how? I did not have the money. I was too young to go in alone. I would hurry home and tell my mother about it.

My mother was busy preparing supper and did not want to hear any of it. I kept at her, asking her if it would be all right to go see this

Laurel and Hardy movie. "Will you shut up and leave me alone?" was her response. Only I did not feel like shutting up and kept bothering her about it. "Why can't I see the movie?" I kept asking. And she kept telling me to forget it.

When the old man got home that evening she recounted my "badgering." That was all he needed to hear. The belt came off and away he went, with everything that he had in him. This was the man's M.O. He couldn't just whack you on the rear, give you a spanking—he had to beat you senseless. By the time he was through (what seemed like an eternity later and he had been forced to stop pretty much due to exhaustion), I had welts all over my body, face, neck—you name it. Black-and-blue. I had been the recipient of yet another savage beating by this barbarian for no real reason that I could think of. Nothing justified it. I was a 9-year-old kid, a kid who'd asked to be taken to a harmless Laurel and Hardy movie. If I had been a pest about it, and there is that possibility—did it justify what this nut had just put me through? Could my old man ever understand why there was nothing resembling love I felt toward him all my life?

Would he ever understand that this is the quickest way to kill off a child's love for his father? Fill a child with fear and you're killing the love that child had for you and turning that love to hatred.

After my beating I was cleaned up, given a white shirt to wear (long sleeves, the better to conceal the welts with), a tie.

The top button on my shirt was buttoned for the same reason as well—and my father and I walked down Rue something or other, to the movie theatre on the boulevard.

As we stepped into the movie theatre I noticed up on the screen (in black and white) Tarzan the Ape-Man was battling what appeared to be a monstrously large tarantula. My father was interested in the film. He had always been a big fan of Tarzan, Johnny Weismuller. From the vague accounts I picked up over the years this is how my father had courted my mother back in Sarajevo, by taking her to Charlie Chaplin comedies and Tarzan adventures.

I sat there, numb from the beating. When Tarzan's pet chimp appeared, that lovable, playful chimp did nothing for me and my state of numbness. I was stiff, stared straight ahead.

My father went out of his way to appear fatherly after such a beating, always; usually if he was out in public—and this occasion was no different. He would, from time to time, look down at me sitting on his right to see whether or not I was enjoying the show. My numbness persisted. Even when my beloved Laurel and Hardy buddies appeared on the huge movie screen in front of us I continued to sit there in a daze. The irony of my appearance, the irony of it all did not escape my 9-year-old mind: a father, immaculately attired in suit and tie, and his equally immaculate 9-year-old boy seeing a movie together, spending some time together. People looked at us, couples, approvingly, giving my father a polite nod of approval: *how nice and decent this man is to be spending time with his young son this way.*

Like I said—the irony of it hardly escaped me. To this day I do not remember much of that Laurel and Hardy movie. I had remained in this limbo-like existence throughout. I do not recall what happened afterwards, how we got home, but I guess we did.

My dream, my great dream, what I wished for, prayed to God for during those years that someday I would be delivered from these unbalanced people that were my parents, delivered from this world of fear and unhappiness that was a living hell my sisters and I were stuck in.

I know I loved the city of Brussels and never wanted to leave Belgium, but the old man (and his wife) were determined to fulfill a dream of their own—that dream was to go to America. If only they could have left me behind. We were in Belgium for a year and a half—and in that short time I was already speaking French. The school was fine, the instructors cared about you, cared that the students learned something, even though the boys had to wear shorts.

When it was time to leave Brussels I wept, but it did me little good. We were Chicago-bound.

• • •

My Own Bag of Rocks

He grabbed her by the hair and yanked hard. She was 14, I was 18. She was my sister. He was our father. He'd been treating his kids like this forever. Always the beatings. He used whatever was handy: belts, switches, his (carpentry calloused) hands. This was how the old man got his kicks, smacking his kids around. And the old lady was not much better, although to her credit, this was one of the rare times she could not be held directly responsible; she hadn't instigated this particular violent episode being perpetrated against one of her youngsters of like gender. Ordinarily, and as a matter of routine, the first thing she liked to do as soon as he arrived home from work was nag him about all the "bad" things the kids had done. And this had him grinning that readily available gargoyle grin (revealing crooked, yellow teeth), because now he had the excuse to pull the leather belt off and start whacking away, start pounding. This was the guy's way of decompressing.

He grabbed my sister by the hair and yanked hard and smacked her in the face, on top of the head. Her crime? Too slow to translate. He'd been watching the news on TV and had insisted she translate. He was either too ignorant or too lazy, or both, to understand what the English-speaking newscaster was saying. We'd been in the U.S. since '61, this was 1969—on Chicago's North Side. The old man was as brutal and ignorant as they come. I'd been in my room in the front that faced Wilson Ave., aimlessly leafing through a Joe Weider muscle-building magazine when my ears first picked up on the commotion going on in the TV room. I heard the TV in the background and my old man saying something like:

"What's he saying now?"

And my sister involuntarily stammering with a partial translation, or else unable to respond at all. And that was followed by a smack or a slap, a whack, and the fast sound of Jemila wincing back in pain.

I could hear it all, every bit of it, coming from the TV room at the other end of the hallway—and it made me cringe. As I craned my neck from where I stood leaning against the dresser I could see my sister in full view through my open door, but only part of the old man, back of his head and neck, shoulders, where he sat in a recliner. Jemila was on the sofa, to his left.

I lowered the magazine and walked down the hallway for a closer look. I ached to catch him in the act itself. I stood in back of where my sister sat on the sofa, but still within easy view and reach of the old man.

Would his mistreatment of his child taper off if he saw me standing there? Would he have enough sense to lay off the abuse? Was there a grain of decency left? Intelligence? at the least, a degree of apprehension knowing that I was present?

Rhetorical thoughts went through my mind as I waited. Part of me would have settled for it, a very small part, the greater part of my being wished he'd strike again. I wanted him to show me the barbaric behavior he was capable of one more time, just once more.

It took but seconds for the obvious to transpire.

"What did he say?" he asked my sister in Slavic. She did not respond right away, had not been able to comprehend all of the verbiage Kronkite was using herself and continued to stare and strain at the television set from her position on the sofa. That time his tone had been rather calm. He'd flashed the gargoyle grin, but hadn't lashed out. He was clearly enjoying himself. Then he asked her a second time, glaring now: "*What did the man say?*" There was venom in the eyes and in the delivery. My sister stammered. She said something to the effect that she hadn't been paying attention and that she did not know what the man was saying.

That's when the bastard struck out with his fists—hitting Jemila on the head several times. Something snapped in me. I leapt at him, yelling at the top of my voice, pulling him away from her and smacked him (but not quite hard enough) and he staggered, reeling back against the far wall (more from shock than anything else). And I do not recall exactly what I said, that the beatings had to finally end. And the old lady standing by in the hallway about to grab either the mop or broom, was muttering something about: "*You shouldn't hit your father.*"

And I told them both to shut the hell up. And the old guy's (he was 49 actually) lower lip was bleeding. And he threatened to kill me, shouting at the top of his voice and shaking a shaky finger at me. "I'm the head of this household! Things go as I say! Not you! I'll get you for this!" he kept threatening. And I told him I wished he would try. Only his yellow streak was a mile wide. A coward through and through. I could see it now plain as day. Why hadn't I taken him on earlier? Why? Wished I could have. Would have spared all of us quite a few beatings. I glared back at him, wondering what kept me from truly giving him the beating that God knows he had coming all these years. I did not, after all, possess the heartlessness it would have taken to go in after him and punch the daylights out of him.

I stood my ground. I could have had the bastard wrapped and delivered. He was mine. No longer would he push anyone around as long as I was in the house. All that exercising at the neighborhood Y had finally paid off for me. I had powerful shoulders, too powerful for him to do anything about.

There would be no more merciless beatings, no more cruelty; a bit of freedom now. No more living in a house of fear. I'd hated his guts all my life. All the beatings came back that moment, the years of living in fear, in Sarajevo, in Brussels and here in Chicago, the mental scars, all of it, as I stood there wanting him to come at me, wanting for a chance to really work him over, to give him a taste of his own medicine, to show him what it was like to get beaten up.

But he never did, as I knew he wouldn't. He was, after all, a coward, a coward who only knew how to pounce on defenseless kids. And he and his wife both knew that if I walked, so would the paycheck I handed over to them every week by working at the corner supermarket.

"You shouldn't hit your father," the old lady admonished from the hallway. "You shouldn't be disrespectful!"

"*What about the both of you being disrespectful toward your own kids?! What gives him the right to hit her for no reason like that?! What gives him the right to punch her in the face when she didn't even do anything?! What gives him the right to act like that?!*"

"Could be you don't have the whole story! Could be she had it coming!"

"She did nothing! I saw the whole thing! I was standing right here, goddamn you both! *He was punching her in the head for no reason at all*!"

"You don't know that." It was clear to me that my raging voice had her quaking; both in fact were quaking. "Didn't you just hear what I said? Are you that stupid? Are you both so mentally screwed-up that you have to keep mistreating your own kids this way? You're supposed to love your kids and show them care and not go around hitting them just because it gives you some kind of perverse thrill! Know what the problem is? The real problem? You are both disturbed! You're sick! The both of you! You should have been locked up years ago! Animals like you don't deserve to have kids!" I faced him. "You should have been locked away years ago! You hear me, you bastard! You should have been turned over to the police years ago! *You ever lay a hand on any of them I will tear you limb from limb! That's not a threat—that's a promise*!" Fear gripped his jaw shut. The barbarian was finally too scared to say anything after that.

My own rage had me shaking. My eyes were about to do their number.

I turned on my heels, and walked out of the house.

A week later living on the streets, away from home in the old neighborhood near Old Town, staying with my friend Gunnar, hanging out with those street punks I had nothing in common with; I had dreams, goals—a need to be like Edgar Allan Poe, a need to pursue literary ambitions, perhaps not in the horror and suspense genre (as I'd had enough of it at home), but to pursue some kind of writing life, filmmaking life. I could relate to Poe's pain, his woes and misfortune, and I knew to pursue a life of books I would need to create plenty of distance from these hoodlums—but before I knew how or when I had gotten involved in a street brawl and hauled off to county jail. I had never been arrested before for anything.

And now I was staring at a possible six-month prison sentence, and all for associating with the wrong crowd, a crowd I had never cared for or understood. After doing a day and a night behind bars somebody put up bail for our release. The next thing I did was to walk to the nearest army recruiting office. And that was the beginning of yet another nightmare called Viet Nam, that was back in '69. And it is '87 now, and with the exception of a brief leave after four months of infantry training prior to going over to Nam, I have not seen or talked to the old man since. And I regret that I did not stick around at home longer, it would have prevented the beatings from going on as they did as soon as I left. It would have helped the other kids in the family.

But I hadn't. I had had to get away. But that's the tragedy of it. This is what has haunted me all these years (even though Emina, two years younger than I, fled at the age of sixteen shortly after I was shipped to Viet Nam, fled to escape the beatings, after having called the police even on the folks once).

And then the other sister, the one I had saved from a beating that time, Jemila, when she turned 15 fled to join Emina. The youngest kids, Zuleika and Emir, were too young to do anything of the sort and remained where they were.

I hear the folks finally had gotten the message and learned to go easy on the physical abuse with the younger ones. *And the emotional abuse*? Well, that never let up.

Sometime around 1970 the folks moved to Los Angeles, settling in the Fairfax District (I later was informed by Emina), somewhere on Sierra Bonita. And then while April and I were living on Flores they relocated once again to the City of South Gate (and eventually out to AZ).

I wished I could have said to my former girlfriend:

What then was my terrible "secret," Dearest April? I am not even so sure that it can be labeled a secret. There was so much buried pain there in my soul that I could not even begin to explain it to you. It was not so much that I intended to keep any of it from you, but more a concerted effort to keep it blocked from my own mind, an effort to seek a new life, a better future and a beginning with someone like you. But this is exactly why I was always so nervous and unhappy—my past, my painful past gnawed at my heart and soul, at my insides. It managed to crush any and every attempt at wanting to be positive and happy around you.

• • •

Where Do the Smiles Go?

I was looking at pictures of Sylvia Plath last night. I had gone to the apartment after work and was leafing through this hardback entitled *Letters Home by Sylvia Plath, Correspondence 1950-1963*. The book was a collection of her letters to her mother and some other people, with enough black and white photos interspersed throughout. And Sylvia is smiling in about a third of these pictures, mostly when she was younger—and then there were some of course when she did not smile or had any kind of specific expression on her face. And I turned back to the pages that contained the photos of her smiling. She had a nice, happy smile—and my eyes filled with tears. "God," I heard myself sigh, " . . . What happens to the smiles? Where do the smiles go?"

Why is it this way?

She had had two breakdowns, undergone shock treatment . . . WHERE DO THE SMILES GO? And now she was dead and no more.

There would be no more smiles because she was gone forever, her and others like her. Look how much pain she had endured, how unhappy she must have been, a gifted woman like that—and she had taken her own life in the end because she was so unhappy . . .

What chance do we have in this world? What is the answer?

Why, why, why????????? TELLLLLLLLLMMEEEEEEEE!!!!!!!

I had my face buried in my hands. DAMMIT WHERE DO THE SMILES GO???!!!

WHAT HAPPENS TO THE SMILES!!!!?????

They're here for a while and then there is nothing left. . . .

Why do smiles leave us? Why does death win so often? *Death* and *grief* always winning. Love and happiness do not stand a chance. They never did.

• • •

It's Times like this I think of Malcolm Lowry and Algren and Knut Hamsun

Somehow or other a job opportunity came up to dispatch at this small, very small cab company (so small in fact, they only had twelve cabs and worked mainly Bev. Hills) started by a group of Ethiopians, former cabbies on L.A.'s west side. I knew some of them as we worked the same hotels: Bev. Hilton, Bev. Wilshire, Beverly Hills Hotel, etc. It would be min. wage (what else was new?). And I mean minimum wage: $4.50 an hour—no more, no less. This was just about the mid-80s, not much money, but plenty of hours. I hadn't been doing that well with Eager Beaver Cab Co. anyway, and thought: what the hell? I'd had a bit of experience dispatching. Let's try it. And did. My hours were 7:00 a.m. to 10:00 p.m., Mon. through Saturday. My Sunday hours were light: 7:00 a.m. to 7:00 p.m. (I needed the time to do my laundry.) Social life? It didn't exist. But that was okay—it was one tribulation after another. Man, I am beginning to hate the word—but I was "resigned" to it.

The dues, the fucking dues. No escape. Most of the people that I knew were paying heavy dues. As heavy as mine? It didn't matter. I saved my money. At the end of four months I had over four grand saved up. There was an opportunity to buy into the company, get a cab of my own—even though this particular cab company was flimsy at best. I raised another four grand and bought myself a hack. So I found myself back in the cab, living in it, in order to pay off the loan. Finally did that—and that's when the video explosion really hit; home video was the big thing—and a couple of colleagues (Red Gunderson and Angus Gladwyn) and I started talking and got the film bug again, not that it had ever left, only now we figured we had a chance: Super 8; it transferred quite well to video tape. Why not?

We'd all attended film school in the early 70s, had had some big dreams and ideas—but lack of money had prevented us from making any progress. This would be our chance.

I would write the script, and direct. Gladwyn would do the photography, and Red Gunderson would act and assist. I would sell my cab and put a few grand into this thing, Red would come up with twenty-five hundred, his wife would match that.

Gladwyn had his credit card, and we also recruited a buddy of Gladwyn's named Mead Fuchs to produce. Fuchs was a bit actor on a daytime soap, frustrated at not getting anywhere; they refused to expand his part from a one- or two-line weekly walk-on—and so it was settled: we would enter the home vid. market with a horror cheapie. "*There's a built-in audience for horror, man!*" We needed a degree of assurance that we would make our money back, that our investors would get *their* money back—thus it would be the genre route.

Fine.

This would be a dream come true. Finally. After all those years of wishing and hoping, knocking on doors and getting knocked on our backs—this would be it! A beginning. Finally; finally, truly a start!

I knocked off a script in a week; weak plot, with plenty of gore—it hurt inside to have to do it, my conscience ate away at me—there was quite a battle there. Just try and ignore your conscience sometimes, particularly when it refuses to be ignored. But it had been so many years—for a while there, due to the pain of it, I'd even forgotten all about film and concentrated primarily on prose: mystery novels, plays, short stories, free verse. Hollywood was a nightmare to stay clear of. Right. Only there we were, making a film.

We bought our props, hired a couple of makeup effects people, our actors, bought our film stock. We shot for a week, and realized, upon paying our actors that our rapidly shrinking budget was about to shrink out of existence. We had wanted to be just and righteous and fair to all concerned—my colleagues and I could easily recount the bullshit and hassles and ripoffs *we'd* encountered over the years in Tinseltown—and we were determined to treat everyone working on the film with respect and dignity and pay them.

Well, we ran out of money, and had to scrounge up some more. I won't go into all the details here, that's another book; shooting without permits in and round L.A., having shotguns aimed at us as well as M-16s by gun-happy cops. "You can't shoot without film permits," they all said. Problem was their permits would have eaten up the entire budget, you see?

Well, we got the damn thing "in the can," and while doing my darnedest, quickest best to complete the editing (you don't even want to contemplate editing single system Super 8 unless you're prepared to lose your mind), I was all out of funds—and the apartment building manager wanted the rent money. I was still on Burnside at this time. Soon—there was an eviction notice being slipped under my door.

PAY RENT OR ELSE . . .

It was then Angus Gladwyn came to the rescue. He may have been one irritable s.o.b. on location, irritable, unstable, ill-tempered, impatient, but deep down the Texan had a heart of gold. I'd been fortunate in this respect: I loved my friends (the few I'd had over the years) and the feeling was mutual. He wanted to stay with family in Texas and offered me the use of his one-room apt. in North Hollywood on Camarillo Street—for the duration of the editing, sound mixing—and sale of the film to a distributor.

I packed my things, the few things that I had (I'd given away most of my stuff over the years: dishes, clothes, etc.). I preferred to travel light. I did, however, hold onto my precious book library and the manuscripts: that was blood and sweat and hard toil—the glue that held this dreamer together. They could have all else—just leave me with my books and manuscripts—and my record albums (only the three hundred or so albums I'd accumulated over the years had been pretty much destroyed by a seismic crew a while back; you see they were making the building "earthquake proof"; so that the owner could double everyone's rent, you understand? They had come into my apartment with sandblasters and had gone at the stucco walls and all that stucco dust had gotten inside the record sleeves . . . and there's no need to go on. It was heartbreaking. I'd had Gladwyn take photographs of the damage to my collection—and I had threatened to sue, if I were not reimbursed. They did fork over five hundred, but that hardly made up for it.).

That same old message knocked at my brain: Don't get attached to things, my friend. But I love music, music and fine fiction. Don't get attached. . . . But if you did not like *something* in this world, what the hell was there to live for?

Even a burn-out-zombie-case like myself had to have something to give him hope. . . .

Don't get attached. . . .

In any event, I was living in North Hollywood now. My belongings remained in cardboard boxes. Gladwyn was in Texas and would send me the occasional five-dollar bill to forward his various contest entries, etc. The man was a contest/lottery fanatic. He entered everything. We were through editing the film, Fuchs and I had gone over the sound-mixing phase together, had raised the money to have it completed—only now there were no takers. Sound and cinematography were weak, some of the editing choppy, not smooth. Well, what the hell do you expect? I felt like saying—it was put together with spit and chewing gum! There was no real money to do anything right—only distributors don't want to hear that. They'll come up with every reason in the world to point out the flaws, in order to pick up the film for nothing. As far as I was concerned the film contained scenes I was proud of—and even the sections that were supposed to be tongue-in-cheek came across that way; they were funny. The performances, generally speaking, were fine—and yes, some of the acting was a bit rough—but I wouldn't hold the actors responsible; there hadn't been enough film to reshoot. That's what happens when all you can afford to shoot is one take of a particular scene. The distributors, the sharks were doing their best to pull the wool over our eyes—and it would not have been that big a deal, except I was starving, literally starving, nothing to eat in that room on Camarillo Street. Two dollars and change of the five bucks that Gladwyn would send went toward forwarding his contest results, and the rest was spent on food—I had two dollars and fifty cents (give or take a cent) to make last for approximately two weeks, until the next five-dollar bill arrived. I couldn't go to anyone about it, it just was too damn embarrassing. Work? Employment? I tried, did my best. I spent a lot of time up at that employment office on Magnolia—without much luck. I was dropping weight, and would have taken anything, anything but a return to the cab. I thought, was convinced that was behind me; anything but that—I'd had enough driving a hack in this town.

I was back at the North Hollywood employment office, yanking on my gray trousers. I'd dropped so much weight that now my pants wouldn't stay up. Now there's an easy solution to obesity: take their fucking food away.

There's no mystery to losing weight: lack of groceries will do it every time. Well, all those weight-loss chains know that, that's why it's such a well-kept secret, you see?

It keeps them in business and oh so wealthy. Don't let the gullible suckers know that all it takes is "not eating." No food, no weight gain. *What a concept.*

And so I kept yanking up on my pants while standing in front of their huge bulletin boards with the 3 by 5 job cards on them. Dishwashers wanted. They were looking for dishwashers. Several places in town were looking for dishwashers.

$3.50 an hour.

That's what I was qualified to do. If that. 36 years old. Kicking around and paying dues ever since getting back from Nam. Dishwasher was about the only thing I was qualified to do. And am not so sure I would get hired on as that even.

What's left?

What to do?

Don't ask me, baby; 'cause I just don't know.

The waiting game goes on. Week after week after week. The waiting. Trying to sell *BLOODSUCKING GEEKS*, the film. The distributors are all jackals interested in one thing—giving you the shaft.

There it is. They want to rip you off. The film was finished on June 8 (over a month ago) and no sale, no money. Got a five-pound bag of brown rice left, three hot dogs—a five-dollar bill and a handful of change. When does this pitiful existence end? If we can't sell the film for a reasonable amount of money well, then we have to form a distribution company. This is what I told Fuchs and Gladwyn. I seem to be the only one who thinks this way. I don't get it. What is going on? One distributor, in fact (VICTORY), asked for all rights, worldwide distribution rights—and offered us no money up front. Incredible. I told Mead that this was "fucked."

There was no other word to describe it. Nothing. No other goddamn word at all. "*You bust your back to put a film together on very little money—finally manage to get it made—and everybody wants to screw you*!" said I.

It goes on. Tinseltown.

Paramour and NCB and Home Cine Entertainment turned it down. We are still waiting to hear from Express/Lizzard, Ronson, and others.

I do not expect good news.

What's left?

What do we do next? Distribute? We may have no choice.

Wish I could at least find a way to finish the *MAD DOGS AMONG US* script, or at least find the concentration to work on it—while the waiting goes on.

Driver's license expired three months ago. It would only take ten dollars to renew it—but when you don't even have the ten dollars, what the hell.

I go up to the library now and then. Not much else to do. About once a week I might get on the ten speed bicycle and take a ride, to get some exercise, to get out of the room. This inactivity is killing me, ruining my health. I am definitely picking up some bad eating habits.

What eating habits? One needs to have access to food in order for that to happen.

Can't say that I look forward to eating the rice. What I do sometimes is put some catchup on it and it gives it flavor and the rice goes down a bit easier.

Yessir, life in the great and good ol' USA. See how we starve, folks. I'll have to use the five-dollar bill sparingly. In fact, came in the mail the other day from Gladwyn (so that I would have postage money to send him all that useless contest information).

Hiram Angus Gladwyn got a ton of mail—and all of it having to do with contests and prize money and giveaway cars and home appliances—that he never won. Never won a dime. How could anyone be such a sucker for these obvious scams? A waste of time and money. I would have preferred to spend it all on food—but could not do that, had no right, since the man expected his contest rules and regulations, contest forms and weekly news sheets. Go figure. My mind was always on food. All else was secondary.

This is the first bit of writing that I have engaged in in a while (other than letter writing). Am currently using Gladwyn's machine (that he let me know about in his last letter. He'd had an electric typewriter in the closet all this time!) Both of my typewriters, in fact, all three of my typewriters are down for the count. So, having this typewriter does help. It gives me something to do. I only wish I had the damn ability, the concentration to finish up one of the mystery novels by now (other than *P.I. FOR HIRE*, as *P.I.* needs an overhaul).

Having looked at *OBSESSED WITH DEATH* again gave me something to think about. A quick way and means to a fast buck. But you know how that goes. One ends up spending more money once again on postage.

Jesus, when I think of all the money I have spent over the years on postage, all those scripts sent to agents and/or publishers!

God-All-Mighty! So after a while, one does get tired of it, one begins to start thinking that it just might be a losing battle. I need a second wind, to regroup, recharge, resurge, reapply, get back, start again, begin anew—AND ALL THAT—but not this way, not like this. Not living here like this with nothing to eat.

Pun intended: it does eat away the soul. Food has to be there—and soul is it—and it eventually starts to go along with your sanity.

Where do all those hungry street people come from? Ask me—ASK ME AND I WILL TELL YOU. I know, dear friend, I know. It's times like this I think of Malcolm Lowry and Algren and Knut Hamsun (during Knut's starving and struggling years).

It's nothing new, is it? Nothing new at all. The way the game is played. The rules of the game, the rules of this particular, mind-twisting game.

I wonder if Miss Scarpitta, my 11th grade English teacher, would find it hilarious.

"*See? What did I tell you? Did I not say that you would never amount to anything?!*"

And withered, old Prunella Stone, another teacher, same subject, might be gloating as well these days, if she were alive—and who knows? She might be. "*You can't fool me, young man! You did not do that assignment yourself! You cheated and you copied it!*"

The assignment had been simple enough really. She had asked the class to compose two letters—an informal letter to a friend, and the other was to be a formal business letter. "It's up to you to do as you wish," she had told us the day before. The business letter had been easy enough to do. Mine was from a bank to one of its customers delinquent on a loan. It was a nice, threatening letter full of big words and bloated, overstated warnings—in fact, the entire letter was bloated, overwritten.

Norm Crosby couldn't have done a better job of it. With my other letter—written by me (from Australia; I'd never been to Australia) to a buddy in the states I had filled with every cliche in the book. The contrasting styles was deliberate—and rather obvious, I thought, only 70-year-old Miss Prunella Stone with the beady, evil eyes did not think so.

"There is no way you could have written the business letter without help—"

"Ah, Miss Stone, I swear to God, I did it on my own—and if you would only give me a chance to prove it—"

"Be quiet and sit down! You get a failing grade for cheating! You were nothing back then—and at 36 you're still nothing!"

Instead of being the recipient of a high mark for being able to pull off the assignment, she had flunked me. *Justice*. I'd almost felt like breaking down and crying in her classroom that day, in front of the whole lot of them. What had I done wrong? What was my sin?

Instead of encouraging me and allowing me to feel proud because of the accomplishment I had managed, the old biddy had gone out of her way to humiliate me—would not even give me a second chance, not even one to explain.

I could have easily written a dozen of those stupid business letters right in front of her on the blackboard. But she would not hear of it, had been quick to dismiss me. She was convinced she was right and no one was going to prove otherwise. She'd been teaching all her life; she had the answers, she had the venom. A bitter old bag of bones, heartless.

Shake the images. I couldn't. I'd been carrying stuff like this around forever. It sticks with you, it sticks with you. Human beings are hard to figure out.

And the pretty blond who sat to my right, the pretty blond I'd been working on getting the nerve to talk to for months, Claire Dodd, who had the power to cause me to break out in a cold sweat without even trying, and my stomach do things; I would simply look at her angelic and perfect face and I was at a loss for words, nervous, in awe of her beauty and natural charm, dreaming, hoping she would one day notice me—and in one quick minute "Old Prune Face" had wrecked it all for me. I stood there, a fool, a brainless jerk; a no good cheater; fraud.

Red-faced, feeling like a worthless worm, I had sat down, head just about bowed, wishing I could have shriveled out of sight. The teacher had gone on about something else; I was no longer worthy of her invaluable attention. All I could keep thinking: *Why?*

Why did you have to humiliate me like that? What was it that I did?

What am I guilty of?

A moment later, and I could not explain or understand why the interest, Claire Dodd inquired if she might take a look at the two letters.

I had nodded my head, finding it difficult to believe that she had actually said something to me, was showing interest in me now during this lowest of low points. I handed her the letters, watched as she read them before her quietly. I waited for some sort of sign, an expression on her face that might indicate she was on my side, that indicated she knew, even if no one else in the classroom did, that I had done nothing dishonest, that I had, in fact, done such a fine job that even miserable Prunella Stone had been fooled.

I waited, and waited. I ached, prayed to hear a favorable word from Claire Dodd, a smile, something, that would confirm she was on my side indeed—but just then the bell rang—my letters were returned to me—and that was the closest I'd ever gotten to connecting with her.

A few years later, upon my return from Viet Nam, I had walked past her in front of an office building in downtown Chicago—and she hadn't even recognized me, or had she? She had kept walking, more beautiful than ever, and I had kept walking—nervous and confused from the war, mentally shaky and scarred, doing my best to put on a face of sanity, to keep going, while working for minimum wage at the Mercantile Exchange.

"*Be quiet and sit down!*" she had yelled at me. "*You get an F for cheating!*" And like I said—today she might very well say: "*You were nothing back then—and at 36 you're still nothing today!*"

Well, who can disagree with that? I might wish to protest—but then would look around at my surroundings—at my pathetic predicament—and well, I cannot respond.

Have not sold *BLOODSUCKING GEEKS* yet. Three different distributors turned it down so far. One place tried to burn us good.

AMIGO said to us: "We'll sell twelve thousand units, at least. We'll need all the rights to the film, worldwide rights."

They offered no money up front—only percentage of sales.

Talk about Royal ripoff. The other distributors like Paramour and NCB and HOME CINE ENTERTAINMENT didn't want it because the film itself looks cheap. Just too damn cheap. The whole look of it.

Now, I know whoever ends up with the film will make close to a quarter million bucks with it (at the least). That's a fact. *We don't—unless we distribute—but it does not seem like the guys want to go into distribution.*

I made several phone calls to that effect. PLUS VIDEO has forty-eight stores in California. THE STOREHOUSE has two hundred. It would be just a matter of selling to these places, a matter of the artwork put together for the printer, or duping some copies of the film and contacting the proper people (buyers) for the major chains.

I figure we get a rough figure how many copies we will need and go off and get them made—and we sell the copies. To begin with we deal with the major chains first. *And we go from state to state.*

Only my partners didn't even wish to discuss it.

• • •

(July 10, '87)

Another Cup of Rice

Saturday. 7:12 p.m. Boiled another cup of brown rice, mixed in some catchup and mustard with it (for flavor) and ate it. It still tasted like wet mud with mustard and catchup mixed in. The survivor is getting sick of surviving. I know, I know; some well-fed son-of-a-bitch somewhere is saying: don't gripe.

Well, this is not griping—and if it is—to hell with it!

So be it. Try living on this kind of menu, pal. It has been going on like this for months now. *For months*. And if it is not I who is complaining exactly, I have a feeling it is my belly. The belly bloating. This is what happens.

Every Sunday night they persist in showing starving kids in Ethiopia and other third world countries on my television set. Well, pal, you are not showing me something I do not know first hand. It has been like this for years for me—*I mean for years—for over a decade or more*. On and off, off and on—the starving goes on. There was a period there when I drove the hack when I could afford to eat and pay rent—but now that the hack is no longer here—the trick is to try and go on without food. A mean feat, if one can pull it off.

Is anyone that great a magician?

No one has to starve in this great country of ours—they will tell you. Well, yes, perhaps—but how did I end up like this? How did so many others? Tell me.

Mead Fuchs came over to pick up the rest of the stills from *BLOODSUCKING GEEKS* (so that he might have a better presentation when he sees other distributors).

Nonetheless, we discussed distribution again. Entity turned down *BLOODSUCKING GEEKS* as well. That makes about four rejections. The film is just not there technically. Looks cheap.

I wonder why. Try making a film (any film) for under twenty grand, and you'll know why. We did what we could. Even spending close to eight grand in audio studio (Harbinger Sound burned us for over three grand for bad work—work we had to do over again at another studio in North Hollywood).

Super 8 is a real bitch to work in. No matter how hard you work, no matter how conscientious you might be, no matter that you have good actors, makeup, all that; a decent script (not that *GEEKS* was) and a director who cares—the finished product will not look very good when you are done with it.

Cheap. That's how it will look. CHEAP. And this is what every distributor thus far has told us. "Thanks, but no thanks. The look of the film is just too cheap. It's not there. Sorry."

What to do?

I keep thinking we ought to distribute the film ourselves.

No one else in the group seems interested (and will not allow me to do it). If I had the means I'd buy the film and go it alone.

I got it from Fuchs that Gyles, the projectionist, will take our film to someone at Valiant Video Monday.

"Well, I am not holding my breath," I said to Fuchs. "Don't expect big bucks. If anyone does offer us anything up front it'll be a ripoff. So what's left, other than going into distribution?"

Fuchs remarked: "If it's so easy to get in distribution, if it's so easy to make big bucks like that, then I would think that everybody and his brother would be in on it. And it just doesn't seem to be the case."

I countered with: "All your major studios do in fact have their own video distribution outlets. It only makes sense."

Mead Fuchs shook his head. "Nope. I just don't see. We don't have the means. It's not as easy as you think."

What were these scared little rabbits afraid of? How could I make them understand?

Fuchs was in a hurry and left.

• • •

(July 11, 1987)

It's Clear Why Ernie Feared this Town

Thursday. 10:06 p.m. Eighteen, nineteen months now spent (wasted) on *BLOODSUCKING GEEKS*. The distributors want the film, but what they really want to do is rip you off. The only way to survive is to get into the distribution business. But then one would have to make sure that's what one wants to do with one's life. And at the moment am just not so sure. I need to get back to writing, real writing. Have spent too much time lately on dumb movie scripts and dumb movies and all that nonsense.

The guilt is eating away at me. Am just hurting my prose by doing this stuff. And yet how does one get out? It will have to be back to another 9 to 5 job. Maybe it won't be so bad as long as I can go back to writing some good stuff.

It's frustrating as hell. Doing a lot of pacing lately. Don't know what the hell to do. Gladwyn will be coming back sooner or later to reclaim his apartment—and then what? Am out in the street.

It's clear why Ernie feared this town. It will piss on your soul. As tough as it was to make *BLOODSUCKING GEEKS* (having M-16s pointed at us by cops in bullet-proof vests, getting kicked out of places in middle of scenes because we did not have permits, did not have hardly enough money to have enough film or fake blood on hand). The toughest part seems to be dealing with greedy distributors. They want it all. That's all there is to it. We can't even get enough of an advance to cover our expenses.

Where to from here?

I still can't get over the small advance the woman offered me for the film.

I keep thinking if only I'd have written a couple more mainstream novels instead of all those detective books. What the hell do I know about detective work? (I'd done my research, but still—hackwork is hack work!—and nothing more than HACKWORK!)

Hack writing destroys true prose! There is no other way to look at it! That's it. It kills art! It kills prose! BALZAC said it! (plain as day!) ERNIE SAID IT (PLAIN AS DAY!) Any writer (any real writer) will tell you the same thing: *shortcuts kill talent*. What do I do with myself now?

Got in the car earlier today, drove up to McDonald's for a Big Mac, fish sandwich, small milk. Drove around in a kind of daze, trying to figure out what to do, my next step, trying to shake the guilt acquired by having written all that trash. Jesus, it's a real problem.

Drove over to Crown Books in Studio City, spent a couple of hours there, going over books, seeing what was out there, the new stuff, hoping to come across something truly worthwhile—and as always—ended up going over the masters—the classics, tried and true.

That's what always happens. Not many contemporary writers are worth spit. So it's always back to the masters of old—*London, Steinbeck, Kerouac*, etc.

Trying to stay optimistic, but it's not easy. What's in the cards for me?

Took the old manuscripts out of the cardboard boxes the other day, looked at some of that stuff. The prose still stands. It's there. Why did I have to get impatient with it back then? Why waste all those years writing the Stone Felsen mystery books?

Confusion had had a lot to do with it. Confusion. Trying to stay on top of things, living the life of a hermit isn't the best way to do it.

Maybe I needed distance. That's it. I needed distance.

How much distance? Did I get far enough away?

• • •

(Aug. 13, '87)

“Madman” Miles F. Moody

I got by on peanut butter when I could afford it, then it was down to Cream of Wheat, while still trying to find a distributor for the film. I was dropping weight, no one to turn to. Bread and water literally. Couldn’t find work. Nothing. This was 1987. Nothing had changed since my move west in 1972. Not a damn thing. I was older not much wiser; about it. The producer Mead Fuchs stopped by now and then to take me out for a burger. It kept me going.

And sometimes one of the neighbors, a guy named Dingo, would drop off a leftover pizza or half a bag of marshmallows he hadn’t been able to eat himself, or a half-eaten bag of cookies. I was grateful for small favors. It kept me alive. I dropped to 140 lbs., down from 169. I’m 5’10". The pennies in the tobacco can amounted to about four bucks—and was all the money I had in the world. A life of paying dues.

It was afternoon. I had the drapes pulled shut, lay down on the sofa to take a nap; it was the only thing left to do, contemplated how to respond to CINEMA FACTORY INTERNATIONAL when Casey tells me no Monday . . . just thought about it. . . . We were almost out-of-the-woods with *BLOODSUCKING GEEKS* . . . thought we had it all figured out—we would have been able to pay everyone off and I still would have had about the same amount of cash in my pocket as I did when we first started the film. . . . Thought about it, pondered my next move . . . what to do to catch up financially, get back on my feet, and make the next step . . . about to doze off . . . when I hear someone pounding on my door.

It sounds like Fuchs, so I get up to open it—only it's not Fuchs. It's the professional bum/creep/playwright/screenwriter/complainer/negative vibes idiot. I thought for sure he'd gotten the message three weeks back that I had no use for his kind. I didn't want to hear anymore about him wanting to kill somebody ("any Hollywood big shot"), because the professional bum/asshole can't make it and/or is really screwed-up mentally.

What do I do now?

Again, it is tough for me to be rude to anybody (unless I'm really pushed beyond my limit); tough to be rude to somebody living in a car—but I cannot get it through my head that this guy has been living like this for many, many years—bummed all over Africa, India, Europe, just all over—been many places like this, using people, looking for and very good at spotting the ones with the soft heart and abusing their kindness and/or generosity. I've been broke all my life (and still never sponged off people)—so now, here is this professional leech/user/full of hatred/bitterness creep.

The easiest thing is to let him in politely. Am wondering what he wants this time. Is he working? Yeah, turns out he worked for All Star Cab for a week. The owner had told him he had B.O., and the creep had told the owner to take his job and shove it. But the creep wasn't all that worried right now because he had a couple hundred in his pocket. *What's he want with me? Why does he keep coming around? Didn't he get the message the last time?*

I didn't like being around somebody like this. I don't like leeches, I don't like complainers, especially when they are writers and constantly blame the whole world for their own either lack of talent and/or failure.

"I'd like you to give me a reference so that I can go to Super-Duper Cab and get a job with them," said Moody.

"No sweat," said I. Anything to help a "friend" get a job.

"Type up whatever you want to type up," I told him, "and I'll sign it."

He put it together (something about having driven my Mojo Cab for a couple of years, something about being clean and dependable, reliable, a good worker with a clean record).

I signed it.

Since he had some money he wanted to buy me a beer. "Fine," said I. "I haven't had a beer in months, only I'd rather get something like food in my belly more than anything else; the Cream of Wheat just leaves me weak."

Since he'd borrowed money from me the last time he was here (and all those self-help books I'd given him to sell), he said: "Sure, I can buy us something to eat." And did.

He came back with a 6-pack of Miller Draft Beer, spaghetti, Newman's Own Spaghetti Sauce, a pound of lean hamburg.

I cooked up the spaghetti and the man was back on the same old track the whole time. Pointing the finger again: "*They kept me out! Those motherfuckers don't want me to make it! They know I'm good!*" It was the same old song. He wanted to kill somebody again, and kept putting away the brew, polished off the 6-pack, got up to buy more. I tried to tell him to take it easy with the brew.

"All you need right now is to get stopped one time and you can forget about getting a job as a cab driver." He didn't want to hear it. "*I can handle it*," insisted Moody.

He walked across the street to the supermarket, returned with a 6-pack, opened a bottle. The venom, the bitterness started pouring out again, like a fountain, a waterfall, like your contaminated kitchen sink backing up into your aching brain.

It was all vile and despicable, anger, hatred. It was making me sick just to hear it.

I had the TV on and I was watching Judy Garland and had him tuned out most of the time. Now I hear him say something about being broke in India, getting busted on a train in the middle of the desert and the conductor kicking him off the train. "I said to him—fine! Leave me here to die!" said Moody. "I really don't care!" And the conductor had told him to shut up and get back on the train. He'd gotten stoned on opium in India, in New Delhi. In Bhopal he'd asked a kid to bring him some water to drink—and apparently the kid had scooped up some real dirty, contaminated mud water and this had given Moody (ruined his liver, anyway) a fit.

"I was taken to the hospital," said Moody. "They gave me glucose for three days. Somehow I lived." Now I hear him shouting, something about San Francisco (he'd lived there once). "*I just might go up there and kill a fag!*" And then I hear about a Czech woman he'd lived with in Germany. "If I had some real money I'd go back and live in Paris!" He had the 6-pack polished off, and I know the man is drunk. He'd been guzzling the stuff. In all that time I'd only had two beers and was slowly working on my third (not that I had really wanted the third one, just to keep him from getting any drunker) but it was too late. It was 11:00 p.m. and the man was shouting, banging his empty beer bottle on the carpet, against a stack of books near the sofa. He pulled up the rocking chair he sat in and was now sticking his booze-smelling mug in my face.

"Why don't you cool it?" I said. "I've got neighbors."

He kept with the noise, shouting: "YOU THINK I GIVE A FUCK ABOUT THAT ASSHOLE?"

"I do," I told him. "They're my neighbors; cool it."

"Mailer is bigger than Bukowski!" said Moody, wanting to know why I liked Bukowski. "Because he is nothing but a bum boozer and a pill popper!" I told him I'd never met the man, only that I liked some of his stuff. I never cared for Mailer (but none of it means a damn. Most writers were sniveling little idiots like this punk screaming at me now and calling me a loser because I'd had the decency to let him come in and clean up.). He'd asked earlier if he could take a shower and get rid of the B.O. I'd said, sure, go ahead, given him a clean towel—and I had been a "loser" three years ago as well in Hollywood when I'd helped him move, loaded up my car with his belongings, as he'd had no other way to get from Burnside to Vine, his new address (that he'd stayed at for a while prior to skipping off to Mexico to blow the rest of his UCLA Film School government loan).

According to Miles F. Moody, he was sure I had been a loser then (he'd thought it, never said it to my face until now); "*and I'm convinced*," he said; "*that you're a loser now.*"

Hmm, I thought, this guy is about as hopeless as they come.

He hadn't liked the way I had knocked his play (the protagonist was a lot like him, a hateful doper, just a negative human being altogether; the action took place in Nam), I suppose, and some other things.

Well, I kept telling him to cool it—and he kept raising his

voice—and me waiting for him to swing on me so I could really make my move and send him on his way.

But he didn't do anything, instead pushed the rocker back, and he was no longer in my face. Then I heard something about Brando. "What do you think about me going up to Brando's gate and trying to talk to him?"

What can I tell this guy? I just wanted him out of the place, out of my life. He was not making sense. I'd tried patience—but patience and decency have a way of backfiring on you—and this is what happens.

"What do you think of the idea?" he insists.

"I don't know. It's up to you."

"In a way," says he, "Brando and me are neighbors." As Moody parked his VW just up the road from Brando's gate every night.

Jesus Christ, I'd met hundreds of basket cases like this when I drove the cab—ten years of hacking in L.A., a lot of nut cases—after a while one learned how to deal with the crazies, how to spot the nuts and stay clear—now there was one right in this room with me! Ranting and raving about nothing! About killing, about talking to Brando, about going back South, about making enough money driving a cab to stay in Mexico. And none of it meant anything!

Not a damn thing.

He was back on his play and my negative review. Only the truth was (and I reminded him)—I had liked certain things about the play, and had not liked others. There was good stuff in it and stuff, like the main character, I could not relate to.

So I said: "Hey, I could have lied to you about it, but I chose not to. *So take it like a man.* I told you exactly how I felt about your goddamn play! All right? TAKE IT LIKE A MAN! You came knocking on my door asking me to read your play! And I did! All right?"

"I'm sorry you said that," he said.

"I'm not sorry I said anything! That's the way it is."

He shot up. "That's it, isn't it? I just ruined your whole day by coming here, didn't I? I RUINED YOUR FUCKING DAY!!!"

Yes, he had—and if he was so damn perceptive, why did he keep coming back?

Again, I tried to tell him to cool it, to take it easy. There's no reasoning with a drunk. He turned to look for the letter of reference, found it, crushed it. "*GODDAMMIT! YOU HAPPY NOW?!*" he shouted. "*YOU THINK I NEED THIS?!!! I DON'T NEED THIS FUCKING THING!!! I DON'T NEED THE FUCKING JOB!!! JUST FUCK IT!!!*"

"Hey, take it easy, man."

He kept the balled up letter of reference, and left.

I got up, locked the door—and thought—so many people in this world are just like this, just as mixed-up, screwed-up. He should not have been allowed to roam freely out there, not a dangerous character like this. He was sure to do something stupid, something crazy. I heard a crash, glass breaking, like a bottle hitting the sidewalk in front of the building. I heard him start up the VW outside, tires screeched as he drove off.

Well, punk, I hope you don't come back—because if you do I believe all hell is going to break out if you so much as attempt to ruin another day for me.

• • •

(Aug. 21, '87)

Why Are You Desperate?

Tues., Aug. 25, '87.

Up at 8:05 a.m. for a piss, to brush teeth, dab cold water on my face, and a spot of hot tea. I parted the drapes, and then sat at the typewriter, trying to come to terms that another day would go down to waste, another day of waiting, of nothing happening . . . feeling depleted, energy waning. . . .

Where am I?

Is the tea ready?

No.

The traffic hum out there was steady and loud. Camarillo Street.

North Hollywood. Got on the scale. 148 lbs., today.

Is the tea ready?

Yes, the tea is ready.

I poured myself a cup, a teaspoon of sugar. This is breakfast this morning. Does this explain why you're down to 148 from 170?

It should. Yes, it does.

I have to get a job and stop worrying about *BLOODSUCKING GEEKS*.

BLOODSUCKING GEEKS is a dead issue. Something not worth the effort I put into it. A lost cause. All that energy, sweat, worry, agony—over a nothing little splatter piece of crap. Jesus.

But then every time I got like this Fuchs would tell me that people actually liked the film. There are people who actually think the film is okay. (Is that all—okay? Well, it ought to be enough.) It was made for under fifteen grand—the other ten grand came later during the audio segment, sound and music editing, and the initial fifteen grand had come in in bits and pieces—because if we'd have even had the entire FIFTEEN GRAND to begin with it would have been a much better film. We would have had better sound, MUCH BETTER EFFECTS! And is any of this getting me anywhere?

No.

Take a sip of your tea.

I will.

And do so.

I rose to open the door, let air in; sat back down at the typewriter. The traffic hum continued out there. What am I doing with my life? What are *you* doing with *your* life? Do any of us know what the hell we're doing? Do the rich, do the poor, do the sick? Do the healthy? Do the in-between? Do the above? Do the below?

Better get up for some more tea.

Fine.

The sugar is giving me strength. I'm getting smart now, real smart, genius-type.

I placed the cup on the table near the typewriter (within easy reach).

Listen, I kept getting knocked down by the whole thing—the writing game, the word game, the book game, the paragraphs, all those sentences, all those commas and periods and exclamation marks!

I did, kept getting knocked down all the time—and SOMEHOW, ALWAYS! ALWAYS! SOMEHOW!!!! managed to get back up.

It's true.

Do you believe me?

I started way back there right after the army. Years ago. Was it '71 or '72? A long time ago, amigo. Am afraid to count the years. But you know, even if one has the ability to keep bouncing back up one cannot always conceal the fact that one is getting punch-drunk, wobbly, and all that. Here it is 1987.

What is Casey Ryder going to do? Does she really give a damn?

And better yet—why should she? What am I to her? Nothing. A nobody, a stranger. So why should she put this effort out to help me? *In Hollywood these things do not happen. They just don't.*

Already told her how much I appreciated all the time she has (to date) spent with me on this thing. I thought that was decent of her.

If she does help sell the film—we are (or I am) going to have to send her a big bouquet of flowers. Something. I'll have to thank her.

More tea.

Got up. Put on Michael Parks' *BLUE* album. There was something about that voice that was so damn soothing.

What I need is a bit of luck to come knocking on my door.

Who doesn't?

But I've worked for it (all those years). I deserve it.

That's what they all say.

No, really, listen. I busted my back all those years, don't you remember? The dead-end jobs, the warehouse? The security guard jobs? The candy bar factory? The trash pickup? The pizza delivery? The apartment painter? The carpet cleaner? Don't you remember? Didn't I pay enough dues?

There is no set amount of dues that anyone has to pay.

That is not fair, pal.

What's fairness got to do with it?—and besides, I'm not your pal.

And what about the hacking job? Ten years on that one? TEN YEARS spent in an oven on wheels! What about that one?

I heard you.

Well, what about it? Do I get a break?

Maybe.

I'm not lazy, I'm not asking to be given anything—just once, just once for things to go my way! I work hard; you've seen me!

You know you have—this isn't right! I can't see it! I can't understand it!

No one asked you to. That's life.

This can't be life.

Says who?

It just can't be.

You're angry—

Frustrated is a better word.

Fine. Frustrated then. But you're just rambling on and on now.

You've got nothing to say.

I do. Only am not connecting! Not getting through! I am sick and tired of trying! Getting weary of the whole thing.

You can't be.

I am. I'm only human.

No, you're Superman.

You've been reading comic books!

You're the "hero" who kept telling that nut the other week to stop complaining and to get a job, any job, and to start writing again—because this was the best time of his life to keep writing (as you are both the same age—so you were in reality saying things to yourself as well, telling yourself not to give up while you spoke to him).

So what?

So what gives? You're good with advice—only now you are copping out.

DON'T SAY THAT ABOUT ME!!!!

What else can I say?

I AM NOT COPPING OUT!!!! I PAID MY DUES!!!! I AM NOT A PROFESSIONAL BUM LIKE THAT JERK!!!! AND LOOK AT ALL THE STUFF I'VE WRITTEN OVER THE YEARS! WHAT'S HE DONE?

Five and a half screenplays. That's what the creep told you.

Look at all the boxes full of stuff I've done over the years!

Would you look at that stuff!!!!

You're getting excited!

I know I am! I have that right! I've paid my DUES!!!!!!!!

But you know you've admitted yourself that the early stuff needed polish! You never could go past the first draft and REWRITE!!!!

You've admitted it to yourself and said so to others as well!

What about that?

All of it did not need a rewrite!

Just about all of it!

Even *P.I. FOR HIRE*?

Yes, pal, EVEN *P.I. FOR HIRE*!!!! Only you did not want to do this—so you're stuck with half a dozen cardboard boxes full of stuff that is not going anywhere for you! What about them apples?

You don't B.S. around, do you?

I don't with you. It'd be a waste of time. Nobody is trying to fool anybody here.

The truth is hard to take.

Well, take it! You've told others that they'd have to take the truth!

Remember? DON'T YOU REMEMBER?

. . . I don't know what to say . . . how to respond to that! . . . just cool it . . . just take it easy . . . I'll take it easy on you if you promise to take it easy on yourself.

How do I keep doing that? I'm 36.

You've got a few years left.

For a while there I was worried that my belly was in a real mess, maybe stomach cancer or something, maybe a bad liver from all that 7-11 black coffee, and from all that crying I did after the split, from the pain.

Elston's birthday is coming up. You better do something nice for that guy, he's a friend, to show your appreciation for sending you that forty bucks two months ago in the mail—and you were able to go out and get something to eat.

What can I buy him?—when I can't even go out and buy a Chicken Little?

You've got three bucks left. A Chicken Little costs only 39¢!

Yeah, but I may have to buy another bag of rice to keep me going, to keep from dying of hunger, from malnutrition.

Cool it.

That word again. You're good with that word—COOL it. Cool what? I'm human. I feel like I'm getting weaker every day. What do I do about it.

Pray.

Yeah?

That all you can tell me?

You've always prided yourself on being a loner—well, LONERS are supposed to be tough people—FACE THE WALL—A-LONE! FACE IT—TOUGH IT OUT, BUDDY! You're on your own and always have been.

That's what April Marie said to you that time, didn't she? Something about never really allowing her into your life. Something like that. She was right. She was close.

I can't respond to that.

Try.

I can't. It's complicated. I loved her, I'd have given my life for her, one of my eyes, I swear it, my whole life—I loved her more than anything in this whole world—just didn't know how to keep it from falling apart. Just didn't know how to right the wrongs. That was all I wanted to do. Had no answers. JUST HAD NO ANSWERS.

That's okay. Drop it. You've beaten that one to death. No more about that. Okay.

I understand. Okay. No more on the subject.

Finish your tea.

I did.

Have some more.

No, I want to live, I want to be back out there on location! I want to be doing something creative and exciting!

You can. You can make it happen.

How?

The same way you did it before. Only this time get the bucks, make sure you've got total control, make sure you don't get chased out of places by the cops and/or rangers, make sure you've got your locations nailed down good, make sure you've got a powerful story! (That was a major weakness, weak story.)

I know all about that! I even tried to tell the guys that the script was weak. But they liked it anyway. I knew it was not very good. I knew I had no plot (because there was no money for a plot, a real plot).

I know all that.

I wanted to make the *GRAVEDIGGER* script. They didn't like it.

You know exactly what you are supposed to do now—polish the *GRAVEDIGGER* script, and do it yourself! Do it on your own! That's the only way. In fact, you ought to be glad they didn't want to do it back then because the script needed work! Do you see now?

Do you get it?

Yeah. Yeah, I do.

What now?

I keep thinking about this wonderful girl I talked to three or four years ago in traffic court in West L.A.

She was from Seattle.

Jesus, there's no hope for you. That was years ago! Why waste time thinking about it?

Because she was wonderful—and all I had needed to do was ask her to have lunch with me and I didn't, chickened out . . . and I think about it now and then because women in L.A. are not much. I have gone years without meeting anybody like that, years. And when I do meet someone genuine—what do I do about it? Nothing.

What else is new? You let April Marie slip right through your fingers. April Marie turned out to be something else, something other than what I had originally perceived her to be. She hated men. She was a libber. She resented all men because of what her father had done.

Prove it.

I don't have to. It's there, all there. She had all these bitter answers, bitter-pat answers that she'd gotten from this bitter "book" written by April Marie.

Your cup is empty.

In more ways than one.

True.

Michael Parks was singing. . . .

I want to be back out on location.

There's always Mr. Ruiz who might back you.

He would have earlier—only not now when he finds out what happened with *BLOODSUCKING GEEKS*. He's a businessman, and not a flake. People don't throw their money around like that—not people with any real brains.

He might take a chance.

Don't know. . . .

Don't have anything to add to that. And if I get up from the table, then what? Pick up Lowry's *UNDER THE VOLCANO*? Turn on the tube?

No.

I have to get a job.

Get up, turn the record over.

I did.

Heat up some more tea.

I'd rather have something to eat.

Food costs money. Do you have any money to spend?

Not this morning.

Get a job.

Easier said than done. Do it.

I tried. The film company warehouse in Hollywood, remember? They had stacks and stacks of artwork, flyers from Madonna's latest bomb. *WHO'S THAT GIRL*. And the guy never called back. You blew it. You were too nervous, too anxious, too desperate. You shouldn't have called him on the phone after the interview. I needed the job. But you were too desperate. I know it. Couldn't be helped. That's what the nerd told you, too. "*Why are you desperate*? You sound real desperate to me." I am desperate, motherfucker, because I am at the end of my rope! Ever walked in my shoes? Ever gone hungry this long? I'm not looking for a shortcut, just to get hired for a lousy warehouse job, a min. wage dead-end warehouse job and you're telling me I can't even get that. How would you feel?

I hadn't laid it on him this way—but maybe I should have. Why were there so many insensitive assholes in this town? What would I have to do? Crawl on my belly and literally beg to be hired (then for the encore slip into a coma due to lack of groceries in said belly)?

So he never called you back. Never did.

That's his problem.

Mine too.

What did you do to intimidate the guy?

Nothing. Not a thing. Really. We talked like a couple of old buddies. He even said he'd tried writing a book—that never got published. All true. Was even from Chicago (claimed to be).

And he never called back?

I had left a colleague's number with him. He never called back.

He never called back?

That's what I said—he never called back.

Never called?

Hey, quit. I have to find work.

You never went back to North Hollywood Detectives, Inc.

I can't be a security guard.

Why not?

I just can't. It's a killer. It's a job for somebody retired.

You're retired.

Enough of this.

That's what happens when you start having conversations with yourself. Things get out of hand, things get screwy, things go nowhere.

I get the message.

Yeah, but you're doing it again—all over again. Stop talking to yourself.

All right. I will.

Get up and turn off the machine. Leave the journal alone.

I will.

Do it.

Michael Parks was doing *YOUR CHEATING HEART*. . . .

A Hank Williams tune.

Right.

And he's doing a nice job of it.

Turn off the machine.

I will.

• • •

Where's My Next Meal Coming From?

Polished off the last of the tuna, the last of the bread, last of the mustard. Returned to the employment office. There were jobs I liked on the boards—but most required experience.

The one that didn't, I was sent out on. Burbank Airport. The Garden Cafe. I parked the Colt at the green curb at the end of PSA. There was a woman in a yellow dress that looked a lot like my former girlfriend that got in a pickup as I pulled up. Nah, I thought, it couldn't be her. The woman had looked at me briefly, then climbed in the pickup. There was a guy driving. She'd had her hair up in a bun, wore sunglasses, her calves seemed larger than April's and there seemed a slight tummy—something she'd never had, as though the woman might have given birth to a kid or two at one time—I suppose this is what causes it.

None of it was worth two cents. I was broke, flat-out busted and disgusted, driving on empty, looking for a job.

I went inside, walked up to the girl at the cash register, told her I was there to see the lady about the job. I was given a form to fill out.

Jesus. It never ends.

Fill out this two-page form. What's your job history? You take the time to fill it out and you know you are wasting your time. It seldom works.

I do it anyway. I need the money. I'm broke, baby. Where's my next meal coming from? Busted. Ever been this busted?

Am not crying the blues here—just stating a simple fact. Without food we perish, dry up, die; without food—whether we like it or not—the body goes through changes, and before you know it, you are dying . . . and there is nothing the best doctors in the world can do about it—because by then it is too late. Malnutrition.

This is how Caren Carpenter died. By the time they found out about it—it was too late to save her. Only I don't have bulimia, or whatever the hell you call it.

The woman takes me to an adjoining cocktail lounge. We sit at a table in back, against the wall. She explains the job to me. It entails loading up food trucks and taking them out to the airplanes and loading the stuff onto the planes. She asks about my past jobs.

I tell her I was self-employed, etc. It's not enough. She needs phone numbers, names, etc., so that they can check up on me. She wants to know if I can get a DMV printout. I tell her yes, I can do that, but only if it's worthwhile for me to do so—otherwise, I'd be wasting my time. And not only that, I can't tell her that I don't have the 75 cents it would take to get a DMV printout.

The job pays $5.50 an hr.

I'm uncomfortable. I don't know what the hell is wrong with me—*and I do know what the hell is exactly wrong with me*—why am I forced to undergo this humiliation? Why am I here? I am overqualified for this dead-end nothing job. I don't want the job. I don't want to be around so many people. I just want to be back in my room typing. My stomach is nervous, nervous and sick . . . and I know that I've got bad breath as well (lousy eating habits, no doubt, Mr. Register?). I feel uncomfortable around this woman, and maybe she feels the same way about me. She tells me that there will be a week-long training course first. I don't want to be here. I feel other customers in the place can hear everything we are talking about—and I don't like it. She keeps pressing about what I'd been doing the last two years of my life. Finally, I have to tell her about the film, etc., and whenever people hear that they don't want to hire you because they are afraid you might be just another flaky Hollywood type with stars in your eyes, a flake with rainbows on his mind, a dreamer, a creative so-and-so—and, of course, they are right.

But so be it.

What else can I say or do or be? Nothing. I am what I am. I am a writer—the same way Van Gogh was a painter. Why do I have to apologize for that? Why?

WHY, LORD, WHY?

Why can't I make a living writing my little pitiful tales? My poems, my pathetic little plays about cab drivers and down-and-out Tinseltown dreamers?

I'm nervous, my belly is growling. . . . I want, more than anything in the world, to end this interview, cut it short, so short; and finally it is over.

I get up, and hurry the hell out of the cocktail lounge, step into the hallway, first take a step or two in the wrong direction, then double back, passing on my way a cafeteria with food, sodas, fruit drinks, coffee, Danish, salads, and people lining up with trays and a pretty woman in tight jeans at the end and I better keep walking and not looking at the food, just ignore the food, ignore everything, in fact, make it outside—and once outside the bright Valley sun hits me full force and I've got one hand in my pocket, due to shaky nerves, while the other carries the envelope with my unemployment office forms, I hurry down past PSA, ask a seated woman for the time.

"Quarter after one," she tells me.

I thank her, unlock my blue Dodge Colt with the dry bird shit all over it, I get in, start her up and slowly, purposefully head back down Hollywood Way, down to North Hollywood, down to the room.

I spend two hours fixing a flat on the ten speed. I clean up, and ride it to the library. I leaf through *THE L.A. WEEKLY*. Nothing in it. I glance through *PEOPLE MAGAZINE*: Sly divorcing Brigette, Joan Collins winning her divorce from Holm. Even the rich have their problems, you see? I leaf through *AMERICAN CINEMATOGRAPHER* and the article on the new James Bond Tim. Dalton—and all of it is putting me to sleep—it is really lack of food, am fainting—and pray not to go completely down in the library. I check out two murder mysteries, and ride the bicycle back to the apt.—and I still don't know who the hell I am or where I am supposed to be going or why even I was ever born. . . .

• • •

(Friday, Sept. 11, '87)

You Got Enough Money for Food?

Rode the bicycle all the way to Tobias Silverman's—Coldwater and Saticoy. Quite a haul. But it had to be done. Not only did I want to chat with him, but kept wondering if he might have a position for me in his downtown jewelry business. . . . I had to try.

There was nothing left. No food money, no gas money. The employment agency bit was not helping. Every job interview I had gone out on proved fruitless, futile. Maybe I could try to sell Toby my color set or just plain borrow enough money from him to try and get my cab permit again. . . .

So that was that . . . worked up a sweat as I pedaled the six miles up Coldwater to Toby's.

I finally got there, knocked on the door. His dogs, all three of them, are barking. Toby puts the German shepherd Nelson in the backyard, lets me in. He was brushing his teeth, gave me a cherry soda and returned to the bathroom. I was sitting in the living room with the two dogs (a Lhasa apso named Zsa Zsa, all white with lots of hair all over, and a Boston terrier named Dixie) sniffing me out. The black and white TV with the bad picture was on, baseball. I think the Mets were playing somebody. The reception was awful. The station kept apologizing and explaining that they were having problems with the audio.

I can't help but notice the stench in the air—dog crap and dog piss, but I don't want to be rude, not here, not now, not to this guy. The room is sparsely furnished, the sofa is thirty years old, caked with grime and dog hair. The carpet is a ragged, worn, filthy thing the color of the dying, hopeless lawn in front, but I wasn't judging, nothing of the sort. The man had lost a kid back in '80, had gone through hell and back, had given up on life back then, not giving a damn about anything.

Toby was through brushing his teeth, got dressed in a bedroom in the back.

We talked.

"I'm thinking of opening up my own jewelry store," said Toby.

"I think that's great, Toby," said I. "Only what about the risk?"

"I'm not worried about it." This would be the only way to eliminate the middle man in this line of work. He was still selling watches out of his downtown office.

Toby asked me about *BLOODSUCKING GEEKS*.

"Same old thing," I said. "The only way to make any real money would be to distribute it ourselves." Toby was curious to a point, but his head was not really into it.

"Too risky," said Toby. We got into his big white Caddy and drove on over to Encino for breakfast. I drank three cups of Sanka and ordered an omelette—ham and cheddar cheese (a bad choice, because it was about the worst omelette I had ever tasted, but I did not let on, was just grateful to have food in my mouth). The egg part tasted fine, the ham didn't, neither did the cheese. The wheat toast was good, so was the jam, the coffee. Our waitress was sexy, too, no makeup, pleasant, about 20 or 21 (or younger, who knows?); either way, too young for me at 36.

We talked some more about his business, some more about my business. I was trying to get Toby interested because I felt he had the ability to raise money—instead, Toby showed interest in putting in the time—but no money commitment. "Money's too hard to come by," said he. True.

I nodded.

What else could I do?

"Stay in touch," said Toby. "I mean it."

We drove back to his house, squeezed my ten speed in the back seat and he dropped me off at the corner of Magnolia and Tujunga (I felt like going to the library). "Let's stay in touch," said Toby. "The only way you are going to get anywhere with this film is to first get the other people's okay to let you distribute, otherwise, forget it."

I knew he was right. I thanked him for breakfast. (Toby was a good-hearted guy. On his way to his girlfriend's a while back he had come across a dog with its belly ripped open, taken the dog to a vet, had it stitched up, saved the mutt's life—one hundred and fifty bucks. How many people would have gone to all that trouble, I thought, as he recounted the story in the Jewish deli, how many?)

"Listen, Chance," he said, "you got enough money for food?"

I hesitated—there I was—flat busted, two quarters in my pocket, fifty pennies and a nickel at the apt. in a tobacco can sitting near the stove. I was more than busted—I was disappearing. . . . After he'd asked me several more times while I struggled to get my ten speed out of his backseat (because the kickstand was in the way, he pointed out), I finally admitted that I could use twenty bucks to go down and get my cabbie's permit. He handed me a twenty bill—and I felt pretty humiliated, embarrassed, rather small and insignificant. . . . *Jesus, don't ever get yourself in a position like this again. What a miserable way to exist. . . .*

Toby pulled away in his used Caddy and I got on my bicycle with the balding tires and rode it on over to the North Hollywood library.

And then later that evening "Madman" Miles F. Moody dropped by—and that was a surprise and I let him in after all. I was no longer pissed off at the poor asshole, no longer felt like cramming my fist down his throat. I could relate to the scrawny slob's dilemma. He walked in with four bottles of Bartles & James wine cooler. I watched as he drank three of the bottles, one after the other. You could say he liked the stuff. I took a sip from my bottle and couldn't hack it, wine these days never appealed to me. As a teenager I'd tried it for a while, the cheap stuff, Ripple, Bali Hi, Irish Rose. Since then I couldn't stand the smell of wine or hard booze. Beer was fine. I liked beer.

Moody kept his eyes focused on my wine cooler. After spaghetti, Moody said it would be a real shame to waste all that wine cooler that I no longer wanted. I gave him a glass. He poured it into the glass and drank it down.

"That was chicken-shit what you pulled the last time you were here," I told the man. "You know something? It's a good thing you didn't come back the next day because I probably would have busted you in the mouth."

He acted as though he had no idea what I was talking about.

"*You don't get drunk in here, you don't talk to me the way you talked to me that day! That's pure bullshit!*"

He knew what I was saying. I'd gotten him pissed off that night, comments I'd made about his main character in that play.

He'd been driving a cab for two weeks now. I said I was looking for work.

"You don't look too healthy these days," said Moody.

"Starving does that to you," I countered. He said no matter how much we starved we would still have no idea what true starvation meant. I replied: "I went from 169 down to 143 in less than three months! If that ain't starvation, pal, nothing is!"

He said nothing.

I told him about the dead-end jobs at 4 bucks per hour that were available. He was all too well aware of that.

"You better stick with the cab," I told him. "No matter how tough it might prove to be. I'm looking for a cab myself—Super-Duper preferably."

He said he would look for a Super-Duper cab for us, and let me know Tuesday. He left at around 10 p.m.

I truly would rather find an apartment building to manage, a place with a roof over my head, a place for my typewriter, maybe a hundred or one hundred and fifty dollars on top for groceries. That would suit me just fine for the time being.

I was preparing what remained of the spaghetti for myself that Sunday morning. I don't know, there had to be some decency in Moody as a human being. I could have been just a bit too hard on the poor slob. And maybe he deserved it, and maybe I'd been too harsh on his play. I ought to remember one of my favorite sayings: PEOPLE ARE JUST PEOPLE.

I missed hearing Merle Haggard's voice. I needed to hear some Merle Haggard. I put his record on. *A kid from Sarajevo who loves Merle Haggard.*

It's all in the movies. . . . He sang with so much heart, a heart that had been busted-up enough times to know that life included a lot of pain. . . .

It was overcast in North Hollywood and Merle's voice was just right. . . . The song is over and I have to get up and press the button on the stereo again. I need to hear the same song again. Sing it Merle. . . .

A plane is flying overhead (from or to Burbank Airport). I look at Gladwyn's plants. They might need water. I better water them. And do just that.

• • •

(Sept. 13, '87)

Blood Bank

So this morning I cleaned up, dressed, got in the Colt and drove it on up to the newsstand at Van Nuys and Sepulveda; bought the *ORANGE COUNTY REGISTER* (75¢) and the *L.A. TIMES* (25¢). And as I paid for the papers I could not help but notice the rows and stacks of *FLING* magazines and others with beautiful, busty, tanned women on all those glossy covers and could not help thinking: *Yes, it would be nice to have a girlfriend, a wife, somebody.*

The reality was I had to drive up to the blood bank and give blood.

I got back in the car and headed north on Van Nuys. Heavy traffic, heat; a busy street. I reached the 6400 block, made a left at the corner, found a meter with fifteen minutes remaining. I shoved another dime in for an additional hour—and I sat in the car for a while.

Can I go through with it? Did they use clean needles and all that? Paranoia was working again. It couldn't be helped. And not only that—there was the added humiliation of having to sell blood for ten bucks, the humiliation of having to go through something so damn pathetic as this is in order to get money to eat.

Did I have it in me?

Could I take the humiliation?

It was not easy.

So I sat in the Colt, went over the CLASSIFIEDS in both papers—not much in either one. Everyone was looking for couples to manage apt. buildings.

I was out of luck (*and out a whole dollar*).

I took the entertainment section from both papers with me, got out, walked slowly back to Van Nuys, paused at the furniture store on the corner, stared at the furniture. Looks like it might be from George Washington's days, who knows? I walked south some more to the next store—a toy shop—they've got cars in the window, teddy bears, trinkets, figurines, trucks with remote controls, etc. I keep walking, passing the BLOOD BANK. I can't go in.

It's too much.

Dammit, I just can't. It's not the fear of giving blood—it's the rest—fear of catching AIDS, the idea that I was, in fact, hitting rock bottom. When you sold blood for money you were in all reality selling your soul, the last vestiges of your victimized, pitiful little soul. Could I sell my soul? Did I have any left?

What soul? Did I know what soul was? Did any of us have any soul?

Christ, man; I kept walking farther south and paused at the Levi clothing store. They had a huge cardboard cutout of Merle Haggard dressed in Levi's, a vest with a name brand on it, holding a beer with some brand on it, a cap, likewise. They had cowboy boots in the store, cowboy shirts.

Dammit, what the hell am I doing standing here staring at this shit? What's the matter with me? You drove all the way out here and now you haven't got the guts to go in!

Wait a minute!

Are you going in?

I want to —

Well —

I should —

What the hell is it? Look at all the gas you've wasted! I know that—but my life is a little more important than that. This AIDS thing is scary—

WHAT HAS AIDS GOT TO DO WITH IT?

I might catch it if I go in there to give blood. The blood bank may not be all that clean. Just scared, that's all. I don't mind giving blood, I just don't trust these people. It wouldn't make sense to catch the virus for a lousy ten bucks.

You're overreacting, man. Just go in. You've got five bucks left.

How long will that last you? What will you do then? I know, I know; DAMMIT, I KNOW.

I didn't move, just stood there in the heat on Van Nuys Boulevard, a lost fool with five dollars in his pocket and the entertainment section from the *O.C. REGISTER* and the *L.A. TIMES*. I felt like a total idiot. And I was.

Where to? What now?

I don't know.

You're not going in there, are you?

No. Fuck it. I just can't. It's too goddamn humiliating. IT'S LIKE CRAWLING IN THE GUTTER! IT'S THE SAME THING! That's what it is.

I walked back to the Colt, sat there a while, went over the job ads again . . . what good did it do?

A Vet, that's what I was, a Nam Vet—not lazy, not a sham artist, not a thief, not a bank robber or a killer—just a busted, broke fool looking for a job—and I couldn't find anything.

Did I predict this years ago? Did I somehow sense even back then that this is what awaited me? How could I have known? Was there some kind of jinx at work here?—some kind of jinx had hit me and stayed with me no matter where I went, no matter how hard I worked, busted my ass to do good? How could I have suspected anything of this nature way back then?

Bullshit.

You're not making sense now. Just turn it off and shut up.

God . . . if you exist and you're watching all this . . . what the hell is going on? And not just with me—not only me . . . what about all those other poor bastards out there going through the same thing?

Huh?

I started the Colt up and headed back to Camarillo St. I ended up taking Victory on toward Lankershim and in spite of all of the money problems and food problems and gas problems and worries, in spite of it all, can't stop thinking about the women I'd spotted on all those glossy girlie magazine covers, and I know that farther down on Lankershim I will be passing a bookstore near Magnolia and I also know that inside that bookstore is a nice magazine rack full of *GEM*,

FLING, *PENTHOUSE*, *HUSTLER* and *PLAYBOY* mags, with pictures of nude women with knockout figures . . . and it's been forever since I'd had my arms around a woman, so damn long since I'd kissed one on the lips, so damn long since I'd held a naked woman in my arms. . . . But I drove right by the bookstore. You looked at pictures of naked women and all it did was get you all worked up—and then what? It's back to the apartment with no one waiting there but the TV set and those 3 or 4 girlie mags you could not bring yourself to throw out along with the stacks of others that you did throw out a while back.

So forget about women, buddy; because when the belly is empty, I guarantee you one thing, that dick of yours is not going to be thinking about pussy at all.

I parked the Colt in front of the apt. building, went in. I read the papers, boiled the remaining two hot dogs.

What's my next move?

You tell me.

I'd gotten cleaned up and dressed and spent a buck and all that gas for nothing. All for nothing.

I added catchup and mustard to the hot dogs and ate the hot dogs.

I poured some lemonade into a cup and drank it. I reached in the refrigerator for a carrot, rinsed it under the tap and I ate the carrot; sat back down on the sofa and went over the job ads again, all of it.

What's the use? How long will that five bucks last me?

There's always the BLOOD BANK. To hell with the BLOOD BANK! I mean it. What if someone from the film sees you? What if someone out of your past sees you go in the BLOOD BANK? How will that look?

Ask me if I care.

At this point in time, at this point in my life—I do not give a damn. Let *them* starve for a while, go without food, let them taste the gutter and then we'll see how everything is. You hit hard times, nothing to be done about it. It happens to quite a few of us. It just does.

You shouldn't have ended up like this.

Tell me something else, tell me something I haven't already told myself a thousand times before. Tell me.

When the money runs out this time what do I do then? Will I be able to go back to Tobias? No way. He did say: "Call me, Chance. We've got to get together, call me. . . . "

How can I call anybody in this state of mind? I cannot keep asking friends for money, I can't do it. That's not what friends are for. I'm starting to look like a sham. I think people are starting to look at me as one. Sam the Sham—and his Cream of Wheat.

I'm stuck. Can't move. Don't know where to go or what to do. Am without direction right now. This never used to be a problem. What the hell.

I'm a writer—but when the belly is empty *writing be damned*!

You can't put the typewriter in the skillet, add salt and pepper and fry it, now can you? You can't eat a typewriter. Some of these jobs I just can't go out on—not at 36. There's the color TV. I can still try to sell it. What's going on with *BLOODSUCKING GEEKS*?

• • •

(Sept. 15, '87)

Reject

The producer, Mead Fuchs, and I shopped the film around to discover to our great dismay that the major video distributors were not interested.

It was tough having to deal with video companies while existing on Cream of Wheat in that small room in North Hollywood; no phone, no food, no gas to get around. Unable to find work, too desperate for my own good to get hired on for anything, I was stuck waist-deep in quicksand and sinking fast. I still had my bicycle, but trying to ride it down to Hollywood and back (the ride back would have been uphill all the way) in the weak shape I was in was out of the question.

At the start of production in '86 I had weighed 165 lbs.

I was down to 139 pounds in that room in North Hollywood.

The employment office was on Magnolia, several miles to the north, and I would go up there 2, 3, 4 times a week to look for work—*any kind of employment*—and I could not get hired for *anything*. I must have looked like hell and nobody wanted any part of me. My pants wouldn't fit now. I appeared haggard, at best, lost, disoriented. Lack of nutrition will do this to you.

What gives?—I kept asking myself. I just put every last damn dollar into this film (it wasn't much—about five grand, as I had sold the cab, paid off what debts I had and plunged what remained—the 5 Gs—into the film)—why can't I get a break? Why can't we sell this thing?

I was in that tiny bachelor apartment for eight months. I really had no one to turn to. My married sister Zuleika had moved to Ohio with her husband and daughter. Zuleika's husband Walt was a lieutenant now in the Air Force. My brother Emir had moved with our parents to AZ (and they were existing on the old man's social security and food stamps). I had not spoken to either parent in eighteen years, and was not about to start now. My other two sisters were living in Chicago with problems of their own.

All this starving was not doing my health much good. I would have to pay the blood bank another visit. No way around it. I got in my car and drove on over to Van Nuys Boulevard.

I was ready to give blood this time. No questions asked.

It had come to that. My back was to the wall. It was hard going in, humiliating, trying to deal with what I had reduced myself to—but if I wanted to get something to eat I would first have to give blood, get my eight or ten dollars and buy the food.

The blood bank was full of street people: junkies, hookers, drunks, homeless, professional drifters. From the waiting room in front I could see them all in the back room sitting in barber shop chairs having their blood pumped out of them.

Now, I had nothing against these people; this was only an observation of what I was seeing inside the blood bank. Actually, I felt relieved, as I figured if they could give blood—so then could I. It would be easy money. They were in there getting theirs, why couldn't I?

A guy in a white frock walked up: clean-cut, all that.

"Fill this out."

Somebody always had a form for you to fill out. Would it ever end?

I filled it out.

Then they had to test my blood first. Okay. They did that—jabbed a needle in me. White Frock walked away with my blood sample. I waited. Just thinking about the food I'd be able to buy had me going pretty good, salivating. My God, a Big Mac would have hit the spot, a Big Mac, fries, a large Coke. I thought about it and thought about it. There was no way to quit dreaming about food. . . .

"Mr. Register?" White Frock was back. "Sorry," said he, holding up the glass tube with my blood sample.

What was he sorry about, I wondered.

"See this? You have too much cholesterol in your blood."

I stared in a daze. It was not the high cholesterol content in my system that bothered me—it was the fact they wouldn't take my blood. *I could not even give blood.* Stunned, that's what I was. Forget about that hamburger and fries and soft drink you were going to get, forget about the real food you were going to taste. Forget it. Stop thinking about food. It was tough. Junkies and whores and winos were giving their blood—but I couldn't. All I wanted was enough money to buy a meal, something to eat—and they wouldn't take me. Those people back there were going to go back out there on the street to buy their heroin and cheap wine and grass—all I had wanted to get was something to eat, a hamburger, a hamburger. I used to dream about being able to buy just a hamburger. . . . Every time I saw a commercial about food appear on the color set back at the room it only made the hunger pangs more acute.

Was this what my old man had left Europe for? Had forced me to leave my beloved Belgium for? Brussels, the good education, the French language that I loved? Was this it?

Land of Opportunity? America, Land of Plenty. Was this it? So I could end up starving to death in a room in the San Fernando Valley at 36 years of age?

Where was the justice? Tell me, damn you! Explain it to me!

All this was going through my mind as "the doc" in that white frock kept holding up that plastic (or glass) tube with my blood sample laden with cholesterol in front of my face.

This is what you brought me to America for, old man Alićahaić?

When would it let up? Hadn't I suffered enough? Hadn't I been put through enough? Hadn't the pain of having lost April been enough for me?

Suicide, I kept thinking, suicide is the answer. That's the only way to end the suffering, the only way to end this non-existence, this poor excuse for a life that consisted of nothing but pain and bullshit.

"Have a good meal," the White Frock advised in a voice that sounded sincere enough. And he suggested exactly what I should eat: well-balanced meals. And just then I felt like responding with: How do I go about buying these well-balanced meals? How do I get this food? But didn't. I heard him say: "Come back to us in two or three days."

I nodded my head, said nothing, and walked out: fighting dizziness and weakness in my knees only made worse by the glaring sun and blinding sidewalk outside. I fought the weakness as I walked north on Van Nuys Boulevard. My eyes were on the verge of giving up a teardrop or two, but I thought: *Hell no*; it's too ridiculous a situation you're in to allow for that to happen. You're not going to shed a tear. I was shaking my head, however, and I believe I chuckled to myself. "You can't even give blood," I muttered, as I walked up to my car.

"They don't want your blood."

I sat in the car in a stupor, unbelieving. "You can't even give blood. Isn't that something? They don't even want your blood."

• • •

(Sept. 20, '87)

Bums

Back in the 70s there was a saying I had: "I'll either become a great success or I will end up a nothing bum," I liked to tell my buddies at Terrance Gullick Academy of Film. I had made an accurate prediction. That carrot that forever dangled in front of my face was of my own creation; my own fantasies and wishful thinking kept that carrot swinging in front of my eyes.

I was the mule that would never get the carrot, the fool who did not know better and allowed it to sink him to despair, dust. . . .

How often over the years and how many bums did I pass on the street, sleeping on bus benches, in parks sleeping on the ground, standing around skid row, hanging around the Greyhound Depot, these people who had hearts and emotions and needs like the rest of us, how did they end up like that? What cruel sin had been committed?

But in life you find out that nothing cruel, no sin need be committed in order for you to get knocked down like that and kept there.

How many had I seen from my cab walking around filthy and barefoot?—the faces covered with sores and crusted blood, clothes caked with dry vomit . . . how many?

It was scary.

Why was it that just a block from skid row, just a block away people were staying at the New Otani Hotel in warm rooms and music and all the comforts of home? What made these people any different?

What a comment to make: "I will either become a great success or a nothing bum roaming the streets with nothing left to lose, not even my mind. . . . "

What a thing to say.

I see that my spot in the gutter is inches away.

• • •

Forget Your Dreams

Gladwyn was back from Texas, and once again I needed to find a place to stay. Toby Silverman's offer was there, the only offer around actually. He paid $900 a month in rent on a three-bedroom, two-bathroom house he was sharing with his three dogs on Wixom Street in North Hollywood. The wholesale jewelry business he maintained in a downtown office (selling watches, rings, bracelets; some gold, some gems, mostly wristwatches) kept him going on many an out-of-town trip; he would fly out to wherever there was gold to be bought, rings, chains, etc., wherever he might find a deal on a load of wristwatches; and the rest of the time he spent in Glendora with his girlfriend Kate and her three teenagers from a previous marriage. Wednesdays and weekends Toby spent with Kate, and by my moving in with him he would not have to worry about his dogs going hungry. Usually, his system was to leave a huge tray of dry dog food on the kitchen floor for them, as well as a tray of water next to it. As the dogs had a way of knocking the water over and, no doubt, hated the dry food, Toby saw my moving in with him as a solution to that. I would be helping my friend out in this respect and he, in turn, would be providing me with a roof over my head and my own room with a bed.

It beat sleeping on the sidewalk.

"You wouldn't have to pay rent," Toby said. "You can write, do whatever you like—as long as you keep an eye on the dogs for me."

It was a big relief for me, needless to say. Toby Silverman and I had always gotten along, there was a longstanding bond there, a friendship that had originated back in the early '80s, when our mutual friend Angus Gladwyn had invited me to the house Toby had been living in in Chatsworth at the time with his ailing dad, a tough Doberman Pincher named Cyrus, Dixie, the Boston terrier, and Toby's estranged wife Kelda. Toby was half Jewish, half Catholic. A group of people had gathered that evening at his and Kelda's house to watch the Hearns/Leonard fight. Kelda had been there, as well as some of her friends.

Gladwyn had brought Chubby Elston and me. The one thing that had struck me upon meeting Toby, the most acute of all observations that had stayed with me over the years: the pain; this human being, this gentle soul had projected more pain than anyone I'd ever met—and rightly so; I had been instructed by Gladwyn, prior to the drive out to Chatsworth, of the tragedy that Toby and his then wife Kelda had lived through: their five-year-old boy had drowned in their backyard pool not many months prior to this gathering.

Well, we hit it off, Toby Silverman and I. There was an instant rapport. We both loved books—and more than anything—there was that pain; we were both in agony deep inside: I, at having split-up with my woman—and he, his loss by far the greater, having lost his only child. There was so much empathy I felt for this man, wished I could have, upon meeting him that evening years ago, eased his agony for him, said something to lighten his burden—but of course, in a situation like that, nothing can be said, nothing can be done.

And we had stayed in touch over the years; not that we had spent much time socializing, my fault that—my own demons and agonies I felt I had no right to burden such a soul with, whose burdens far exceeded mine already. The truth of it was I couldn't even help myself then (nor now).

I'd been taking it a day at a time, from 1980 on, fighting off suicidal tendencies, walking that tightrope—with nothing but a prayer for a safety net.

So now, after that eight-month stay at Gladwyn's place, Chance Register was on the move again. And what of *BLOODSUCKING GEEKS*?—what of the film? Well, we had a distributor, but it would be months before we saw any money.

I had my paperbacks and manuscripts packed in cardboard boxes and moved into the house on Wixom Street with Toby and the dogs: Dixie, Zsa Zsa and Nels (the Boston Terrier, Lhasa apso and the German shepherd, respectively). Several months later Toby introduced me to a friend named JoJo Ripley who cleaned carpets for a living. Eventually, I ended up going out on some jobs with JoJo in an effort to make a dollar or two, at least to cover postage for the short stories I continued to send out to various publications—stories that continued to get sent back to me with accompanying form rejections. What at times bothered me more than the rejection slips was the way people couldn't wait to tell you that you ought to forget your dreams, you ought to forget this creative thing—(these people have had a dream or two themselves, you see, and realized that they couldn't go the distance—for whatever reason—maybe lack of talent, maybe lack of drive, maybe no guts, maybe lack of discipline, maybe did not want to pay the dues; it goes on) so they are always the first to tell you that you should consider doing something else, clean other people's carpets and/or toilets. This is all the non-creative mind knows. Get a 9 to 5 dead-end job, like they are chained to, get a nothing job, a job that will drain and eventually kill you, a job that you will hate—but it will be a job nonetheless that will make you some money, put food on the table, pay rent, etc., all that. Forget the creative thing because they don't understand it, can't relate, or even if they could they probably would hate to see you get anywhere with it—because only then they would have to deal with the fact that they sold out, didn't have it, never had it—whatever it took, to make it away from the 9 to 5 grind—so they resent, envy, etc. There it is.

I am not saying that these people are not good human beings, am not saying at all that these people do not have commendable qualities—but it is frustrating because they all sing the same damn song.

I have worked since the age of thirteen; nobody, but nobody, has a right to tell me about work, about going out and working for a paycheck. I have worked all my life, man! I can even recall as a kid of twelve helping the old man carry sacks of potatoes, apples, etc., down in Chicago (at the sidewalk market on the South Side we used to go to) about ten miles from our apartment on Halsted, near Armitage, and can recall hauling that stuff back, either on the bus and/or little red wagon. The old guy did his best to stretch a buck, feed his five kids. I worked, all my life I worked: stock clerk, warehouse jobs, security guard, drove a cab, was a dispatcher (fifteen hours a day, six days a week, plus twelve hours on Sunday during that four-month period there while living on Burnside), was a grunt—*so how dare these people put me and my dreams down? How dare they mock something they do not understand?*

That first day we went out to strip-and-wax a woman's floor in Ladera Heights, JoJo Ripley (who is 45) saying: "Yeah, I realized I didn't have the talent to make it as a musician so I quit, gave it up, couldn't make a living at it. I'm much happier now." This was back in '69 that the man had given up on his dream, and I imagine he was hinting at something, suggesting that I ought to do the same. Look, it's fine if JoJo does not feel he has talent; great; terrific for JoJo Ripley.

But that is not me. That is not Chance Register. Because no matter what anyone tells me, I will never accept it. Never! Ever!

No matter if I don't ever sell anything! That's just the way it is. I feel it in my bones that I do have something, that I can do it—if only given a chance—an opportunity to make it happen. I realize that asking for that chance, that break in this screwy town is asking a lot—for the impossible.

Later that day when I recounted Ripley's message to Toby, Toby came back with: "Do you think he was trying to tell you something?"

"Toby, of course he was trying to tell me something—he was trying to tell me more than one thing, at least that's what I read there."

It's tough to openly disagree with a man who has given you a place to stay—a bed, a roof over your head, and peanut butter sandwiches—because if one were to keep on disagreeing one would eventually find oneself out in the street, at least this is the vibe perceived.

Stands to reason. You're living under Toby Silverman's roof so you must accept Toby Silverman's logic even if that logic only makes sense and applies to Toby Silverman.

Respect the host. I do my best.

How do you say to these "well-wishers" without appearing arrogant and/or ungrateful that you do not care what anyone's assessment of your talent is, because you believe in yourself? And always will—no matter what? How do you verbalize without causing an argument? The best that I can do is not bother with topics of this nature. It seems people are hinting that I may be afraid of physical labor—and I just don't get it, because that could not be further from the truth. Just today I raked leaves in the backyard, filling up 11 large bags full of leaves and dog crap. Spent the last three days doing that—which brings the total to 25 bags and a couple of blisters. I mean it's work. Cut the grass, trimmed trees back there. Work. And I don't mind. In fact, I like paying my way. I do not like handouts, and am not looking for any. When Toby needed to move those heavy jewelry cases from a store near Claremont to the house here—I was there with a positive attitude. And then last week we moved a case down to his office.

I cleaned up the place, vacuumed, picked up crap off floor, picked up dog crap off patio floor, etc. And I always tell Toby: "Look, if you need my help in anything, all you have to do is let me know."

I tell the guy: "Let me help while I'm here, because I won't always be here."

At the moment he is contemplating moving to a bigger office in the same building. I said to him: "Fine; I'll help. Whenever you're ready."

So it truly bugs me when people belittle the many hours I spend at the typewriter—often 12 hours a day (often 7 days a week); there are times I know I worked more than 12 hours a day—so where do people get off by making light of that? And as I have said, I do a lot more than that. I do *work* when there is work to be done. I have always paid my way. Never took advantage of anyone, ever.

Never took advantage of my then common-law-wife. Even though I kept writing I hacked all those years to make the writing possible. But people can't relate—those who are not into that, all those who hate their 9 to 5 jobs—but somehow feel that you ought to be as miserable as they.

How do you figure? How do they figure?

Why knock writers and filmmakers? Why put down the novelist, when as far as I am concerned, that is the noblest of professions.

I said to Toby: "If I am able to get a loan, will you at least help me buy some accounts? Will you go out with me?" He was hesitant, but said that he would. As good-hearted as the man is, as grateful as I must be for his kindness, *why is it everything is so difficult*? Why must Toby keep putting things off? I don't get it.

He says he is not able to get into the cleaning now because his present business is taking up all his time. "Fine, but will you at least help me get started with this thing?"

If people are convinced (or even so much as think) that I am about to give up on my dream of becoming a writer—well, they could not be further from the truth! I am and will be a writer until the day that I die.

How many years has it been now? How many? I started right out of the army. I was twenty back then—am about to turn 38 next month—am still at it—and even though I have yet to sell something, I am more determined than ever to make it, to stay with it—no matter what it takes. These putdowns have had a very positive effect on me. I am more determined than ever now to BE A WRITER. I feel (finally) that I am a writer. Even though I have written so much stuff over the years—I wondered if I could truly call myself a writer—to me *BLOODSUCKING GEEKS* does not matter (it's low-grade crap, I must admit—water under the bridge), but I have other things that I am proud of—and I will keep right on going.

So there you are—my detractors. Thanks for the push. Thank you for making me want it even more now than ever! How about that? Can people like this understand what I am saying here? How I feel? And what I am going through?

I doubt it.

It has been a good day after all.

• • •

('87)

Make It Look Like Hard Work

Shaved the beard off. I'd forgotten what I looked like underneath all that hair. Had the beard for years.

Nice day. Got the German shepherd in Toby's old Caddy and took him to the park on Strathern, and then afterwards drove by North Hollywood Park at Magnolia and Tujunga. Drove by Valley College, ran a bit with the dog. Felt good to be out. Thought about driving out to the beach—have not been out there in years, would be a good idea to get some sun (vitamin D)—instead, headed back here (due to lack of gas money). Might make it out to the beach next weekend. The old Caddy uses up a lot of gas. It's scary how much gas that thing eats up. Should fix the Colt.

It really is time to get this puny body back in shape. All that starving on Camarillo St. (eight months' worth), and then another eight months of it here at this place has dried up what muscle tone/tissue I had, sucked it up, shrunk it. Have to start doing some light workouts, et cetera; all that. I'm only thirty-eight. I can't stop taking care of myself at thirty-eight. It would not make much sense. Well, things get you down and then your body knows it. Life takes its toll—don't it? *It sure do.*

Well, fine. I have this feeling that it is time to start anew, to rejoin the living. That's what kept going through my mind all day today: REJOIN THE LIVING. GET BACK INTO THE HUMAN RACE. Get with it! Start going out more, start thinking about finding a girlfriend. Yes. It is about time. For a long time there did not think I'd ever get with it, did not think I'd ever want to. . . . I swear to

God, when you are down, down so far you wonder what's the use? Why waste the time?

I want to get my second wind now. And I have a feeling I will keep the whiskers off for a few years now. It is time to start over. A new beginning. The beard had served a purpose—a kind of mourning; that's what it all meant, that whole phase I went through. A limbo life. And it seems all that is behind me, I hope.

Knock on wood.

Where's some wood? Find wood. Knock wood.

I did (or do).

When I find myself thinking more and more about getting a girl, well, that truly is a good sign. Did not think I would ever want to go through that pain again, but am now thinking I can handle just about anything. Am stronger for having survived the last romantic fiasco. I do not know what anyone can do to me now. I have gone through all of it: the toughest, the meanest, cruelest of ordeals.

8:01 p.m. It feels like summer out there. So it has been nine years now since the breakup with AMV. I think about her now and then—and this is strange, peculiar, funny, not easy to describe—never thought I would be able to think about the breakup without ever feeling a good deal of pain—and yet, AND YET (TIME HEALS!). Here I am, and there is no pain. . . . And is it possible that that person, that man, that human being years ago, that mess in agony could have been me?

Was that me back there that time in 1980? Was it? Of course it was. Am trying to be clever here. But it was me, had been me—in such sad shape because I had split up with a woman (girl actually; a twenty-one-and-a-half-year-old, immature bottle blond) I had loved so much. Lord, I found out what pain was.

And here I am now pain-free. Of course, I've still got my financial problems, do not exactly know where I will be staying—but at least am looking forward to falling in love eventually with a decent lady.

So now looking back on it, it almost seems that guy in pain back there all through the early '80s, in fact, up until about '85 (nearly '86)—a lot of pain—and it may seem (intermittently) that guy in pain may have been someone else, that it had all happened to someone else—but I know it was me it had happened to.

Sometimes people chuckle (find it amusing) when I let on it had taken six years to get over the breakup. All I can say to that is go out and fall in love with somebody, and I mean really love that person, *give your heart*—and then break up with that person and come and tell me what it feels like. If you feel no pain, all I can say is that you never loved, do not have the capacity to love (not all the way).

(March 25, 1989) 2:45 p.m. Saturday. Cleaned out the old Caddy yesterday, and I mean cleaned the damn thing out: the trunk, under the seats; scrubbed, scraped grease and grime off the steering wheel, doors, handles, dashboard. Filled a trash bag full of garbage. Drove by McDonald's for a Big Mac and a regular Coke, returned videotapes. Tank low now. How much change can there be left in Toby's drawer?

Stayed up until after 3:00 a.m. last night typing query letters to literary agents. Put six of them together. All I need is stamps now. Have the queries ready to be mailed. All I have to do now is finish the novel. What happens when I get a response from one of these people—and do not have the book finished?

(March 28, 1989) Tuesday. JoJo Ripley had more work for us. First we drove over to see that woman, that short, squat lady with a froggy-sounding voice to clean a number of "expensive" rugs. The squat lady who always sounds like she's got a frog stuck in her throat runs her own storage/restoration business. JoJo and I laid the carpets out on the driveway outside the warehouse and cleaned them by hand. We were on hands and knees with damp rags dunked in a bucket of chemically treated water that ate through the skin on your fingertips and felt like sharp bee stings. Ripley frowned on the idea of using gloves, gloves cost money and hindered efficiency, or some such loony notion. But there we were, senselessly dipping our exposed hands into this chemical solution and brushing down carpets (that hardly needed it).

"Get the dust, Chance. You getting the dust?" Ripley carried on like he never felt the bee stings, or else he was simply used to it after years of exposure, better yet: psyched himself to ignore the pain; his strong sense of smell for green easily overwhelming all other senses (primarily the common one) and further fortifying his immunity to this discomfort.

"Make it look like work," JoJo Ripley kept urging underbreath. "We're paid for the work we do, Chance." I would look at JoJo with a chuckle and a shake of the head, and JoJo straight-faced, always, not bothering to return the glance, red-faced JoJo, his face forever red like the color of his receding hairline, thinking about all that money he was taking in, and about all that money he was spending on remodeling his Chatsworth home, kept his head down, running that damp cloth over the rug and saying to me: "Keep brushing in the same direction; hear me?" It was 95 degrees in the Valley. Hot. I did not always feel like responding. "Chance?"

I would look up. "What is it, JoJo?"

"Are you listening?"

"Of course, JoJo; I'm always listening."

"What did I say?"

"You're kidding?"

"You said you were listening."

"You know what, JoJo? You're starting to sound like my old man."

"We're being paid to do a good job here."

"Keep brushing in the same general direction," said I. "Am I right, Mr. JoJo Ripley? Huh? Are we the Dynamic Duo, or what? You'll be a wealthy man, yet—unless you end up pouring it all into that house of yours in that ritzy Chatsworth neighborhood."

And this would always have JoJo Ripley chuckling. JoJo shook his head, returned to the task at hand. "You're a character, Chance; a real Ace."

"Yeah," said I; "I'm a champ, going places. Stick with me, kid, I'll take you to the top."

The Valley heat was merciless. Sweat dripped from our faces.

And then we drove on out past Magic Mountain to clean a woman's house. Evidently her '77 Corvette had caught on fire the day before in her garage; fire had destroyed the garage and parts of the kitchen. This was an insurance job. JoJo Ripley was salivating at the mouth. He would explain later why. The rest of the woman's two-bedroom house was spotless—and I mean *spotless*.

Everything was white. The woman must have spent all her time cleaning the place. So while JoJo worked in the kitchen he had me go in the bedroom with the steam cleaner and vacuum the ceiling. I felt like a fool. There was nothing to vacuum. No dirt anywhere, nothing. I looked at JoJo, the woman was doing something in the living room, and I said, under a guarded tone: "You serious? Vacuum what, JoJo? *The house is spotless*."

"Get in there and make it look like hard work," said JoJo; "like you're really doing something."

And so I dragged the steam cleaner into the immaculate bedroom with me in search of dust, something to justify JoJo's instructions. I vacuumed the carpet in search for dust, feeling like a complete fool. And then JoJo rushed in, grabbed the vacuum from me and aimed it at the ceiling and walls. I stood there looking at him quizzically.

"What?" said I.

"Make it look like hard work," said JoJo Ripley, as he ran the nozzle across the ceiling. The woman was eyeing us through the half-open bedroom door uneasily, needing to make sure that the bedroom got cleaned. Okay, I thought, but what is there to clean?

"Watch me," said JoJo. "Chance, you watching what I'm doing?"

"Sure, JoJo," said I. "You're vacuuming the ceiling."

"This isn't funny. We're here to do a job."

"I feel just like a jerk pretending to be doing something."

"Never mind that. Just do it. Make it look good. She's watching our every move." And he thrust the vacuum in my hands. "Go to it," said Ripley.

"Ten-four," countered I, to JoJo's dismay. He was back in the kitchen. I ran that vacuum all over the ceiling, the corners—in one of the corners I discovered the tiniest sign of a cobweb—Hey, I'm actually doing something here. I ran it up and down the spotless pink curtains, up and down all four walls; and then JoJo was back in directing me to get in the closet with the vacuum. "What?" I stood there looking at him. "It's clean, JoJo."

"*Do it anyway*." And he was gone. The woman stood in the

doorway with a displeased look on her face; I was not working hard enough to search out the nonexistent dust in her bedroom. I felt uncomfortable, not unlike a certified idiot.

What am I doing here? To break the ice, I complimented the lady on how well she kept her home and how beautiful it all looked. That pleased her.

"Thank you," she said.

"You must take pride in it."

"You're right," said she; "I do."

"I'm curious—how did the fire break out anyway?" That's when Ripley walked in, started up a conversation with the woman, asking her something about the kitchen. She walked back to the kitchen with him. I was relieved. The closet was spotless, shoes in order on a rack below a line of hanging white and pink dresses and blouses, beige summer jackets; all in perfect order. Cleanliness was all right; there was nothing the matter with being a neat person and having a clean home, but this was too much; this lady was clearly a fanatic about it.

And so the entire day was spent this way. We got the living room, two bathrooms, hallway, other bedroom.

Finally, I just needed to feel like I was actually accomplishing something worthwhile and JoJo Ripley allowed me to work in the kitchen, cleaning soot off ceiling, walls.

Figurines, trinkets (and this lady had dozens everywhere you turned) were brought down from atop cabinets, wiped off with a cloth, placed back up.

The woman stayed there the entire time, watching us.

She was in her 40s, tall and thin-faced, plain-looking, stolid and reserved, on the constipated side. Was she concerned that we might steal something? She seemed cordial and all, still it was a bit unnerving to have her there watching our every move while we acted like we were actually getting something done. It was a scam, a big scam. She had insurance. JoJo got the gig and the big payday, that's why he had to kiss up to her and make like we were doing something. The kitchen had been damaged by the fire—that was obvious; what the woman needed was a cabinetmaker, somebody to replace the cabinets and redo the ceiling, counter and tiles, not a couple of guys like JoJo and myself dusting things with a damn cloth. But JoJo was remodeling his own place and he loved these insurance jobs for the big payday they provided. And what was I getting? $7 an hour.

JoJo Ripley was getting hundreds, maybe over a grand or more—he was not telling. Afraid I would move in on his turf, not unlike my dear friend Toby.

"You probably won't really feel at ease until you've had your carpet cleaned," said JoJo understandingly to the woman.

The lady nodded readily. "You know, you're exactly right."

I'm looking at the living room carpet: spotless. You could eat off it. But the lady is agreeing with JoJo.

And they decide that we will be returning to clean the carpet tomorrow.

It was after 3:00 p.m. by the time we finally left the woman's house. And then I find out from JoJo, since this was another one of those insurance jobs, the woman who got the account (and passed it on to JoJo) was making at least five grand on the job. "At least five grand," JoJo Ripley repeated. I looked at him. "You heard right," he said.

"Big bucks," said I.

"Why do you think I'm in this business?"

But he would not tell me what his cut of the action was. By now I'm trying to talk JoJo into getting more jobs like this and going out and making some real money. "We'll see what happens," said JoJo noncommittally. I said, "As foolish as I felt pretending to be accomplishing something in that woman's house—it's not half as bad as going hungry and having no money for a hamburger." JoJo and I both laughed at that. "What a screwy world we live in," I said. "What she needs is to have the kitchen redone, cabinets replaced, new tile, all of it, not a couple of guys dusting her knickknacks."

"You worry too much," said JoJo. "She is having all that done."

Yep. And JoJo Ripley was getting a good chunk of all that insurance money too.

• • •

(March 29, 1989)

The Bus Bench Is Too Close

Tuesday. 7:47 p.m. I may have overstayed my welcome here. Feels that way. Hard to climb out of this hole I got myself dug in. JoJo still owes me $70.

The man wasn't about to pay me what I was worth. The way it goes. Everybody was afraid you were going to take away their livelihood, cut in on their action. *Life. And people, man. People. Go figure, go figure.*

Not much made sense anyway. Toby looking pretty glum these days—all the time, every day. I figure he'd like to be on his own. If only he hadn't expressed interest in going into the carpet-cleaning business together—that's the only damn reason I remained when I had that opportunity to take over my brother-in-law's mom's property down in South Gate. My brother-in-law Walt had phoned (long-distance from Ohio) with an offer to manage his mom Faith's three houses—located fifteen miles southeast of Downtown L.A., as she had a strong desire to relocate to the state of Ohio to be near her son—and I would have been able to live in one of the one-bedroom houses at half the rent. But I had passed on the best offer I'd had in years, an opportunity to leave this nowhere existence behind and perhaps get back on my feet. I had allowed Toby to convince me to stay on with him, I had allowed him to convince me that we would go in business together. . . . So much for that.

Live and learn. So what happens? I put myself in a real jam. So fine—am ready, willing and able to get into the cleaning on my own—if only I could scrape up enough funds to buy a steam cleaner, go it alone. . . .

I want to get out of here, move out somehow. How? What's the answer?

Stuck. Just stuck. I'd rather be by myself than live like this. Man, I'm tired of being a charity case. But there I was, working hard, busting my back cleaning those carpets and floors with JoJo Ripley, ruined my Adidas sneakers (and no bucks to show for it). Can't get a break. And Ripley smiling his money-grubbing little smile and saying: "You know, Chance, nobody owes you a living. I tried to help you out."

Right, JoJo; thanks for your help. Stay with the toilets—because with your mentality that's where you probably belong.

Before he left the house for his horse lesson, Toby said: "A customer offered me 25 grand for a thousand watches. I turned it down."

"You turned down 25 grand, Toby?" said I.

"It wasn't enough," said Toby. "I can make five to ten grand more on it."

I couldn't understand why Toby treated his friends as though they were his enemies. He was telling me about all these money deals, the buying and selling, the large sums of money that go through his hands (and I realized the man had worked hard to get where he's at), but all I had needed was enough money to buy a used steam cleaner.

I would have paid him back. Did the man consider me a friend?

Would a loan of this nature have broken him? I was not asking for a large sum of money, just a break to get started. I was not asking for a handout either. . . . I just couldn't seem to fathom the various mentalities I was surrounded by these days. . . . I was totally baffled. Puzzled. How quickly people's attitudes changed.

However, I could see where Walt was coming from, and I did understand. They had needed my help back then and I had been unable to come through—no matter the reason—I hadn't done it—and I had let Toby talk me into staying here on this dead-end street just so he'd have somebody take care of the dogs while he went on all those out-of-town business trips—and by doing that I had put myself in this crazy fix.

I am not pointing the finger at anybody here—just trying to figure a way out of this jam. It was clear I was up against the wall—and the people who knew me knew that fact. What was I asking? Just to be dealt with fairly. Was that so much to ask?

JoJo was getting these thousand-dollar jobs and there I am working just as hard and the man can't even see to it to pay me enough to get my car fixed. It's the little people that are always this way.

The world will always be full of little people—not physically little, mentally. In their mentality, in their approach to others around them. The self-centered little minds trying to cling to every penny and every dime—needing to take it all with them when they go. The fact that nobody lives forever has never occurred to these mental midgets.

What's the next step for me? I'm staring the gutter right in the face again. There it is—the sidewalk an inch from my nose.

Damn. Thought I was getting away from it. I swear to God I thought I was putting some distance between me and the sidewalk, the bus bench, sleeping on the grass in the park . . . scrounging around in garbage cans in back of greasy spoons . . . but there it is again . . . (has it ever left? How long now? How many years? How much longer?)

And now Mead Fuchs is saying I have to fill out IRS FORM 1065 and that my Federal number is 95-4197361 — INDIVIDUAL PARTNERS.

"*Why are they doing this to us, Fuchs*?" I said. "*I'm a homeless person, man. This is a joke. I don't get it.*"

• • •

(April 11, 1989)

Peanut Butter Days

Just finished viewing *THE YEAR MY VOICE BROKE* (on tape), a fine Australian film starring a talented young actor named Noah Taylor; in fact the whole cast was truly fine.

A well-made film, a film about human beings, a film about things that are/ought to be important to us, that ought to be written about, filmed.

This is exactly the type of film that hits you where it hurts.

It makes you think about your own past, your own childhood—the pains of growing up, and of course, the pains that we never seem to shake, the hurts, that stay with us always. This is life.

Reminded of the way people can hurt one another without ever meaning to (misunderstanding will often do it, lack of communication, misinterpretation).

It becomes somewhat tiresome, the phrase: "We weren't communicating." Am just weary of that expression. But,yes, it comes down to people's inability to articulate their thoughts, feelings—pain results.

What am I getting at? The film brought back memories of April Marie Voss. Could not be helped. The picture got me. The eyes were wet. . . . *If even love cannot save us, help us—what can? What is the answer? Why do people have to find ways to rock the boat?*

Why do they look for it? Why does it happen? Why are they doomed?

That pendulum feeling is there again (when did it ever leave?). The pressure on, the pressure to find work, move out. Thoughts of hitting my 40th and not living, not having any kind of life at all.

My peanut butter days in North Hollywood, my peanut butter days and ice water to wash it down with in North Hollywood. These peanut butter sandwiches are beginning to taste like mud. Have to wash this stuff down with ice water. Even jam no longer helps.

Toby has been kind enough to allow me to dip into his dresser drawer full of change from time to time. Bought a fish sandwich down at McDonald's on Sherman Way last night. But how much longer can I keep spending the man's change?

I need to have my own money. Was looking for work when the Colt broke down. I know I have to do something. When I spoke to LEECH last week (over the phone), thought Thordis mentioned she had sent Fuchs a royalty check for fifteen hundred. Well, that picked my spirits right up. Only here it is a week later and no bucks.

What happened to the check? Did I hear wrong?

I called up LEECH yesterday, asked to speak to Thordis. A man had answered at the other end: "Thordis is on vacation. Would you like to speak to Geraldine?"

"No, thanks." I had nothing to say to Geraldine, nothing at all to say to someone like that.

Well, I had hoped to get my car running again with that royalty check.

What's left to do? Wait. There is always the waiting. And more waiting. And when you get tired of waiting—what's left? You wait some more. Life on Wixom Street (with three dogs and a bicycle and peanut butter sandwiches).

Yeah. This is what it's like. And every time you hear someone remark how they always wanted to write you just want to tell them about all this—about living like a hermit, about having to put your life on hold for twenty years so you can hope to get better at what you have chosen to do with your life, to get published, get somewhere, make a living at it, hopefully. Every time you hear:

"That's great. You're a writer? I always thought I might write a book someday. It must be great to be creative that way."

No, you've got it all wrong. It gets so lonely sometimes you just want to scream at the top of your lungs. It gets so frustrating at times because you can feel the walls closing in, not unlike being in a prison cell: on top of all that the words not clicking, not making any sense—and you hear the clock ticking and see yourself aging . . . and nothing going on . . . and you put your life on hold for so many years and for what?

"You still want to be a writer?" (You would like to ask them then.)

Bullshit. That's what these comments are. Pure bullshit.

You get up and find yourself talking to the dogs (at times needing somebody to talk to). So you talk to the dogs. (It could be worse. You could be talking to spiders and flies and dead moths.)

How about that?

• • •

(July 27, 1989)

Be All You Can Be at Bink Security

Spent a day at Bink Security on Riverside Drive. Took test, filled out piles of forms.

They gave me my uniform (the individual supplies his/her own black shoes).

I guess they want me to work Paramour Studios. The last place I was interested in. But it's union over there, so it's okay. Am geared for a two-year stretch of playing Rent-A-Cop. As long as they give me plenty of overtime, that's fine with me. Will try to get 12 hours a day, seven days a week. Anything over forty hours is time-and-a-half; over sixty hours it is double-time ($10 an hour). As long as I get it I will stay with it.

Need to get away from the typewriter for a while. That is all I have been doing for over two years now, nearly three years (without a break). Am grateful to be working again (for money). It took me a long time to get a job (the toughest hurdle was psychological, getting used to the idea that I would be working for someone this time—no freedom—the kind of freedom I had in the cab). At least it will be steady employment.

Play along. Get your rest away from the typewriter—and go back to it in a few months. I will still be able to write during the day while pulling guard duty at night.

So it is not all that bad at all.

Attitude is everything. Keep right attitude about all of it.

FIRST DAY AT PARAMOUR STUDIOS

Got into my Bink Security uniform. Nervous about it all. Will I be able to take the people? Will I want to? Will I last even one night? I took a deep breath, exhaled; drove down to Paramour Studios at 9:00 p.m. Reached the main gate by 9:30, parked Colt in A lot. Entered studio security building, walked up to second floor—waited while dispatcher (tall, middle-aged woman) handed me my work sheet.

I looked at the work sheet.

NIGHT — CLEANUP — STANDBY

In the hall one of the walls was covered with framed black-and-white photos of Paramour head honchos (people I'd read about in "The Trades" for years); the real "movers and shakers," studio executives with power to make things happen.

They looked like ordinary human beings to me. In fact, there was nothing that set them apart from all the other struggling ants out there—and yet they pulled in a million (or more) in yearly salaries.

I stood there, studying the faces. Most wore eyeglasses, plain looking, everyday Joe Schmoes. But I was fascinated—not by anything I was seeing— but by what I was not seeing. How did they do it? How did these ordinary-looking characters get such high-ranking positions? Who did they murder? Maim? What was the con? There had to be a con for a bunch of unremarkable faces to be running a motion picture studio of this enormity. And there I stood, in a cheap Bink Security uniform, waiting to pull a night shift, my first with the company, at slightly above minimum wage.

It was a puzzle to me, the whole thing was a puzzle. I didn't even bother to try and figure any of it out anymore; I wouldn't know where to begin. One thing I was sure of—these dorks should have been *working for me*—and not the other way around. These two-bit, criminal-looking four-eyed bastards should have been down here where I was in their cheap Polyester Bink Security uniforms getting ready to pull guard duty instead of up there in their posh offices in that high-rise glass structure with well-equipped and quite accommodating secretaries.

I turned away from the photos. What's the use? To them you don't even exist, you don't even rate. Did it matter?

I believe I was well beyond the point of even asking: Did it matter?

A "mobile unit" was called for me. I walked downstairs, clocked in, and waited outside for the mobile unit. Ten minutes later a white Bink security car showed up with an Hispanic lady at the wheel.

"I'm Chance," said I, extending my hand. She said her name was Lana. We shook hands, and rolled, heading uphill to the Tours Security Office. I'm discovering this back lot is huge, lots of hills and narrow paved roads, lots of trees, shrubbery, fake storefronts. I spot a couple of raccoons crossing the road forty feet up ahead, a coyote can be heard in the distance, or is that a wild dog? I couldn't tell. Did coyotes howl? I didn't know. I'd gone on a tour of Paramour many, many years ago upon first arriving in Los Angeles—only they never showed you this part of it; the tourists only saw the dollied up, fancy attractions. Paramour was like a small town, it lay over that much Southern Cal. real estate.

"So what's it like working here?" I asked Lana. She made a sound, like a chuckle or a giggle in her throat. She seemed all business, this Latina. She was not my type, but I was genuinely curious about the job, edgy and nervous was more like it, and I was also trying to be pleasant, ease some of the discomfort at being in a car with a total stranger.

"You don't want to know," was her reply.

"That bad, huh?"

She glanced at me. "*That bad*," she underscored.

I got the hint, but said, "Are you saying it's not a good place to work? Is that it?"

"You catch on real fast."

"Thanks," said I. "So what's so bad about working here?"

She paused before answering: "The people. They're a bunch of backstabbers."

"Oh yeah?" said I. "Well, I always try to keep a good attitude."

"That won't do you much good around here. We got a bunch of backstabbers working here," she said. "Place is all bullshit. They pretend to be nice to you—the minute you turn your back they can't wait to badmouth you. I'm telling you it's bad, it's really bad. If you think being positive is going to make a difference you got another think coming. That shit don't make any difference around here. The people they got working here are a bunch of bad apples. That's what it is—they got all bad apples working in this place."

I looked at her. "Well, you seem all right; what are you doing here then?"

She laughed. "I'm studying to be a nurse—and I'm getting the hell out. Who needs this bullshit?" Lana's not so complimentary comments had only managed to add to my existing state of trepidation. But you've got to be brave, my son.

You have to at least get through one night—no matter how bad it must be. *One night—at least*. You've got that much in you. Come on. Do it. I wished right there and then we could have turned the car around and had her take me back to my lonesome Dodge Colt. The Colt needed me, wanted me to steer it back home to the dogs in that house on Wixom Street. But no, we make it all the way to the hill (more like a mountain) to Tours Security Office. Fifteen minutes later we're there.

"Thanks, Lana," I said, "for the ride as well as the warning."

"No sweat," said Lana, gave me instructions on how to find the office among the maze of gift shops and hot dog stands and other tourist traps, and was gone back down the hill again.

I pass dozens of tourists, all on foot, scrubbed and clean and happy looking and me totally out of place this way, among people. Crowds scare me. I've lived the life of a recluse so long now that this is all new to me, strange and intimidating, but I keep walking, do my best to get to my destination. What am I doing in this uniform? This monkey suit? A flunky and a failure on his way to nowhere.

(Am aware of switch to present tense, so be it.) I find the office, go in. A balding, middle-aged guy wearing glasses (probably a former LAPD cop or ex-military lifer) sitting in a swivel chair behind a desk at the far wall. There is a counter as you first enter the office. Two women in uniform (everyone up here wears white Bink Security shirts and gray trousers, instead of the blue I've got on) are doing something behind the counter, paperwork. One of the women is in her late 40s, the other in her early 20s. This, too, is a dispatch office. The group of guards here are called the A-Force. The starting rate here is $5.76.

Someone tells me to sit and wait. I do.

A worried woman tourist walks in with her teenage daughter asking if anyone has turned in a camera. A moment later another woman with her daughter comes in, asks if anyone has turned in a wallet.

Night Cleaning Crew appears. Janitors. They've got their mops with them, buckets, brooms and rags. I am assigned to go with these guys to one of the gift shops and stand guard over them while they clean and wax the floor. I am there "to make sure nothing gets stolen." The gift shop contains custom-made cups with various Paramour logos as well as logos from various television shows shot on the Paramour lot, T-shirts, videos, cameras, film, posters, cheap jewelry, postcards, figurines of stars like W. C. Fields, Chaplin, Laurel and Hardy, Lucy, Ernie Kovacks, Little Rascals, Harold Lloyd, Buster Keaton, James Dean, Bogart, thousands of trinkets, knick-knacks, all with the world-famous Paramour logo on them—adding up to what, I wonder?—other than money? What?

They were here, they made their mark—but they were all gone now. Gone . . . with the dust and the wind.

I spend the rest of the night pacing, bored, watching as the two Mexican workers sweep the floor, strip it of wax, mop it, give it several coats of new wax. My feet are killing me. I don't have the right shoes for this job, the heels are digging right up into my feet. Time moves slowly in these situations. I stand outside the gift shop, keeping an eye on things through open door and large shop windows. I refuse to come on like a warden or a prison guard and wish to appear casual about it—and truly, do I care if anybody steals anything here? Do I? Ordinarily I might—but here? With Paramour? Paramour, the studio that wouldn't give an inch? On top of that, what irks, all the goods are way overpriced. I don't care if the Mexicans decide to walk away with the whole store. They were paying someone minimum wage to keep an eye on thousands of dollars worth of merchandise. Makes sense. Only Paramour could not be blamed entirely. They paid Bink handsomely for our services (I was to find out later); only Bink was sucking the guards dry, ripping us off. It was Bink Security. It never ends.

The bloodsuckers were not to be found in horror films, they existed in real life. Everywhere you turned—the bloodsuckers were there sucking the very lifeblood out of you—from Morris-Royce (warehouse owners I once worked for) and on and on.

I am relieved by one of the other minimum wage slaves and go off to eat my two peanut butter sandwiches I have brought with me.

The supervisor in charge (actually a roving supervisor) of guards like me keeping an eye on the broom and mop gang is a slight Vietnamese male named Antoine, a young kid of twenty-three. Goes out of his way to be personable, which to me, by this time, means a great deal.

Any sign of a friendly gesture at this point does mean a lot to someone stuck in this Twilight Zone type of setting where the clock drags on and the night is going on forever and my damn feet are killing me. I should have had the heels repaired. From the way I have of walking both heels were worn down on the outer edges and therefore it never felt like I was stepping on a flat surface—because I wasn't. My feet wobbled with each step I took (more so than was usual for me).

A couple of hours later this Antoine hands me a walkie-talkie. They have codes up here for the various shops and guards. I am #A-45, Antoine is #45; the shop I am guarding is Post #45.

All these codes and uniforms and rules and regulations and badges and walkie-talkies and I had left the army for this very reason. I'd made buck sergeant at nineteen in Nam. Upon my return to the states they had attempted to get me to re-up: "Reenlist," the lifers all said, "you've got a good future ahead of you." But I had left (with an honorable), wanting out of the olive drab fatigues, wanting my freedom to pursue my dreams; convinced I could and would do better, much, much better—and the irony was, here I was in a cheap Polyester, ill-fitting uniform still taking orders and playing the old vacuous army bullshit (for minimum wage, at that).

But Antoine is helpful, and that cannot go unnoticed. I ask if it is okay to talk to the workers. "Sort of," says Antoine. "They don't like you to, but I don't mind." And he hurries off to check on another team or two of broom-pushers.

I remain standing outside the gift shop. It is nearly 2 a.m. A guy in rubber coveralls and knee-high rubber boots is hosing down walkways. I greet him with a nod and ask how long he has been at it. He tells me six months.

When the mop-pushers go to lunch and the guy with the hose is done and gone it is very quiet, too quiet. Nothing to do but pace. It's a game. A game called life. So much is pointless. A brown cat appears looking for food. And then a couple of skunks. No kidding. There's skunks in the area. I'm thinking: Well, fine. They look cute enough, only you never want to let a skunk spray you, because then you might as well burn your uniform. I stay out of their way. The skunks can do whatever the hell they want is the way I genuinely feel about it. The skunks leave. I'd never seen a skunk before. Ever.

I talk a bit with a short black woman who has been a guard with Bink for a year now, makes $6 an hour.

She is pleasant enough. The first time we start talking we kill half an hour. Which is fine. Breaks up monotony.

She's got three kids. Used to work a double shift but could not take it. Needed to spend more time with her kids.

Everybody is struggling financially, except the fat-cats (I don't mean felines either). The Vietnamese guy is working eleven hours this night; about to receive his degree in engineering.

When finally 4:00 a.m. rolls around the night clean-up crew is done and it is time for Antoine to lock doors.

Time to go home. I clock out. Am taken down to gate. I say goodnight to the woman in the security office, go downstairs, walk to main gate, walk a block down to Lot A to my car. Get in. Am aching. My legs are aching all over. It takes effort to move my legs to use the clutch pedal on the floor.

I drive slowly up Lankershim. As soon as I hit the sack I am out like a light.

• • •

(Aug. 17, 1989)

Farewell, Zsa Zsa

Tuesday. Dear, sweet Zsa Zsa passed away this afternoon. 6:30 p.m. Got a call from Doc Shane. Said they were in the process of treating Zsa Zsa, nursing her back to health (complications due to diabetes) when she died. I had taken her in the other day. Zsa Zsa's eyes had gotten badly infected, etc., loss of appetite, etc., consumed excessive amounts of water.

For three weeks I had been waiting to take Zsa Zsa to the vet's, only I'd had no idea where to take her, what the address was. I kept asking Toby about it, the rare times he set foot on the premises, but Toby had a way of shrugging things off, postponing the inevitable, saying that it could wait. I phoned him at work with same fruitless results, likewise when I was able to get hold of him at his girlfriend's place in Glendora, Toby kept putting it off, stalling for some reason, not in any hurry to attend to the matter (as he had not believed it to be as serious).

"Look, Chance," Toby had said, "I need to stay focused on this New York trip I have to make in a few days. I'll contact the vet about Zsa Zsa when I get back from the East Coast."

All the while, I had attempted my best with Zsa Zsa, having to reopen her eyelids with warm water (crud build-up due to her illness), trimmed the dog's hair around both eyes, but her eyes unfortunately kept closing up on her. It had all looked pretty bad to me.

Finally, when Toby returned from N.Y. I got the vet's name and address, called for an appointment—that took a week—and drove Zsa Zsa down yesterday. I had no idea that Zsa Zsa would pass away.

They were going to take blood samples, all that. The doc had said that the Lhasa apso's liver was enlarged. Took her temperature. . . .

Well, the phone call today did it. Zsa Zsa is gone now.

Hell, upon first witnessing this dog, this overweight, hairy, low-to-the-ground Lhasa apso just about three years ago I thought she was about one of the least appealing dogs I'd ever laid eyes on. But Zsa Zsa sure had a way of growing on you. I got to care for that dog, got to love her. Always treated her fairly, gave her bones (same as the other two dogs).

So now, at nine years of age, almost 10, Zsa Zsa has bought the farm. I wonder if the other dogs will miss her.

Life, this is the way it always works. You fall for something, you love something, someone—and they always leave you.

They either walk, or they die on you. And you are left there with nothing but memories.

It did not take much to make Zsa Zsa happy: a bone, something to eat, some affection—and she was truly happy. She was a loving dog.

Farewell, Zsa Zsa, my friend. . . .

• •

Went out. Bought paper. *L.A. TIMES*, *VALLEY NEWS*. The search for work goes on. Have been with Bink at Paramour just about four weeks now. Getting used to the job, its restrictions, all that; but the problem is at $5 an hour a man working only forty hours a week cannot make it. It is tough. So I thought—(I have spoken with other guards who manage to work plenty of "O.T.") *I will work seven days a week, 12 hours a day. If I cannot make it one way, I will do it another.*

Right?

I'll work for minimum wage, I'll work eighty hours a week.

I will do what I have to to survive. I am willing and able to work. But wait, that is not good enough. I phoned in today at 3:00 p.m. (am supposed to phone in every day in order to be assigned work for the following day), to get placed, and the guy tells me: "Well, you've already put in five days and we have some other guards who need hours." I said: "*Look, my check for last week was for only a hundred dollars. I can't make it this way unless I get some real hours, unless I work O.T.*"

He tells me he knows it isn't fair, but that's the best they can do right now.

Bull!

Why are they constantly running ads in the paper that say you can work overtime? Why are they running ads that say top pay!

Why is their turnover so big? Why do employees not hang around? This is exactly why.

I had hoped to find a second job—but Bink's constant changing of my hours prevented it. What is it now? Back to the cab? The other jobs did not pan out. The guard job at emotionally troubled teens school, the limo job, the Tyler & Tyler video warehouse job—and forget all the rest. Too numerous to count.

Is it really back to the cab?

If so—fine. I will even go back to that. If I have to. So be it. I just need a chance to work and make a living. What the hell is happening to this country? What is going on? And I explained to Toby: "*Look, I'm not even looking for excuses not to work. I am not some schmuck who does not want to work—I want nothing but to work! I will work overtime every day! There it is. They won't give me the hours.*"

• • •

(Sept. 12, 1989)

Out in Malibu

Friday night's post was midnight to noon the next day. Twelve hours. Left here at 10:00 p.m.

Reached Paramour Studios by 10:30, got my work order and then set out for Malibu to find the nighttime location for *TIME TRAVELER*, way out there in Trancas Beach; took a good hour and a half. Made it to the location. They had one guard (a woman who'd been a guard for 13 years. Bless her. Give this lady a medal) by the market watching vehicles belonging to cast and crew.

My job was to go to the actual location on the beach, a house on the beach. I pulled out of the market parking lot, was back on the Pacific Coast Highway taking it north a bit to the traffic light, made a left turn and stayed on a bumpy road a ways that curved to the north and ran along the beach homes there.

Shortly, I came across more crew vehicles, meal trucks, honey-wagons, prop trucks, grip trucks, several Porsches. Since there was not much for me to do until these people wrapped and left, I merely stood around, got a plate of food when the meal truck began serving. I would get a good meal out of this. At the meal wagon I said hi to a well-known actor who had portrayed a mafioso type in a send up of East Coast mobsters.

The meal they served was good (a lot better than I can do: salmon, potatoes). They had a whole table outside loaded down with food: salads, jello, pastries, cake. I stuck with the salmon and potatoes (I did not want to overdo it and draw undue attention: Aha, there's a hungry individual; lookit him wolf that food down. Man sho is hungry.).

I stood around, not much to do, while they shot their scenes. *TIME TRAVELER* was a television show about a couple of guys who travel through time defusing various world crises and/or solving people's problems. I had never been interested in the show.

These people were collecting huge salaries and driving Porsches and I was making five dollars an hour to guard their equipment.

At around 4:00 a.m. they packed up, left. The location manager gave me my instructions: "Watch the plants, the tower," he said. And there were some other things they wanted me to watch, but the man spoke in that affected Tinseltown way—Tinseltown fakery, tone and mannerisms. It turned my stomach. I said nothing, nodded my head.

"Did you hear what I said?"

"Sure."

"I didn't hear you," he said, leaning in. I could have slugged the overfed Hollywood ninny right in the mouth. "I got it," said I.

"I hope so," said he; "that's what you're here for, to watch the studio's property." Take the studio and its property and shove it all, including yourself and the rest of you punks, I thought. The tone and attitude sickened me. I was the lowly Bink guard, he was the production manager on a successful television show. *TIME TRAVELER* sucks, I felt like saying—and all you people are doing is collecting a hefty paycheck. The show is crap, pure crap. I had written, directed and edited a film and this nothing production manager was telling me to stand guard over some artificial plants on a beachhouse porch. I sighed to myself and kept it all to myself. What's the point?

"That rowboat out there belongs to the studio," he said, then pointed at the tower (about two stories high, consisting of steel poles, a platform, with a ladder); actually this was some sort of camera set up for high angle shots. "Don't let anybody climb up there," said the production manager; "if they got hurt the studio could be sued for millions of dollars."

That would just break my heart, buddy. "Is there access to a phone?" I asked, my primary concern.

"What was that?"

"*TELEPHONE*," said I.

"The lady next door has okayed the use of her phone. You'll have to knock on her door if you need to use the phone." He pulled a business card from his billfold, wrote down a phone number. "That's my beeper number," said he; "should you need to contact me." And he handed me the card that said MCA on it, LOCATION MANAGER and his name: Bobo C. Fenoglio. And he climbed up the sand knoll toward the road. I was glad the man was out of my face. One by one, the vehicles pulled out. They were gone, and I was relieved to be alone.

There was no one in the house. It was under construction.

Fine. I parked my Dodge Colt inside the driveway, closed the gate. I stood on the porch, walked on the sand a bit. . . . Not a soul in sight, nobody else around, save for a sea gull or two now and then that flew overhead. The 50ish woman who lived next door waved to me and I waved back. She asked if I needed coffee. I thanked her; did not want any. We exchanged a couple of pleasantries, made comments about how much work and how expensive it was to film these television shows: "When all the stuff that they'd shot here would only, at the most, add up to a few minutes of screen time," said she.

I nodded. She was right. "Show biz," said I.

The woman was well-coifed, had dark blond hair.

A pleasant sort actually, and yet I merely wished to be on my own, left alone with my thoughts. In moments like this, feeling so far down, a lost cause, all the hopes and dreams I'd had over the years non-attainable had left me scarred and insecure, nervous even that I quite did not know how to behave around cheerful folks such as this woman living in the beachhouse next door.

It's best to keep to yourself. People can always pick up on how edgy and off-kilter you are; and then due to your self-consciousness you begin to appear shifty. That's all you need. Keep to yourself. It's best that way—if the loneliness doesn't eat me up, dry up my insides, as well as my brain and leave me for dead. . . .

So many people loved the ocean, being on the beach, living on the beach—and yet there I was staring at the fog out there, a thick blanket of fog, hearing, but not being able to see the water and feeling like I was near something evil and threatening.

This was limbo mixed in with fear. I'd always been afraid of the water. Being in a swimming pool and paddling around was fine—but this beach business and ocean business meant nothing to me, but gave me the feeling I was at the edge of the world and the chunk of beach property I was on would soon break off and I would end up down there in the deep murkiness of the water with all those slimy creatures down there.

I spent time in my car. When dawn broke I reached for my two peanut butter sandwiches and walked back onto the porch, lowered myself into a chair, sat there, ate my dry-as-dirt peanut butter sandwiches. Sat some more on the porch with the Bink Security jacket on; it was a bit windy out there.

"Good morning," said the lady next door from her own porch, offered coffee again. I turned it down. "Can't handle the caffeine," I explained. She smiled, nodded. "When I saw you sitting there, slumped down I thought you could use a cup of coffee."

"Thanks," said I; "but I'm okay."

The hours dragged on. The fog cleared eventually. Out there along the water several joggers appeared, ran past, one or two with dogs. I thought of Bridget, our German shepherd. Where was she now? Still alive?

Or passed away? If she were alive I wondered if she were happy at last? Had a master who treated her kindly?

At noon a young kid in one of those white-shirted A-Guard Bink uniforms relieved me.

"Good morning," said I. The kid complained about one of the supervisors—Selma Birch (who did, in fact, have a nasty attitude; I'd had run-ins with her myself). Only this morning, after logging in twelve long hours I was in no mood to listen to tales about Selma Birch. But this young guy in his early 20s went on. He had a long list of complaints concerning Selma "The Bulldyke" Birch that never let up. They all complain. All the guards you meet.

"Why not just shrug it off?" I suggest to the kid. It goes right past him. He's still complaining. "I tried shrugging it off," said he. "Only with that bitch it's impossible. She stays on your ass all the time.

She's nuts, I tell you. I came this close to punching the rotten bitch right in the mouth."

"You don't want to do that," said I, and handed him my work order. I drive off. I have a long way back now. I drive down PCH to Sunset Boulevard, I take Sunset to Sepulveda and take it on north into the Valley. At Ventura Bl., I make a right turn, all the way down to Paramour Studios. When I pull into A Lot, alight from my car and walk over to the turnstile I find it locked again. This is a new thing Bink Security is doing now; they want this gate locked on weekends. It is tough, but I am just too beat to walk around to the main gate after pulling a twelve-hour shift, and driving for nearly an hour and a half I am too tired to walk the distance, to move.

I climb over the twelve-foot chain-link fence. Clock in.

Turn in my work sheet. I walk back out, climb over the fence again—and this is a tricky proposition, as the top of the fence has barbed-wire on it—one slip and there go the Bink Security trousers, or worse—the family jewels. I make it down the other side intact. Am back inside my Dodge Colt, make it to the house on Wixom Street in thirty minutes. Only it is after 2:00 p.m. now.

Too tired to sleep. What gives? I need sleep, but am too tired to fall asleep. I should have been in the sack by 7:00 a.m. My body clock is out of kilter. This is the way it goes. I know I must get some rest if I intend to stay awake for Saturday night's shift out at BUTCHER HOUSE FLATS. Finally, I manage to doze off and sleep for six hours.

I spent the night at the Butcher Mansion; yes, the motel and Butcher home on the Paramour lot. Did it get spooky out there?

Yes, it did. Coyotes screamed, dogs barked the entire night.

I sat in a white limo part of the time (this limo and other vehicles were part of a television show I had been left to guard); part of the time I spent in the makeup trailer while the coyotes cried and howled out there. I walked the grounds with my flashlight, checked out the Butcher Motel, just a shell, nothing more (a fake front); same for the house—this spooky old house that had scared the hell out of so many movie audiences over the years—no floors, no rooms, no cellar—just a shell. That's what was inside—but spooky as well. Was relieved to get the hell away from the post when

6:00 a.m. rolled around. No one out there but me and the scavenging coyotes.

• • •

(Sept. 24, 1989)

20 Years Later: Wondering What Happened?

Saturday. 9:35 p.m. Rain last couple of days. Cold.

Scrounged up enough change to buy a cheap pack of cigars ($1.19).

Sitting here smoking up a chimney, thinking—thinking about it all. The past. Going over it, as usual. Wondering, well, maybe if I had taken a different road here, a different road there, you know? Wondering, could it have worked out any different?

Thinking about the two or three different women I'd known in my life; if I had settled down, married, had a family—if things would have turned out better? Just wondering.

Smoking my cigars. Working on my fourth.

Had a couple of hot dogs.

Chubby Elston called to let me know that he had just spent four days in Phoenix with our old buddy from film school Dale Smith. "I have a copy of that horror script Dale's written, with penciled-in corrections," said Chubby Elston. "I'll be sending it off to you." Then I heard him clear his throat.

"The other reason I'm calling," said Chubby, "money's been tight. It may be a week before I can send you anything."

Well, I understood that. Hard times hitting all.

"That's okay, Chubby," said I. "Thanks for trying."

We say goodbye, hang up.

And I'm wondering why I can't even sell one damn book. Like I said—just wondering. Lack of money has me chained to this damn place. Inactivity.

And I can recall being in the army, 19 years old, eager to get the hell out and start living my life, eager, couldn't wait to get out and conquer the world! Man, I was going to do some things!

That was me! I WAS REALLY GOING TO ACCOMPLISH A LOT! ALL OF IT! DO IT RIGHT. AND EVEN FALL IN LOVE WITH A GOOD-HEARTED WOMAN AND MARRY, HAVE KIDS. ALL OF IT.

I was going to do it. Yes, I was. Going to make my dreams happen.

So here I am—twenty years later—*wondering what happened*.

39th birthday a month and a half away. Twenty years of writing.

And not a dime ahead. Nothing going. Nothing doing. No wife, no kids. No gas in the tank.

Hell, not feeling sorry for myself—*just doing my best to face the face in the mirror, you know*? Just doing my best to face it, the truth, the way it finally turned out for me.

Wondering if I ought to return to Chicago? Yes, the cold is there. Mr. Hawk. But L.A. is a far colder place.

In spite of it all—I still am attached to my typewriter, to the written word—to books.

Can't be helped.

So how then could any of it have turned out any other way? Somehow, even back then when I was 16, always, ALWAYS DID SUSPECT it would be hard, so very hard to get anywhere. My destiny. A bumpy road. Man. But it sure is bumpy for so many others out there as well. Not just writers, my man, not only for writers, for typewriter pounders—but for so many others.

9:48 p.m.

Lately am just writing out of sheer loneliness, doing my best to beat it, deal with it. No one really to talk to. Lately spending very little time in the living room. Most of my time spent in this bedroom pacing, pacing—familiar territory. Pacing the dark corridors of my mind.

What else.

TV bores. No concentration to read anything. Need to get back to that. Reading. Books. Good prose.

I keep thinking: One of these days, one day I will put it all together. It will come together somehow. And a year ago the fortune in my fortune cookie said:

> YOU ARE ENTERING A TIME OF GREAT
> PROMISE AND OVERDUE REWARDS

Right. A joke. But that's what it said. And I had it taped to the lampshade on my makeshift table in front of me.

Just tore it off. Tossed it in the trash basket.

• • •

(Feb. 17, 1990)

Whatsa Matter, Huh?

It was a typical East Hollywood bar full of cigarette smoke and stench and lowlifes not going anywhere and not giving a damn. Roy Purdy took another look at the drunks, the junkies, the pimps—losers all of them, and it made him sick. He didn't belong here. He shouldn't have been here.

He didn't want to be here. Mary and the kids is where he wanted to be. Forty-five years old he was, a grown man, moderately successful, and he was mixing it up with the scum, losers.

He felt like throwing up. His skull ached. After a moment, he picked up the glass with the whiskey in it and shoved it down his throat. The liquid ripped away at his insides. Poison, that's what it was. He was killing himself with the poison. He clenched his jaw. The pain was ripping away at him again. The goddamn pain. His head weighed a ton. Goddamn her, Roy thought, goddamn that woman, and he shut his eyes and fought it, but there was no winning, the tears slowly made their way out into the open and rolled down his face.

"Dammit," Roy sighed. "Dammit. . . . "

The young bartender walked over and asked if everything was all right. Roy nodded, and asked for another double.

The bartender supplied the double and just stood there.

"T' hell you looking at?" Roy said. "I told you—I'm fine."

The bartender shrugged and walked to the other end of the bar.

Like hell you're fine, Roy thought. You've been in this shithole over three hours now. *Three hours*. Go to your room, get the hell away from this sewer. His hand reached out toward the glass, brought it up to his mouth and down the poison went, burning his guts up, tearing away, killing the pain—only it wasn't killing *the pain*.

Roy wiped his mouth with the back of his hand and grunted for another.

"I think you've had enough, mister."

"Make it a beer then?"

The bartender shook his head.

"Come on, just a beer? A lousy beer?"

Pausing, the bartender shrugged, and brought one over.

"It's your funeral," he said.

Roy took a good gulp and banged the bottle down against the bar.

"How old are you, kid?"

"26."

"Ever been married?"

The bartender shook his head.

"Don't ever do it, kid. Don't be a sucker."

The bartender didn't say anything.

Roy swallowed beer. "Been married ten years," he said. "Ten years. Never fooled around—no young filly on the side—ever. I got two of the most gorgeous kids you ever saw." He took his wallet out. There was a picture of a boy and a girl. "Tommy's the youngest, you see? He's 6—and Jenny's almost 8. Almost 8. . . . " More teardrops formed and rolled and landed on the countertop. He wiped them away and stuck the wallet back in his jacket.

"Bright kids . . . both of them." He pulled on the bottle.

"Don't get to see them much these days. The wife's got them, you see? She's got them. I'd like to get my hands on the asshole who put the law together." He emptied the bottle and motioned for one more. The bartender came up with another bottle. "Thanks," Roy said. He took a pull. "She got the house, the car, the business, the kids . . . goddamn her." He had another pull. "And if that wasn't enough—I don't get to see the kids unless it's convenient for her. Is that fair? You think that's fair? You think that's right?" The bottle was raised again. "Hell no, it's not right. But she's doing it. Goddamn bitch is doing it and getting away with it too! Hell yes, she gets away with it! The hell am I supposed to do now? We had a nice house, yard, garden . . . I got shit now. It's gone, all of it. Gone. . . . I'm staying in a fleabag, one lousy room. You ever stayed in a fleabag, kid? Huh? Know who I talk to in that fleabag, huh kid? I talk to the roaches. To the goddamn roaches! See what that bitch has reduced me to? 45 years old—I got shit! SHIT! From a family to no family—TO SHIT! Why I'm hanging around in this stinkhole—only fucking reason." Then he shook his head. "Hell, in the old days you'd never, I mean *never* find Roy Purdy in a stinkhole like this. NEVER! And here I am, day after day—month after month—no better than the trash—I'm no better. You still got your health, my attorney says to me. You got your health, Roy—and you do get to see the kids now and then. They love you, Roy. You know that. They care about you. Nothing will ever change that. Start another business. You can do it. Your credit's good. You got friends who'd do anything to help. You even got some money in the bank—take a cruise—live a little. He said that to me over a year ago, my attorney did. Over a fucking year ago. He don't know what it's like. None of them do. They look at you and smile their sad smiles—but they don't know. THEY DON'T KNOW!" Roy emptied the bottle and requested another.

"I'm sorry," the bartender said, "I think you've really had enough. I'm sorry." And he left to tend to another customer.

There's only one thing to do, Roy thought. Only one thing. . . .

I can't go on like this. I can't. I want my life to be the way it was, the way it was before that bitch ruined everything, before she took my kids away. She'd like to see me die, well maybe I'll accommodate her. Maybe I will. . . . I wasn't good enough for her, the witch. She didn't need me, she said. Too domineering, Roy. I can't live like this. I have to live my own life.

I gave her everything. Everything. And this is my thanks. I'll end it, he thought. I'll fucking end it. See how she feels when I'm gone. See what she does then. I'll drink myself to death. I'll do it. She wanted the kids—well, she's got them.

They're hers. They never loved me, none of them ever loved me.

They never needed me like I needed them. I was used. They used me. We'll see who has the last laugh, we'll see. . . .

And the tears came on stronger than ever and Roy got weaker and weaker and his head just kind of lowered itself against the counter and he sobbed in great big sobs. Oh God, he thought, what am I going to do? Dear Lord, what am I going to do? I don't want to kill myself . . . I don't want to die. What will my kids think?

What will they think . . . ?

And after a while, a voice from behind said, "Whatsa matter, pal?"

Roy Purdy wiped his face and gradually raised and turned his head. His eyes blinked nervously and he couldn't be sure what he was seeing. He was looking at a man in a wheelchair. It was obvious the man was an adult but he was only 30 inches tall; the head was normal size, but that was all. The bespectacled face staring up at him rested on a diminutive torso, short arms and legs that would have looked more appropriate on a child's rag doll. The man worked a lever on his armrest with a toddler's hand and his seat rose to about Roy Purdy's belly, and the man in it said, "Whatsa matter, huh?"

• • •

A Piece of Advice

"I wanna fuck him up," Sonny Charnofski said; "cut his nuts off; something like that; know what I mean?"

"Yeah, I know what you mean, kid," the older guy said, and called the bartender over for another beer.

"*I'm serious, man. I wanna kill the bastard.* He fucked Millie, man. *He fucked her.* I can't live with it. I can't let him get away with it."

"Right, kid," Charlie Gripp said, and poured beer down his throat.

Sonny Charnofski ordered Jack Daniels with beer chaser. He drank it down, winced, and sighed, "Shit"; shaking his head.

"Goddamn, that's powerful stuff," he said. After he'd recovered, he got the Camels out, offered one to the old man; lit them both. "You ever had it happen to you?"

The older guy inhaled, nodded.

"What you do?"

"Nothin' . . . "

"*Nothin'*?"

Charlie Gripp drank his beer. The kid continued to shake his head. "*Nothin'. No fucking way I'm gonna do nothin'.* Man puts the meat to my old lady he's gotta pay, all there is to it. I wanna put him in the hospital, fuck him up bad. Maybe not kill him—fuck him up bad, though. Break his bones, cut his motherfucking dick off—see how he likes that. Let the cocksucker try an' fuck somebody's old lady without a dick."

"You ever do some steppin' out on the old gal?"

"Who me? Huh-uh. *Never. Not once.*"

Charlie Gripp looked at him good and long.

"Not one fucking time, man. *Never.*"

"You a rare one then. Most men I know, that's all they know. Nail anything that moves—an' when they catch the old lady at it—they go nuts, start screamin' about how they gonna kill her or the sumbitch that put it to her."

"You sayin' I ain't right? I'm wrong? No fucking way I'm wrong."

"Ever ask yourself why she let it happen? Huh, kid? Ever ask that?"

"How the hell should I know why? She was sweet-talked—the cocksucker's good at it. Hell, this ain't the first time he's been caught fuckin' a married woman."

"How about this—ever give her the kind of attention she needed? Huh, kid? You think about that? Were you always there when she needed you? You take care of her?"

"I ain't got no hangups, if that's what you're talkin' about. Hell, I gave it to her whenever she wanted it. Three, four times a night sometimes. Shit—that wasn't our problem. An' I ain't braggin', but I ain't small, no premature ejaculation, whatever the hell they call it, nothin' like that. Nope. I got control, always have. Know what I mean?"

"Maybe that ain't what I'm talkin' about . . . "

"What then?"

"How about other things, kid? Flowers and stuff. . . . Women like that, you know. Hell, who don't? A gift now and then, stuff like that. They like a pretty dress now and then, dine out now and then . . . "

"Well . . . I couldn't. It takes money to do all that. Don't it?"

The older guy nodded. "It sho do . . . "

"So what's a man to do? Hell, we had a hard enough time just makin' the bills . . . "

"Neglect, kid. That's what it's called. And you're just as guilty of it as I was. Just like all of us. An' when they leave us we go on actin' like we don't know why it happened."

"Maybe you're right, maybe you are. I'm still gonna get this motherfucker. . . . An' if I gotta blow my own brains out . . . that's O.K. by me, man. It's O.K. . . . " And he turned away, pressing a thumb and index finger into his eyes, then slowly took them away.

Tears rolled down his face. "I need her. I . . . "

"I know it hurts, kid. I know it . . . surely do. But you best forget about doin' anything stupid. Not only will you end up in the can for it—but if she's got any feelings toward you now—she won't if you go out and do somethin' stupid. She'll despise you the rest of your life—and it's somethin' you won't be able to live with . . . even if you don't end up killin' the sumbitch, even if you don't end up gettin' the chair . . . it'll eat away at you, this woman that once loved you . . . hating your guts, not wanting to have anything to do with you . . . even after ten, fifteen, twenty years . . . still not wanting anything to do with you. . . . "

Sonny Charnofski looked at him and didn't say anything.

The old guy turned away, pulled on his bottle, then set it down.

He stared straight ahead, his eyes hollow and glazed.

"That's right, kid. You may not think you'll want her after what's happened, you may not be able to deal with it now . . . but if what you had was real . . . you'll get another chance. But if you go out there and do somethin' to this poor bastard, or if you lay a hand on her, you might as well hang it up . . . she won't want anything to do with you. *Ever.*"

Sonny Charnofski wiped his eyes. Charlie Gripp took a slow pull at his bottle, ran the back of his hand across his mouth.

"I didn't kill him," he said. "Came mighty close . . . he lived . . . he's a cripple now . . . but he didn't die . . . "

"She marry again?"

"No . . . she never married . . . an old maid . . . she don't want nothin' to do with me . . . " After a while, still looking away, the old guy added: " . . . even after all these years, she don't want nothin' to do with me . . . " And he choked on something in his throat, suppressed it with a convenient cough just then whatever it was that had attempted to surface, then Charlie Gripp carefully rose from his stool and proceeded to walk outside into the East Hollywood night.

• • •

I like my reasoning better.

you know the ones I really give a damn about?
the Sextons, the Hemingways, the Lowrys, the Mishimas, the Kerouacs—
all those suicide jockeys; they had the guts to end it, they had
the guts to put a stop to it, the bullshit, the games; they had
the answers finally in their mad states and were tired of the con.
the sane ones will shake their heads and say
something profound like: "They were crazy and couldn't cope with
life."
I like my reasoning better.

BARS

lonely people
struggling for relief,
respite,
struggling,
smiling (trying) looking for friends in
crowded bars;

lonely, lost people
searching for love
something true
something to hold onto.
the path to love
is a winding one,
and even then
how can you be sure?
how do you know what awaits you?

and should you get lucky

pray to god that you are not so battered and weary
and without life
that you should scare love away;
sadly, this is what bars do to one's soul.

another scream from hell

LOVE WAS THE CROSS
i did not know what horror was
until i met up with love

blood and carnage left me in limbo
love put me on the stretching table
love yanked my guts out and wrapped them
around my neck and choked the breath out of me!
love nailed, hammered a stake into my soft skull

love did this, and more
love, sometimes called AMOUR, a fancy term for
incredible pain.

fairytales

I used to think: I'm not getting anywhere;
the written word has backfired on me; the love I've had for
books, and all the respect has not done me a bit of good.
36 now and look around and see men my age with families,
with kids, a wife, a sense of belonging.

I used to think, when I was much younger, it's o.k.,
they can have theirs now: love, money, the good car &
all the rest—I'll get some of it later, maybe not all of it,
but at least some kind of decent family life, something I'd
never had.
I used to think like that. I'll work now, and
work real hard and it will pay off later on.
I will give it my youth and it will be fine
later on. A writer has to put in the time to learn his
craft. A doctor does not become a doctor overnight. I spent
the years in tiny rooms, first in Chicago and then later in
L.A., just barely existing and not really minding it, be-
lieving someday it would all change.
You pay your dues and things work out.
You won't always appear to be a bum, you won't
always be driving a hack and making just enough to cover the
rent and groceries and a new tire for the bicycle now and then,
and someday you'll even have enough money to
date (and who knows, find a mate? a woman to be with) someday
. . .
I used to think: that's all right. I will be
patient; it will happen and I won't be thought of as a bum;
women won't be embarrassed to go out with me because of the
way I live.
I used to think this way years ago
when I was green and naive.
And when you're 36 you realize it's time to stop playing

games with yourself,
time to stop telling yourself lies.
Writers and/or poets make it or they don't make it. And if
they don't make it a writer is just another word for BUM. What
          kind of life do you hope to have now, brother, at
36? What's left? Can you go on?
          What kind of fairytales do you tell yourself now?

the sidewalk is waiting

the sidewalk is waiting, keeps getting closer and closer.
I keep trying to push it away—but the goddamn gray concrete is
persistent, can't do a damn thing about it—there it is!
maybe a stretch of dirty cement not far from the New Otani Hotel,
maybe a space near Little Tokyo, maybe a stretch in front of
the Greyhound Depot, maybe a cardboard box close to the
Mission—the Skid Row Mission.

only stay out of alleys and doorways. remember how
often you saw winos being rolled by other winos late at night,
how often you saw, unable to do much about it, as you cruised
the streets of downtown in your cab?

stay out of alleys, out of doorways, stay alert, if you
care, maybe you don't—people who end up down on the row,
ON THE NICKEL, I don't suppose are going to worry about that—
not much to lose—that would be the least of your worries.

the sidewalk is there waiting for you, pal . . . and it keeps
getting closer and closer. the only way I know how to prepare for it
is to make sure that all my important manuscripts are in my one
suitcase—and as far as what happens to my book library, well,
that's not as important as the manuscripts, the poetry, the stories—
just have that stuff packed and ready in case the sidewalk
turns out to be a lot closer than you figured.
—thoughts on this December 6, 1988 Tuesday at 9:59 A.M.

for Sylvia

well, here we are (you and I) and nobody else. it's 2:10 in the AM and just can't sleep. am thinking about Sylvia Plath and wondering if she had similar thoughts about someone else or if she ever wondered who would (if anyone) feel empty and sad once she took her life?

did she ever go over it in her head? did any of this occur to her? that people would miss her? mourn her suicide? people, total strangers would feel saddened and cheated at not having ever met her, at not having been able to help her?

but, Jesus, am 36 now; where the hell was I when she took her life? how old was I?

and how old were you when I took my life?

did I ever consider what your thoughts and feelings would be on the subject when suicide entered my mind? well, now you can say that I did.

but you couldn't help me anymore than I could help Sylvia Plath, you see?

Life's A Bitch,
Then You Die

spent seven backbreaking hours
cleaning other people's homes;
mopped floors, vacuumed carpets,
cleaned mirrors, windows, picked up
lint, dusted expensive furniture,
cleaned shower doors.

for $35.00

while ten novels sit in my drawer
collecting dust,
ten novels, stacks of poetry,
short stories, plays, movie scripts —

35 bucks.

my 39th birthday is five months away.

(10:20 pm Nov. 22, '89)

A Poem For Christine M.

You lived two blocks over and every chance I
got I'd ride down your street, past your building on a
borrowed bicycle hoping that I might
catch a glimpse of you. It wasn't often that I would
see you—now and then walking home after
school with your younger sister, usually with
your best friend Roberta.
There you were
this particular afternoon in front of your stoop
with your friend. I was across the street, too nervous
to approach you; perhaps if you had been alone . . .
PERHAPS . . .
and what would I have said?
My English was STILTED at best; I was HARDLY ELOQUENT
to make an impression, hardly knew enough
to give me courage to walk up and say anything . . . when
it
took all the GUTS I could muster
to STEAL a QUICK LOOK
or two as it was.
All those times, those months and (eventually)
years WONDERING WHAT YOU THOUGHT OF ME,
if anything . . .

I paused and PRETENDED to be checking my front tire
for something. What was I doing? Checking the tire
pressure? Who knew? That's when you spotted
your dad walking up the sidewalk, coming home after a
day of work . . .
Your FACE, Christine, LIT UP like a
HUNDRED WATT BULB. It was incredible. What was this
MAGIC FORMULA your father POSSESSED
that brought such JOY and EXUBERANCE to your BEING—and

was there any way at all that I might get my hands on
just a smidgen of it?
I stood there, TAKING IT IN. There was
a DEEP ACHE in me even at that young age, there was no
denying it.
You were all I could think of. I was PRE-
OCCUPIED with thoughts of you night and day, racked my
11/12 year-old mind how to get you to show interest
in me.
I did not have the words, nor the way. The X-Mas
cards, get well card (when you returned to school
from summer break that time with your leg in a
cast), Valentine's Day card during Miss Kessler's
math class we were both in (unable to overcome
my damn SHYNESS and hand the card to you myself, instead
I had pleaded with your sister standing in the
hallway outside our classroom door to hand it to
YOU for ME)
and the CARD had been
INTERCEPTED by the TEACHER, whereby she conceived
of that GAME/CONTEST in her effort to bring a couple
of bashful kids together: it was down to my CHOOSING
either YOU or HOMELY SARA (all the other kids
had been picked at this point and were STANDING
AT THE BLACKBOARD; YOU and Sara sat in your seats among an
otherwise SEA OF EMPTY DESKS . . .) and I recall STANDING
there
AT THE TEACHER'S DESK
feeling uncomfortable, ON THE SPOT, in a
NO-WIN situation; there was nothing I could do that
would be THE RIGHT CHOICE. Finally, I did not
have the heart to pick you over Sara; I could not select you
(SOMEONE SO PERFECT IN MY EYES IN EVERY WAY)
over someone as PLAIN as Sara. I felt compassion
standing there in the SECONDS I had to DECIDE
and when I CHOSE HER I knew I did not endear myself
to you (nor Miss Kessler, disappointed Miss Kessler, who

meant well . . .) My good deed, one I was BOTH PROUD
of DEEP INSIDE and in AGONY over at having EMBARRASSED
you as well in FRONT OF THE LOT OF THEM,
that did not get me any closer to you.
I thought, felt,
surely you would soon UNDERSTAND, surely you could tell what
I was doing, the situation I had been stuck in.
Spending my afternoons at the neighborhood public library
after school as often as I could and trying to read Dr. Seuss
(I liked his funny tales) simply because I knew YOU WOULD
BE THERE (even though you and Roberta were always
preoccupied: talking or giggling about something).
I wondered if you were aware of my existence. How
BADLY had I EMBARRASSED YOU in class that
Valentine's Day? How could I ever explain PROPERLY why I
did
what I did? I thought, believed you'd be able
TO TAKE not being chosen by me a lot better than a
girl who did not have your golden hair, who did not have
much going at all . . .
I was convinced, all those times
in the public library as I pretended to be reading the
books before me if I CONCENTRATED hard enough, thought
about nothing else but YOU, how I felt, how much I
WISHED TO BE SITTING BESIDE YOU . . .
but that never got me
anywhere either. (So much for telepathy.)
And here was your dad,
with the Midas Touch. How did he do it? By virtue of being
your dad? Was that all it took? I wished it was I
with the ability to bring such happiness to you.

You RAN down the sidewalk toward your father. Your
father wore a suit, white shirt, tie; (he may have been
carrying a leather brief case, I couldn't
be sure —) but the rest I see so clearly
in my head . . .

sitting alone in this room this quiet X-Mas Eve
nearly thirty years later . . .
you doing a MAD DASH toward HIM, arms REACHING OUT,
your BRIGHT BLOND PONYTAIL swinging from SIDE to SIDE . . .
your father with the big smile on his face, so
happy to see you —
you LEAPT UP hard enough to
wrap your arms about his neck, letting your body
dangle loosely this way to your father's surprise and utter
DELIGHT. He paused to give your waist a SQUEEZE, KISS YOU
BACK, then prior to taking another step,
saw to it that his arms were bound around you
to make sure you did not accidentally fall off
as he SPUN you around.

I recall GAZING (more like a
series of STOLEN GLANCES) and not being able to
ignore the PANGS of JEALOUSY and LONGING that surged through
ME and WISHING, secretly, that was me you had
your arms locked around,
ME your FACE was SO CLOSE TO and SMOTHERING
with KISSES;
wishing it was I who could bring such unbridled
JOY to your big blue eyes and freckled face.

And then a fortnight later
while with my folks and baby sister
visiting someone the old man knew from work, a
cabinet maker named Anton and his family (German im-
migrants, like your parents, who lived on
your street, same block) I discovered to my
shock and amazement, that my other sisters "Emina"
and "Jemila" were spending time with you at your
place across the street. (They must have met you
through Anton's daughter, I didn't know exactly).
It was evening, getting on, and the folks were
ready to leave, only someone was

NEEDED to go fetch my sisters first. And there I was up on my feet volunteering to run over to where you lived to go get them.

What an unbelievable break, I thought. I had this rare chance to go to your residence with a PERFECTLY GOOD REASON—

I'd get to see you, at least; an opportunity to get close enough and say: HI, Christine . . .

I crossed the street. Breaking out in a cold sweat, and with SHAKY HAND, I knocked on your door—

and who should answer but you.

Your eyes WIDENED, and your JAW DROPPED as you FAKED/EXAGGERATED losing consciousness; your mouth AGAPE, seeing me, you appeared stunned, fell back comically to the floor as you shut the door in my face, but not before I'd been able to let you know the reason I was there: to pick up my sisters. You might have been shocked to know we were, in fact, related. You probably had no idea.

I stood there, waiting. Soon, your mother appeared at the door, big blond hausfrau. I repeated what it was I was doing there. She walked off inside the apartment to let my sisters know.

Walking my siblings back to Anton's I could not contain the feeling of having been LET DOWN by Emina. How could she have kept KNOWING YOU FROM ME? She must have been aware how smitten with you I was, and yet had made no effort to HELP ME OUT in this area, hadn't so much as mentioned knowing you at all. She had actually been INSIDE YOUR HOME, played with you, spent time with you, where you lived.

The younger sister I didn't bother with because she
was too young to discuss it with. HOW COULD THIS HAVE
HAPPENED?
"I hardly know her," said Emina.
I don't think
I ever forgave her. If I ever favored one of her girlfriends
she never, or at least seldom, made the effort to help
me out.

Our families moved to different parts of the
city, we attended different schools and lost contact. We lived
on the North Side and I went to Senn
High. Got a job at Del Farm stocking shelves
and bagging groceries. Years went by. Things were far
from pleasant at home. Turned 18, said hi to Uncle
Sam, who, in turn, shipped me to Uncle Ho's killer booby-
traps, triple-thick canopy jungles and polluted rice
paddies. Somehow, not sure how, finished off my tour with
limbs intact, about all that was intact;
subsequently had my heart stepped on
by a blond in Abilene, Kan.
(won't even go into the other one later here in
LA LA that nearly crushed me out of existence,
nearly put me in the ground
way before my time.)
Finished out my two years and left with an HON-
ORABLE (only there hadn't been anything HONORABLE about
any of it). Returned to Chicago. Always HOPED
I'd see you again, run into you sometime . . .
Later in life, over the years,
all those years, it became quite clear to me
nearly every woman I was interested in/drawn to
RESEMBLED YOU.
First CRUSH true CRUSH
LEAVES THE DEEPEST IMPRINT.
The last time I saw you
you were a full-grown woman, filled out

all over: TOP and BOTTOM.
What a BEAUTY you turned out—
but I wasn't surprised—you always
had been in my eyes.
Stayed with my two
sisters, didn't want to, had no choice,
for a while, there in New Town (right after my discharge).
I had that blue (used) Fiat convertible by
then purchased with money I had
saved up while in the Nam boonies;
bought it in Junction City, Kan.,
for $1,400 (from a used car dealer
who had been asking $2,300). Surely,
I thought, I got a deal. I was wrong, because
it was Fix-It-Again-Tony, and again and
again. It was by far the worst lemon
I ever had.
But it was pretty. Ditsy women are drawn
to pretty cars (that wasn't why I bought it; however,
that was the reason I got rid of it eventually).
That day we drove to a beach, possibly Foster,
on the north side of town, my two sisters
and I, circa '72.
I was 20 then. We spread our blanket
out, had the sun screen out. It was a bright sunny day.
When I looked up I must have thought I was seeing
a mirage, my eyes must have been playing tricks on me,
because there you were, walking
up. Towards us.
Christine? I recall saying to myself.
Can it be? After all these years? I hadn't seen you
since I was 13 or 14; anyway, enough years
had gone by — and now, someone, a blond (who
strongly resembled you) in a one-piece swimsuit
with blue and yellow flower patterns
was on this beach
approaching us.

I sat up and stared, couldn't help it. Was it
you? Where had you been all this time?
Were you finally
going to say something to me? Say hello? Ask how was I? What
have I been up to? Thank me for the
Valentine's Day
card (and other cards?)
How did you recognize me? Know where to find me
on this beach, Christine? Will you sit down
and have a chat? Have you thought of
me as much and as often as I had of you?
No one could touch you, Christine. You must
have known
how it was I felt all those
years and were finally coming to share
these thoughts with me . . .
or was I entirely wrong? Were you simply coming over
to see my sisters?
I had no way of knowing...
kept hoping that you would keep walking
our way.
"Look," I said to my sister Emina, not able to take my
eyes off of you, "it's Christine. She's
coming this way. My God . . ."
My sister never bothered to look up, she was pre-
occupied applying the sun screen to her arms and shoulders.
"*It's Christine*," I underlined again. "*Mina* — "
My sister looked up briefly, said nothing. What was going
on here?
I always suspected she didn't think I was good
enough for her friends.
What the hell was this? Some kind of screwie (uncalled
for) jealousy? I had attended the same classes with you
as a kid, I'd known you first,
I had been the one with the UNBEARABLE/
INCREDIBLE crush
on you.

I made no comment, waited with baited
breath, truly —
my breath was BAITED; I had trouble
breathing. You continued to approach us. Then when you were
within 30 to 35 feet, you STOPPED, TURNED AROUND,
and WALKED BACK, walked away . . .
I didn't get it. Couldn't
understand it.
WHY?
CHRISTINE?
I watched, STUNNED, as you disappeared towards the rock
wall, walked up the cement steps to the parking lot
and were GONE.
I never saw you again.

CHRISTINE? You couldn't even say hello? Christine?

Eventually my sisters found their own
place up around Bryn Mawr. It was just as well. The room
on Wellington had been too small, way too small for
the three of us. And can't say as I cared for the
creeps they dated, hadn't cared for the way they
relished
dissing the nicer guys they saw on
occasion. They enjoyed bad-mouthing these poor
bastards who had gone out of their way to show them a good
time, spent their hard-earned money
to take them out;
they dissed them, gossiped late into the night,
every night —
no different from all the bad experiences I'd had
with females of like nature.

Shortly after that
I tossed my few belongings into
the back seat of the
Fiat (mostly books) and headed West,

to L.A. — and that nightmare.

Never to see you again.

I never got the chance to explain I nodded in Sara's
direction in Miss Kessler's class that time
because she didn't have
your looks, I settled on her because she was un-
assuming and I felt a need to act in a kind way,
but in doing "the right thing"
I must have hurt
your feelings as well; this was something I
realized even back then in that classroom:
I just did not know how to get out of the dilemma
Miss Kessler, well-meaning Miss Kessler, had put me in;
that
sweet old maid of a woman's well-intentioned ploy
to bring
a quiet boy and girl together that
Valentine's Day
had backfired on her so miserably and left us
feeling
befuddled and embarrassed. I wished I could have
crawled under her desk, prayed you understood,
that some day
you would, how awful it was this 6th grader felt. You
walked out of my life and I never had that chance—no
hellos, no goodbys
were ever exchanged.
Never saw you again.
And what would any of this mean
lo these many years later? Why even bother to think about
it? Wish I had a better answer
then: certain memories stay with you no matter where
you end up or how old you happen to be. You were in my
sphere/life for such a relatively short period . . .
and yet

cast such a LONG SHADOW. There's no explaining it, other
then to say that FIRST CRUSH (everlasting crush)
LEAVES THE DEEPEST
OF IMPRINTS ON THE MIND.
I must have spent my life
searching for your equivalent (and not ever coming close).
It is my conclusion
in the end we get to own nothing of
value
other than
the occasional (cherished) memory
and (occasional)
dream . . .
(I have doubts even they belong to us.)

Here I sit reminiscing hopelessly about such
(ADMITTEDLY HOPELESS) things
this X-Mas Eve downing a beer, in this room (not
mine)
in a house (not mine)
with hardly enough space for the king-size bed
and large dresser (once belonging to my friend Toby's
since departed father, who stares down at me
from a large framed portrait on the wall above);
my un-
published manuscripts in cardboard boxes—all that I own and
care about (of my few possessions) with a wooden plank placed
across two stacks of these boxes for a "table"—
my makeshift table, truly,
that my
Olivetti sits on, against the wall . . .
thinking of you.
Professional transient is what I feel like lately (&
is EXACTLY what I am). Getting late here now (could be
later than I dare to know), my beer bottle
empty, and it's quiet. My friend Toby in another part of
town for the holidays with his girlfriend and her TRIO of

TEEN TERRORS. The only SOUND I hear is Toby's tiny
Boston terrier SNORING in the other room (she sleeps on the
carpet and the RHYTHMIC snoring sounds RESONATE) and the
CLACK CLACK sounds of this typewriter
as I TAP the KEYS
wondering what you look like these days, what you're like
as an adult: your interests and opinions . . . all of it,
Christine, all of it . . . but I had such an impossible CRUSH
on you, my God . . . had I a photo, yours is the one
I would have carried in my wallet through the swamps
of Nam and everywhere else throughout the years
wherever I went . . .
I wonder what your life has
been like . . . I think of you . . . close to three decades later . . .
I wonder about you . . . the FIRST GIRL
I'd fallen so hard
for
and were the REASON I had started PARTING MY HAIR
EVER SO CAREFULLY each morning as I set out for school,
Newberry Grade School, hoping one day you'd notice me,
walk over and say hello, hoping you'd reach out to
hold my hand . . .
What I wouldn't have given
to have you run up and throw yourself
at me
the way you liked to
RUN UP AND THROW YOURSELF
AT YOUR FATHER —
a man I envied
more than any
man alive.

Merry X-Mas, Christine.
This one is for you.

(Dec. 25, 1989)

VvG

walking down that yellow brick path
of Vincent's
and wondering, cannot help it, just how much
blood went into painting those pretty red flowers.

(Dec. 25, 1989)

another one for Vincent vG.

tacked up your calendar
up on my wall
above my typewriter
open to the month of January
1990
A Group of Cottages 1890, Vincent;
Oil on canvas 61 x 73 cm.

you put your heart and guts into it
one hundred years ago
fighting loneliness and despair
here it is 1990

and nothing ever changes much, Dearest Vincent.

(Dec. 25, 1989)

Don't Panic

The notice said.
The multi-millionaire owner of the apartment building
was raising the rent from 375 to FIVE HUNDRED;
but DON'T PANIC the letter said,
we're doing it to all the other tenants as well
and city hall has approved it because of all that money we had to
spend on Seizmick Proofing and all that.

A year & a ½ ago the rent was 350—now they want FIVE HUNDRED,
plus I got to pay the electric.

DON'T PANIC
the cold-blooded MONEY GRUBBING LEECHES
are telling me, it's not so bad —

How would you muthers know about that?
I'm down to 20 bucks and 39 cents, muthers!

And all you can say is DON'T PANIC.
Are you people trying to be funny? Try eating macaroni
& cheese for two months and an occasional carrot for dessert, try
eating rice every day, maybe an apple for dessert, if you're lucky.

DON'T PANIC, you say?

Just tell me this—when will your bellies be full enough, when will
your wallets be fat enough before you stop jacking up the rent?
When will you be satisfied? When will you have enough? or is that
a rhetorical question? Perhaps there is no limit to greed (as it
goes on and on) like a festering sore, like a bottomless pit—all
the money, all the riches in the world would not be enough. Do
you go on being this way until the ground swallows you up?
How do people like you ever become like this?

DON'T PANIC, you say?

Well, I'm looking at my 20 dollars and 39 cents . . .

I'll *try* not to panic, is my best response to that.

lonely days

sometimes the need to hear a woman's voice, to hear a voice,
someone to talk to, someone to hold, to feel human warmth
and you've gone so long without it, so many years, now nine years
without love, without it, all those years, and you don't
know how to go about reaching out for it, are convinced it was
never there, but that need creeps up on you and you can't
do much about it, can't deny it, can't ignore it . . .
it brings on the blues . . .
and you find yourself trying to hold conversations with the
Boston terrier—
lonely days . . . on Wixom Street in North Hollywood.

Surface Kind of Love

surface kind of love
here today gone tomorrow
        it never lasts
            seldom makes the home stretch
no one loves all the way anymore
   they don't know how.

Soulmate

i dream of you
of your smile
of your heart
that is so kind

i dream of you
night and day

and i know
alas, i know
that you will
never know
about me at all

we will
never meet.

We Can *Use* You

Thursday. 8:31 p.m. March is here. Looks like I'll be going back to driving a cab. These other things are just not working out. Drove down to Vine Street to see about a job as sound mixer. NO EXP. NEEDED, WILL TRAIN, the ad in the *L.A. TIMES* said. So I thought: Okay. I'll check it out. The building is at the southeast corner of Hollywood and Vine. I walk in, take the elevator up to the 8th floor. I enter the anteroom and am greeted by two young, Hispanic-looking ladies, secretaries. The phone rings and one of the secretaries picks it up, while the other secretary hands me a form to fill out. I fill out the form. It's the usual. And then am ushered to an office on my left. There is a middle-aged black guy sitting there at his desk. He is immaculately dressed in suit and tie. "Have a seat," he says to me. I do.

I notice the man staring down at something on the floor, on his side of the desk. I'm sitting there waiting for something to happen, for the man to say something—but he doesn't. He keeps staring down at the carpet—only I have no idea what the man is looking at. I'm waiting and wondering what is going on. He looks at me, finally says: "I have a baby down here."

What's he talking about? "A baby?" I ask.

"That's right," he says.

I get up to take a look—and sure enough—there is a baby in a type of makeshift cradle on the carpet by the man's chair.

"I was wondering what you were staring at," says I. "Guess that explains it."

So the guy and I talk a bit. He wants to know about my background. "I attended film school here in Hollywood for a couple of years back in the early 70s. I've done some writing; never made much money at it; did have a low-budget horror film produced that's in video stores. I did my own editing." The guy keeps watching the baby in the cradle, looks up at me from time to time, nods. He says: "Do you like music?"

"Sure," says I. "I love music; always have."

He's looking right at me now, when he says: "We can use you."

"I'm not a sound-mixer," I explain. "I'm surprised you're not looking for someone with experience."

"Oh no, we can train you. No problem."

"Will I be paid while I'm being trained?" I ask.

"Ten dollars an hour," he says, adding: "However, there is a period of nine months of training that you'll need to go through first." Smooth as silk, that's what this creepo is. Another slick con artist. A bloodsucking leech. But I'll play along. See where it takes you. This three-piece suit is convinced he's got another gullible fool on the hook.

I nod my head. He hands me a piece of paper. "Our recording studios are across the street. Show them this piece of paper and they'll take you around, show you the layout."

I can't believe my luck. It is too easy. I have never been hired this easily. Never. Never have I had this kind of luck before. This is too good to be true. The man says: "After you've completed your training with us you'll be making $60 or more per hour and working with the likes of Michael Jackson, Melba Moore, all the top rap groups."

I can't believe my good fortune. I say: "This is just what I've been looking for, a chance to make some real money." And go to work on my next film.

"Well, you've come to the right place," the man says.

I thank the man. We shake hands. I'm gone. Take the elevator down. I park my car on Selma (as the parking on Vine is quite limited time-wise), walk up Vine Street, enter the building. When I reach the "recording studio" I finally get the picture. *This place is a school*! Get it? A balding-type shows me around. The place consists of various "studios" with sound-mixing equipment, pianos, even a motion picture mini screening room, a room with a VCR and monitor where mixing is taught. The problem with these "studios" is that they all resemble rooms, classrooms—because that's exactly what they are: *classrooms. This is a school.* I further discover that in order to get all this training I would have to obtain a government loan (which they would gladly file for me).

I felt like cursing. I wanted to explode. This is the exact same type of film school con Terrance Gullick ran twenty years before!

The very same thing! Made his promises to unsuspecting, desperate dreamers aching to make a dream or two happen—bled them dry, stomped on their fragile egos—never helped a soul get a job or actually learn the business. What we learned we did so on our own, for the most part. All those Super 8 student films Angus Gladwyn and Red Gunderson and Bo Aldin and Rico Rogozenski, the Stubb Brothers (and others) and I had made had all been done on our own meager savings and blood and sweat—and now, twenty years later, the same con was being perpetrated on other unsuspecting dreamers, newcomers to Tinseltown. A rage boiled deep inside of me. What right did these scum-suckers have to con people like this? What right? Where was the law?

How could they? Would the bullshit ever end? Of course not—not in Hollywood.

"Wait a minute," I say to the balding-type: "You're saying I'd have to obtain a government loan to get my training?"

"Yeah," he says; "but it's no big deal at all—we do all the paperwork for you. It's very simple, actually. Nothing to worry about."

"Oh yeah?" is my response to this. "Just how big a loan are we talking about?"

"Seven thousand," he says. "Which you can start paying off once you go to work."

"*Seven thousand dollars, is that what you said?*" I ask. "*Which I can start paying off?*"

"Sure," he says, calm as could be. "With the kind of money you'll be making you'll have no trouble paying it off."

"*Seven thousand dollars that I'm supposed to pay off?*" I say again. "I come here looking for work and you're telling me now I have to attend this school and get a government loan for seven grand before I can get a job? Why then did the other guy in that building across the street make it sound like I was already being hired to go to work then? He said I would be paid ten dollars an hour—"

"All that is right," says he; "but you have to be trained first."

"Look, I'm not some novice off the damn Greyhound bus. I've been in this town for twenty years now, I've got a film under my belt—it's in video stores—I don't need to be conned like this."

"Nobody's conning you," says he; "just giving you the facts."

"The other guy couldn't have given me the facts just as easily over there and saved me the trip?"

He's nodding. "I don't know why he didn't."

"Because this is a con, man; it's a con job. You get me? You're ripping people off—and somebody should do something about it."

"I think you're wrong about us," says he, then looks up as a buxom mulatto lady walks over. She's a looker in a short dress, high heels that show off her sexy behind and muscular thighs.

He introduces me to the woman, then the balding type leaves. The woman sits down at the desk, is looking over my application form. "You know," she says, looking up; "you'd be passing up an excellent chance here. You're obviously talented and you have the knowledge to go far in this field."

"Thanks for the compliment," says I, "only I'm not about to go into debt for you people. I don't need nine months of more schooling here with you. I've had all the training I can stomach."

She kept doing her best to talk me into it and I wanted to say to her the only thing about the place that interested me was her. I wanted to ask her out, but did not from fear of coming across as too forward—and, in fact, did phone her once I got back to the house. "I do have your phone number, don't I?" she asked.

"You do," said I.

"I'll call you," said she.

Sure, I thought.

• • •

(March 1, 1990)

Yoo-Hoo, Taxicab Man!

I made the move to South Gate. Alone again at last, and living in a one-bedroom house. I was also back in the cab, making a living, dealing with it. It felt all right to be working the streets again.

It was 11:00 a.m. Sunday. I had dropped off a fare up on the Strip and was making it down San Vicente, toward Santa Monica Bl. The Century Plaza was busy, for a change, and I thought I'd hurry on back there before fifty other cabs showed up. That's when I noticed a stacked, black woman with long hair pushing a bicycle up the hill across the street. She was waving and calling:

"YOO-HOO, TAXICAB MAN! YOO-HOO, TAXICAB MAN!" I did a double-take. She did look fine in white hot pants and a tight-fitting, red T-shirt—and I thought: Hell, help the poor thing out. In addition to that, I'd been making every effort to meet women, been giving out my phone number and all that, just tired of living alone, tired of the single life. I'd been celibate too damn long now, too many years.

I kept thinking: She sure is hot. And she could be single.

She might be interested in you. You just never know. Have to keep trying. Well, I didn't have Redford's looks, but even some of us guys with average features needed someone to hold in our arms now and then. We had desires. I was desperate to want to make a U-turn right there in the middle of the street, but then thought better of it, knowing about West Hollywood sheriffs always being around, tough and liking to write out traffic tickets.

There was a vacant parking lot on my right. I slammed on my

brakes, pulled into the lot, drove south toward the alley, waited for a car to clear it—looking back there at the foxy black woman, and I couldn't help it—my groin was stirring inside my trousers. Like I said, it had been too many years of celibacy. Pumping the old hand was getting old. I was finally together enough emotionally after the breakup to start looking for a replacement, to look for female companionship; better yet, a mate. I was finally ready and willing to think about having sex with other women.

I turned my head—there she was—still standing there, waving, smiling, swaying those great hips. My God, what a pair of shorts she had on. And those tits. Damn. Incredible. Maybe, some luck was finally coming my way. There would be some loving in my life. Maybe. I'd been passing out my number to potential single women to call—but they seldom did. I couldn't tell you why they hardly ever called. Too nervous? Feeling it was the man's job? But if I didn't have *their* number (I was always too damn uneasy about asking for *their* number, not that many women would give it around here in L.A.)—how could I call them?

The car cleared the alley, and I pulled into it, took it out toward the curbing at San Vicente. I kept looking at the sexy woman with her bike. But I had to wait for the traffic to clear before I could pull out and make my left turn and shoot up toward her.

I got my break, made my turn, and sped up to her and pulled up to the curb. I couldn't see her face just yet, she was wearing large sunglasses, but I could see that well-shaped behind, part of her buttocks hanging out, the dangling breasts (no bra, mind you). I'm only human. My groin stirred some more.

I hadn't had any poontang in too many years. I needed it bad and wasn't embarrassed about admitting it either. At forty I'm too damn old to lie to myself about things like that.

Horny and hard-up, that's exactly what this cab driver was.

"I'm so glad you came back for me, taxicab driver," the woman was saying. "So glad. I'm in a terrible fix, just a terrible fix. I got to get together with my sister before it's too late. Thank you for helping me out, thank you so much. You're very kind."

I kept looking at that rear end and that large chest hanging there inside that red T-shirt with no bra while she was bending over and trying to pick up her bicycle. What firm, muscular thighs, I noticed. Sexy. This woman was *built. Solid.*

I liked them this way. *But would she go for me? Was she even available*? Most were already taken, of the ones that I was interested in. Taken. What was a guy to do? Keep trying. What I truly wanted and was ready for was to settle down with a decent, good-hearted woman. A one-man-woman. Monogamy was for me. I'd always been this way. Square, maybe—but so what? I liked things this way.

I got out of my cab. "Hi," said I.

"Can you please open your trunk so I can put my bicycle in there? I'm sorry, but I'm really in a hurry."

"Wait a second," said I, trying to be a gentleman about it, "don't lift that bike. I'll do that for you. Here, let me unlock the trunk first—*I'll do the lifting*. That looks like a pretty heavy bike."

"You are very kind," she said. "A true gentleman. It's rare around here. A nice man. Bless you." That's when I noticed the hip shaking and all those apparently feminine gestures with the hands, the waving, the walk, looked strained, fake. This "woman" was trying too hard to be like a woman. Was this a female? Was it? I looked harder at the face, tried to—hell, I couldn't see much. The dark glasses covered too much of it.

The hair was long like a woman's, but it could have been a wig, and probably was. I glanced at "her" groin area—there was no bulge there. If she wasn't a woman, where was the male sexual machinery? Tucked away underneath someplace? I didn't know. Possibly a sex change.

But Jesus, look at the tits—large tits, bigger than what most women had—about 38! And would you lookit those hips—that behind—just like a woman's! *How did they do it*? Incredible.

My own groin had gone down dramatically by then.

I'd been suckered into it. This was no woman, not a natural one.

Shit, I thought; what a damn fool I am. Conned again. I wanted to get back to the Century Plaza Hotel and try to make my rent that was two weeks overdue, and now I was obligated to follow through with this thing. Gotta be a nice guy. So now you're stuck with it.

"Where you going?" I said.

"Two places," "she" said, "First, I have to go drop something off, and then I have to go somewhere else. Don't worry," she insisted, "you'll make lots of money. It's a good ride for you."

I had the trunk open. At least I'd be getting a decent fare out of it. No love or romance, but at least I'd be making some money, making a living. She was still trying to lift that bike, had it off the ground. "Can we get my bicycle in there?" she kept saying in a real hurry.

"Here, let me do that," I offered just the same, only my own actions by now had slowed by about 50% with the disappointment of realizing that this was not a real woman.

I got the bike in there and couldn't close my trunk all the way.

"That's fine like that," the fake female voice said to me. "Really. Don't worry about it, honey. That's fine that way. You can let part of it stick out like that."

"What about the cops?"

"Police won't bother you, sweetheart," the voice said. "You can take my word for it."

Yeah, right. I still remained unhappy about one thing—our destination. It hadn't been exactly clear where it was she/he needed to go (truth was I was far unhappier about discovering the truth about "her" anatomy).

"It's a good trip, honey; don't worry about it. You'll make good money. I'll take care of you."

"*Look, I need to know where you're going.*"

"Okay, I'll tell you. First I need to go up to Sunset, drop this off—"she was holding a folded-over Manila envelope. "I need to talk to my sister, and then you can take me to Western. *You'll make good money, trust me. I'll take care of you.* You're such a *nice man.*"

Was I being conned? What was going on? I hated not being given a straight answer. But it was too late to back out.

Gotta follow through, my man. Initially you sure were acting like a decent guy, trying to be. Tough to back out of it now. *But she's not a woman! This is not a woman!* So what.

"Can we go, please? I'm really in a hurry. I have to see my sister. She'll be so happy when I show her my cosmetology diploma."

"Oh yeah?" I said perfunctorily. I had the key in the ignition, turned it. We pulled away from the curb.

"I'm so excited. Just graduated from cosmetology school today. You have no idea how happy I am."

On a Sunday? I almost said, but didn't. It seemed to me whenever I happened to ask a hooker what she did for a living (the times I got them in my cab, which was often enough at night) the answer had been—more than once: "I'm a cosmetologist." Or: "I'm a dermatologist." *And yet they always had the worst complexions* (loaded down with much too much makeup: rouge, blue eyeshadow, fake eyelashes, etc.).

"I can't wait to tell my sister," came from the backseat. "But we have to hurry up before she leaves. I told that bitch to wait for me—excuse my language—I love my sister, but I asked her to wait for me. She said she would, but you never know. She had to go someplace. I'll be pissed if she's not there. We have to hurry up and make it to the corner. I need to talk to her."

I said: "You know, when I saw you back there the reason I stopped is because I thought you had a *flat tire*." That was partly true. "I just wanted to help. I thought you had a *flat*."

"Oh no, honey," said the fake voice. "I just don't like riding my bicycle up the hill like that. Can't do it. It's too damn hard."

"*Wait a minute—that's why you flagged me down*?"

"I just couldn't ride my bike up that hill like that."

"You couldn't push it two blocks?" That's how long the drive was—all of two blocks. We were at the corner of Sunset Bl., and San Vicente. And I heard her curse. "Oh shit. Damn, damn, damn! I don't believe it. The bitch is gone! She left already. I knew it! I knew it!"

I turned, looked at her. "So what's the big deal?"

"*I don't see her van anywhere. She's gone*."

"You were having me take you to Western anyway—it's only about ten bucks on the meter. You worried you can't pay me the ten bucks?"

"No, honey; I'm not worried about not being able to pay you the ten bucks—*I'm worried about what you got on your meter right now*."

I glanced at the meter. It was only $2.30. *Two dollars and thirty cents*.

She hopped out of the backseat. "*Thank you so much, honey. You're a sweetheart*."

I got out.

I was calm, collected, but I hadn't liked what was being done to me. Nobody likes to be taken. No more than two weeks prior to this a crazy black woman had offered me a chocolate chip cookie in lieu of a twenty-two-dollar ride. I didn't like being burned this way. My landlord accepted cash money only, as did the guy down at the grocery store and all the rest of them. Cash money.

"Wait a minute," I said, and saw her reaching for the bike. "*You don't have money to pay me? You don't have the $2.30?*"

"Sorry, honey. I told you we had to hurry. My sister ain't here. Her van's gone. If she ain't here how am I supposed to pay you? I was gonna get some money from her."

Bullshit, I thought. I was shaking my head. "How can you get in a cab without money in your pocket? How can you do something like that?"

"I'll take care of you, I promise—if you'll just give me your name and cab number. I'll take real good care of you."

That's what the other woman had promised, as did several others over the years. I'm still waiting to get paid.

"Come on," said I, "this is not right. How can you flag a cab down without money to pay the fare? I don't get it."

"You were a big help to me," "she" insisted. "I just couldn'ta made it up that big old hill without your help."

I kept looking at her, still shaking my head. As I reached in for the bike I thought about just taking it back down to the bottom where I'd picked her up and leaving it there.

It would have served "her" right. People just didn't have any goddamn character around here. Goddamn dregs; that's what you got. Dregs. But I did nothing of the sort. I was getting old or something, because I did nothing about it. I could have gotten the cops involved, taken the bike to the sheriffs station at the corner of Santa Monica Bl. and San Vicente—but the amount of the fare just wasn't worth it. Again, it wasn't the amount that bothered me, but the way "she" had pulled it off, the blatant con job "she" had pulled off that irked me pretty good.

I'd helped out people in the past during all the years of hacking, even given some rides without charging a dime, only because they had been special cases, folks in trouble, in need of a helping hand. However, this was something else. Not to mention that I was now beginning to realize where I'd seen this face before—not once, but several times—years ago—hooking on Sunset Bl., in fake blond braids. She had attempted to hitch a ride and I had turned her down. And then another time she had gotten in my cab with a white prostitute, stiffed me for my tip and part of the fare.

I let her have her bike.

"You're the best," she sighed. "Really the best. I'll remember this next time I see you. I'll take care of you; that's a promise."

Yeah, and Santa Claus really does exist.

I said: "So how will you make it to Western Avenue now?"

"Oh, no problem," she laughed. "I'll just ride my bike all the way. It was just that hill I was worried about. I can make it the rest of the way. No sweat."

She pushed it several feet to the corner, got on the bike, and was gone with a wave.

What crap, I thought.

I got in my cab, cursing underbreath, backed into a lot there, and was back on San Vicente, heading south, south toward Santa Monica Boulevard.

That's what you get for trying to be a nice guy. You got burned. Plain and simple—or else you could say you got burned because all you saw where those great tits hanging there, and that rear end in those tight white shorts. Hell, how did they do it? Hormone shots? Built just like a woman. I wouldn't kid you. And then I was smiling, shaking my head. I was laughing. I had to laugh. When a forty-year-old cab driver got pulled into a con like this you had to laugh about it. And I did. And when later on in the Holding Lot at L.A. International I recounted the story to a cabbie buddy of mine who is from China—Duke—he found it hilarious.

Duke is 55, speaks pidgin English. He was working on his waybill, filling it in, but he had a hard time concentrating as I told it.

"Don't make me *wraf*," he kept saying. "You make me *wraf*. Woman turn out to be something else. That's L.A. Funny stuff. Stuff *rike* that *arways* happen *alound* here. You make me *wraf*. I can't do waybill you make me *wraf* so ha'd."

• • •

About the Author

Kirk Alex, born Nusret Alijagić in Sarajevo, Bosnia-Herzegovina, 4/3/51. "'Nus,' rhymes with moose, is what I was known as in the Old Town part of Chicago we lived in when I was a kid."

He was brought to the U.S. at the age of 10. "Lived in the Windy City for the next 8 years. Served in the army. Did a tour in Viet Nam. In the summer of '72 moved to Los Angeles to pursue a dream or two—where, instead, a twenty-five-year stretch of dead-end situations followed: factory worker, shipping clerk, movie extra, mattress salesman, did TV repos, was a house painter, hauled trash, delivered phone books door-to-door, was a print shop gofer, janitor, carpet cleaner, security guard, furniture mover, taxi driver—to name a few—and generally starved on and off for over two decades.

"Paid hard dues and proud of it. Didn't have a rich daddy to pave the way one damn bit."

Kirk Alex started writing at age 20, and collected rejection slips for the next 26 years, until *WORKING THE HARD SIDE OF THE STREET—SELECTED STORIES • POEMS • SCREAMS* ("written from between 1980 through 1990; the eight additional years spent fine-tuning and getting it published not withstanding") his first work to appear in print.

"It's been a hard, bumpy road, no doubt about it; but you can also be sure of this: I was in it for the long haul. It was do or die for me. Once I start something I have to stay with it. I'm a long-distance runner and could never relate to those who aren't. Were there any truly bleak times somewhere in there? Plenty. What keeps you going all those years without a bit of success or so much as a sign that you'll ever get anywhere?

"You do the thing because you love it, it's a part of you; and because you've got no choice. My used $30 Olivetti/lettera typewriter provided the only light at the end of that long, dark tunnel. Granted, it may have been a weak light—still, it was the only lifeline available. Without books/writing, I might have easily ended up in a straightjacket in a rubber room somewhere, or dead.

"And so we thank the gods up there (whoever they are) for providing us with a much needed ray of hope in the countless lonely rooms over the years (when there was nothing but struggle and brain fever and hunger pangs to look forward to) all over this sun-bleached, soulless hellhole known, ironically, as City of Angels, via lasting literary gems created by these fine writers I remain forever grateful for and indebted to: Jack London, Nelson Algren, Edgar Allen Poe, Knut Hamsun, Charles Bukowski, Henry Miller, Eugene O'Neill, James M. Cain, Sylvia Plath, Carson McCullers, Elie Wiesel, James Jones, Nathanael West, August Strindberg, John Steinbeck, Tennesee Williams, Ferdinand Céline, Malcolm Lowry, Jack Kerouac, John Fante, James Ross (who outdid nearly all with his one and only novel entitled *THEY DON'T DANCE MUCH*, a true American masterpiece), Jim Northrup, Ernie Hemingway, Vinnie van Gogh, et al."

ORDER FORM

TUCUMCARI PRESS

P.O. Box 40998
Tucson, AZ 85717-0998
USA

Please send me the following:

______ copies of ***Working the Hard Side of the Street, Selected Stories • Poems • Screams***, by Kirk Alex, @ $14.95 U.S./CAN. plus shipping/handling (see below). Arizona residents, please add sales tax of 7%.

NAME ____

ADDRESS ____

CITY, STATE, ZIP ___________________________________

I understand that I may return any book for a full refund if not satisfied.

Shipping Charges. Inside the U.S., please add $4 for the first book and $2 for each additional book ordered. Overseas Air Rates per book: Europe $8, Asia and Africa $9; Pacific Rim (New Zealand and Australia) $10; Mexico and Canada $5. Outside U.S. surface rates $3 per book. Price subject to change without notice. Mail check or money order — **no cash or COD's**. All international money orders (including Canada) must be payable in U.S. Dollars. Allow a few weeks for delivery.

Please complete your shipping label

(Do not tear this form out if public library property, please make a copy instead.)

-- Tear here --

FROM:

TUCUMCARI PRESS
P.O. BOX 40998
TUCSON, AZ 85717-0998
USA

TO:

____

____

____

____